Tune Up Your PC

Send Us Your Comments

To comment on this book or any other PRIMA TECH title, visit our reader response page on the Web at **www.prima-tech.com/comments**.

How to Order

For information on quantity discounts, contact the publisher: Prima Publishing, P.O. Box 1260BK, Rocklin, CA 95677-1260; (916) 787-7000. On your letterhead, include information concerning the intended use of the books and the number of books you wish to purchase.

Tune Up Your PC

In a Weekend

Sunrise Midday Sunset

Sunset Evening Sunrise

FAITHE WEMPEN

PRIMA
TECH

A DIVISION OF PRIMA PUBLISHING

A Division of Prima Publishing

Prima Publishing and colophon are registered trademarks of Prima Communications, Inc. PRIMA TECH and In a Weekend are trademarks of Prima Communications, Inc., Rocklin, California 95677.

Publisher: Stacy L. Hiquet
Marketing Manager: Judi Taylor
Managing Editor: Sandy Doell
Acquisitions Editor: Rebecca Fong
Project Editor: Melody Layne
Technical Reviewer: Keith Davenport
Copy Editor: Kelli Brooks
Proofreader: Theresa Wehrle
Interior Layout: Marian Hartsough
Cover Design: Prima Design Team
Indexer: Johnna Van Hoose

Important: Prima Publishing cannot provide hardware or software support. Please contact the appropriate hardware or software manufacturer's technical support line or Web site for assistance.

Prima Publishing and the author have attempted throughout this book to distinguish proprietary trademarks from descriptive terms by following the capitalization style used by the manufacturer.

ISBN: 0-7615-2451-7
Library of Congress Catalog Card Number: 99-06893
Printed in the United States of America

00 01 02 03 04 II 10 9 8 7 6 5 4 3 2 1

To Margaret

ACKNOWLEDGMENTS

Thanks to the wonderful editorial and production staff at Prima Publishing for another job well done.

ABOUT THE AUTHOR

FAITHE WEMPEN is a A+ Certified computer technician and the owner of Your Computer Friend, a computer training and troubleshooting business in Indianapolis that provides beginners with one-on-one help with their PCs. She also holds an M.A. in English from Purdue University, where she has taught English Composition and Business Writing. Her eclectic writing credits include not only computer books (40+ titles), software documentation, and training manuals, but also magazine articles, essays, fiction, and poetry.

CONTENTS AT A GLANCE

CONTENTS

INTRODUCTION

Almost everybody who has a computer wishes it ran better. Perhaps your beef is a game that won't run, a full hard disk, a printer that no longer prints, or some other difficulty. Or maybe your computer just runs sluggishly in general, and you wonder whether there's anything you can do to speed it up.

Tune Up Your PC in a Weekend can save you hundreds of dollars in PC consultant fees. It's a step-by-step walkthrough of the process that I use when professionally tuning up a client's computer. You can follow this easy weekend-long formula yourself and, less than 72 hours from now, end up with a trouble-free PC, optimized for peak performance.

Why a weekend? Because that's when most people have some free time. This book is structured so the average reader can work through the entire process before it's time to dress for work on Monday morning, but you are free to take as much time as you want to actually complete it. In some cases, in fact, you won't be able to complete the entire process in a weekend. If you decide to order some new parts from a mail order supplier, for example, you might need to wait a week for them to be delivered.

Why Tune Up?

Most people who think they need new computers would be happy with their existing ones if they only worked right. But Windows-based PCs

typically gather all kinds of frustrating, hard-to-troubleshoot errors and problems through normal use. People shell out hundreds of dollars for a computer repair shop to reload everything, or even buy whole new systems. That's like killing a fly with a sledgehammer. Your old computer might be just fine with a little tweaking and a few corrections.

Tuning up is a three-part process. First, you solve the problems with your PC. Then, you run a series of utilities and change certain settings to configure your PC for peak performance. Finally, if the system is still not performing at the level you would like, you invest in (and install) some new parts, such as memory, an upgrade processor, or a new drive. This book walks you through that entire spectrum.

How to Use This Book

This book is divided into six sessions that you should complete in roughly the order in which they appear:

- ⚙ **Friday Evening: Assessing Your System**. This first session explains how to find out what components you have and how to decide which components are causing the problems you experience.

- ⚙ **Saturday Morning: Fixing Problems**. Here you learn how to troubleshoot problems with Windows, with specific devices, and with individual programs.

- ⚙ **Saturday Afternoon: Enhancing System Performance**. After solving your obvious system problems, you learn what utilities to run and what settings to adjust to make your now-healthy PC run better.

⚙ **Saturday Evening: Starting Fresh with a Clean Install.** This session is optional. If the morning session fails to solve your problems, turn here to learn how to reinstall Windows, wiping out any leftover tough-to-troubleshoot errors and problems.

⚙ **Sunday Morning: Planning System Upgrades.** Here you learn about the various upgrade components that you can buy to enhance your computing experience, and where to buy them.

⚙ **Sunday Afternoon: Installing Upgrades**. If you want to try installing upgrade parts yourself, this session gives you some tips and pointers to get you started.

Conventions

Several special elements in this book will help you on your way:

TIP   Tips offer insider information about a technology, a company, or a technique.

NOTE   Notes provide background information and insight into why things work the way they do.

CAUTION   Cautions warn you of possible hazards and point out pitfalls that typically plague beginners.

Assessing Your System

- ✿ What Makes a Computer Work?
- ✿ What Have You Got?
- ✿ What's Your Problem?
- ✿ What's Your Solution?

So you aren't happy with the performance of your PC? You're not alone. PCs are complicated machines with hundreds of interrelated files and many intricate electronic components, and most people don't clearly understand how everything fits together. By the end of this evening, however, you'll have a much better idea of what makes your computer work (or fail to work!) and what you need to do to tune it up.

What Makes a Computer Work?

Before you think about what needs fixing in your PC, you need to know a little bit about its innards. Throughout this weekend, you will read about the components that make up a computer and how one or another presents a bottleneck to peak performance. Here's a brief summary of the important components.

Hardware

Hardware refers to the physical parts of a PC, usually made of some combination of metal, plastic, silicon chips, and electronics. As a computer ages (and these days, three years old is considered very mature), various pieces of hardware can wear out, break, or become obsolete, and require replacement. The main hardware parts include the following:

- **Processor**. The processor is the brain of your computer. A processor has two measurements: its type and its speed. The types include 386, 486, Pentium, Pentium Pro, Pentium II, Pentium III, Athlon, K6-II, and K6-III. The speeds are measured in megahertz (MHz), anywhere from 16MHz for a very old and slow 386 to 700MHz for a high-end Pentium III. If the processor is old and slow, some programs might not run, or they might run slowly.

- **Memory (RAM)**. Memory is the workspace in which your computer operates. The more memory you have, the more and bigger programs you can run at the same time. If you don't have enough memory, your programs might run slowly or not at all. (More about this later in this session.)

- **Motherboard**. The motherboard is the big circuit board inside the case that everything else plugs into. The capabilities of the motherboard you have determine the processors you can use, the type and amount of memory you can have, the video card type, and more.

- **Case**. The case is the metal or plastic box that holds the innards. It must have enough bays (storage compartments) for all the drives you want to use (hard, floppy, CD, and so on). It also must have a power supply with enough wattage to supply all the innards with power.

- **Video card**. (sometimes called the *display adapter*). The video card is the interface between your PC and your monitor. The card interprets the PC's instructions and sends codes that tell the monitor which pixels (dots) to light up with which colors. If you have an old, slow video card, or you are not using the right video drivers, your screen might not refresh quickly, causing your monitor to flicker.

- **Hard drive**. (also called *hard disk*). The hard drive is where you store most of your files. If you run out of hard disk space, you have to delete something, or use a disk compression or cleanup program before you can install a new program.

- ✿ **CD-ROM drive**. This drive reads CD-ROM discs. Most programs come on CD-ROM these days, so a CD-ROM drive is almost a necessity. Some CD-ROM drives have extra features, such as the capability to play DVD movies or to write CDs.
- ✿ **Sound card**. The sound card plugs into the motherboard and enables you to hear sound through speakers. If you don't have a sound card, you miss out on the sound effects associated with most games and on the audible warnings your computer issues from time to time.

There are other pieces of hardware that aren't physically located inside the box but are still important to your total computing experience. These are called *peripherals* because they are associated parts of the system, usually with a separate casing and power supply. They can be divided into two major groups: *input devices* and *output devices*. Input devices help you get data into the PC; output devices help you get data out.

Input devices include the following:

- ✿ Keyboard
- ✿ Mouse
- ✿ Scanner
- ✿ Joystick
- ✿ Digital camera

NOTE Keyboards and mice don't have their own power supplies, because they don't draw much power and can drain a little bit off of your main PC without causing a problem.

Output devices include the following:

- ✿ Monitor
- ✿ Printer
- ✿ Speakers

A modem is both an input and an output device, because it enables a two-way exchange of information between your PC and other computers through your telephone line. The same goes for a network card; it handles both incoming and outgoing data on a local area network.

Operating System

Windows is by far the most popular operating system today—more than 90 percent of all PCs have Windows 95 or Windows 98 on them. Therefore, I'm going to assume that you fall into that 90 percent. If you have Windows 3.1, your PC is probably at least five years old, and you really should think about replacing it; upgrading it is not cost-effective, and tuning it up will not do much good.

What about Windows 95 versus 98? Windows 95 is a lot like Windows 98, and it works fine for many people. However, there are two reasons why you might want to spend the money to upgrade from Windows 95 to Windows 98:

❖ Windows 98 comes with better system management tools than Windows 95.

❖ Windows 98 supports a lot more of the newer hardware, so if you buy a new device and it doesn't work very well with Windows 95, an operating system upgrade might help. In particular, earlier versions of Windows 95 do not support USB (Universal Serial Bus), a type of connection that many of the newest scanners and other devices employ.

If you are interested enough in system performance to have bought this book, I strongly suggest that you upgrade to Windows 98. It has the tools and utilities you need to make your PC run at peak performance. You can follow along with most of this book with either Windows 95 or Windows 98, but the exact steps might be different in some cases if you still use Windows 95, and not all of the utilities are available.

NOTE There are a few cases in which it is better to stick with Windows 95 than to upgrade to Windows 98. For example, suppose you are using some off-brand hardware device in your system that does not have a Windows 98 driver available (perhaps the manufacturer went out of business before Windows 98 came out). The Windows 95 driver you have for it might work fine in Windows 98—or it might not. You won't know until you try. If you try Windows 98 and that device no longer works, you might want to go back to Windows 95. Windows 98's installation program gives you the opportunity to save your system files so you can return to Windows 95 if needed.

Application Software

Application software is software that helps you accomplish a specific task, such as typing a letter, storing information, or entertaining yourself. In contrast, an operating system, such as Windows 98, actually keeps the PC running. Your computer might have come with some applications, and you have probably bought and installed more.

A few years ago, there were two types of programs available: Windows-based and DOS-based. DOS-based applications could run on a Windows system, but not always flawlessly. Nowadays, however, almost all applications are Windows-based, so you don't have to worry about getting the right ones. See "Configuring a DOS-Based Program" in the Saturday Morning session if you have an old DOS-based program that you can't seem to get running under Windows.

What Have You Got?

It isn't necessary to identify every single component in your system to tune it up. However, some of the fixes and improvements you learn about this weekend involve adding hardware, so it's good to know what you have already.

The following steps show you how to identify your hardware in Windows 95 or 98:

1. On the Windows desktop, right-click on My Computer and choose Properties from the shortcut menu that appears.

2. On the General tab (see Figure 1.1), make a note of the following:

   ✿ **System**. This tells which version of Windows you have.

   ✿ **Computer**. This tells what processor you have, and how much memory.

3. Click on the Device Manager tab.

4. Click on the plus sign next to each category, or double-click each category name, to expand its list of components.

5. Take note of the brand and model names of each component. For example, in Figure 1.2, you can see that I have an AccelStar II 3D Accelerator for a video card, a Creative CD-RW RW6424E CD-ROM drive, and so on.

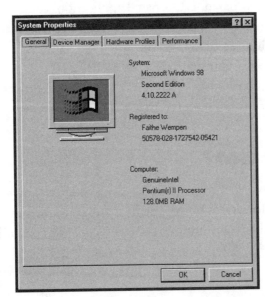

Figure 1.1

Check the General tab to see your processor type, memory, and Windows version.

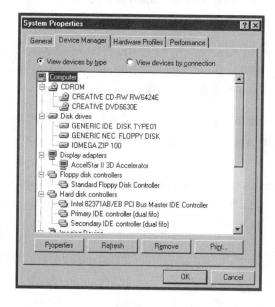

Figure 1.2

Identify the specific models of each component from the Device Manager.

6. Click on Print. The Print dialog box appears. See Figure 1.3.

NOTE In the Print dialog box, you can choose between System summary and All devices and system summary. The former, which is the default, should be fine for your purposes (and it is much shorter). If a particular device or class is selected when you issue the Print command, a third option, Selected Class or Device, is also available, but you do not want to choose that for this exercise.

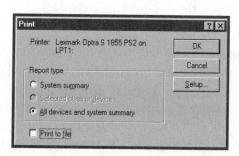

Figure 1.3

Request what kind of report you want to print.

7. Click on OK. The System summary prints.

8. Click on OK to close the Device Manager.

Keep this printout handy; you might need it in later sessions, especially if you need to troubleshoot device problems on Saturday morning. This printout includes the following information:

- **System Summary.** This lists your Windows version, your machine type, your processor, your BIOS information, and some other details.

- **IRQ Summary.** This lists the system Interrupt Requests, or IRQs (00 through 15), and tells what devices are using each one. This is handy to have when troubleshooting device conflicts with new devices you add (see the Sunday Afternoon session). You'll learn more about IRQs on Saturday morning.

- **IO Port Summary.** This lists specific memory addresses that store input/output information and tells what device is using each section of memory. Again, this might be good to know when troubleshooting why a newly added device isn't working.

- **Upper Memory Usage Summary.** This lists the memory addresses in an area called upper memory and tells what devices are using the addresses. You probably do not need this information for anything.

- **DMA Usage Summary.** This lists the DMA (direct memory access) channels that certain devices are using. Devices such as sound cards and floppy disks typically use DMA channels, and each device must use a unique one. This information can be useful when installing and troubleshooting new devices (see the Sunday Morning and Sunday Afternoon sessions).

- **Memory Summary.** This tells the amount of conventional and extended memory installed on your PC. This is useful when deciding whether your PC could benefit from a memory upgrade (see the Sunday Morning session).

- ✿ **Disk Drive Info**. This tells what disks are installed in the PC and what their capacities are. It also tells how much free space is available on each hard disk. This information is useful when evaluating how full your hard disk is. It can also be a great reference if you ever have to set up your hard disk manually in your BIOS program (see the Sunday Afternoon session).

You also need to identify your current peripherals, such as your printer and scanner. However, these devices typically have their brand and model emblazoned on the front, so that information is always readily available.

Take a Break

Break time! Take a 10–15 minute time-out to refresh and relax.

Suggested break activity: Call a techno-geek friend on the phone and compare your computer's specifications with hers. Your friend might be surprised and delighted that you are taking an interest in her hobby and might even offer to come over and help you with this tune-up process!

Don't have any technically-savvy friends? Resolve to make some.

What's Your Beef?

Now that you know what makes up your computer, the next thing to ask is, "Which part is causing the problem?" Answering this question is probably the most difficult part of tuning up your PC. Obviously, if you knew what the problem was, you could fix it a lot more easily! Unfortunately, many symptoms have a variety of causes, any of which could be causing the specific difficulty you are having. In the following sections, I address some general problem categories and tell you what might be behind them. I don't attempt to solve your problem right here, but I point you to the section in the book that can help.

Overall Slowness

It's possible for a computer to operate slowly overall due to an operating system or application problem, but it's not likely. In most cases, a computer is slow because its hardware is old.

Let's talk for a minute about old hardware. If you never buy any new peripherals or software, your hardware will never be obsolete—in theory, anyway. Hardware is only old because it doesn't work (or doesn't work well) with the latest whatever-you-have-just-bought.

So, for example, perhaps you have a nice little computer, circa 1994, that has been running Windows 3.1 happily for years. Last week, you bought and installed Windows 98, and suddenly the computer is running slow as molasses. It's not the computer's fault; you simply asked it to do something it doesn't have the oomph to do. You can go through the software-based tune up routines in this book but, realistically speaking, it won't help much. What you need is an upgrade—or a whole new computer.

Overall slowness is caused either by an old or slow processor or by a memory deficiency (or, most likely, both). Here's an easy way to determine which it is. When you are waiting for a program to do something (like perform a search), watch the hard disk indicator light. Does it flash on and off a lot? If so, it's a memory deficiency. Is the PC eerily quiet with no lights flashing? If so, it's the processor maxing out. (Note that starting up the program does not count as "doing something" for this test because the hard disk indicator always flashes when a program starts.)

Another giveaway is whether the PC is slow all the time or only at certain times. If it's slow all the time, it's the processor; if it seems to get slower and slower the longer you work, it's the memory.

Out of Memory Errors

Do you get Out of Memory messages, or does your system start running very slowly when you have more than one or two programs open at once?

If so, you should probably add more memory to your PC. Windows 95/98 likes to have at least 32MB of memory. If you have less than that and you try to open several programs at the same time, you might sometimes get Out of Memory error messages telling you to close some programs, or everything might slow to a crawl.

Ironically, if you get Program Too Big to Fit In Memory or Insufficient Memory messages at a DOS prompt, adding more memory to your system is not likely to help. The first message is usually the result of a defective program file. You can usually clear it up by restarting your computer and reinstalling the software. Other messages from the DOS prompt, such as those that say you do not have enough free memory, refer to a lack of conventional memory—that is, the available memory below the 640K mark. Later, I explain how to fix this problem, but adding more memory to such a computer does not help.

If you get a message that your printer is out of memory, that's yet another story. Adding more memory to your computer does not fix that, either. You might get some relief by adjusting the printer driver settings in Windows, but you probably need to add memory to your printer (if that's possible; not all printers can accept memory upgrades) or consider investing in a new printer altogether.

■■■■■■■■■■■■■■■■■■■■■■■■■■■■■■■■■■■■■■

TIP If you have a PostScript printer, it probably can work with either a PostScript or a PCL driver. If you get Out of Memory error messages for the printer in PCL mode, try the PostScript driver instead. To do so, use the Add Printer Wizard to add the PostScript driver as a separate printer. See "Installing a Printer Driver" in the Saturday Morning session for details.

■■■■■■■■■■■■■■■■■■■■■■■■■■■■■■■■■■■■■■

Out of Disk Space Errors

If you get warning messages that there is no space left on your hard disk, the obvious solution would seem to be buying a larger hard disk. That is certainly one good solution. But there are other, less expensive solutions.

See "Saving Disk Space" in the Saturday Afternoon session to learn about some utilities that can help you out by deleting unneeded files or by changing the way files are stored on your drive.

General Protection Faults

General protection faults, or GPFs, are error messages in Windows. Almost everyone sees an error occasionally. It usually says something about a program performing an illegal operation and being terminated. If you see such a message, click on OK, restart your computer, and don't lose any sleep over it.

However, if you frequently get such messages, or if you get such messages every time you run a certain program, you might want to do some fix-up work in Windows. Saturday Morning's session is all about fixing problems. My first action is to run ScanDisk, a Windows utility that checks and repairs the file storage system. See "Correcting Disk Errors with ScanDisk" in the Saturday Morning session.

Missing File Error Messages

To run, some of the more complex programs require that dozens of inter-related files be in the correct locations. When you try to run a certain program, and see an error message about a missing file, it's likely that one of these files was deleted, moved, or corrupted. See "Locating a Missing File" in the Saturday Morning session to see if there might be a copy of the file still on your system that you can relocate to solve the problem.

Data files can also turn up missing. For example, in some programs, the last four files you worked on appear at the bottom of the File menu, and you can open them by selecting them from there. But if the wanted file was moved or deleted, that link is no longer valid.

Lockups and Freezes

I just hate when this happens, don't you? You are merrily typing along, or surfing the Internet, when all of a sudden your computer just stops. Perhaps the mouse still works; or perhaps it freezes too. But nothing you do seems to revive the computer. So you end up turning off the PC and restarting it, with an uncomfortable feeling that you have done something horribly wrong.

Well, you haven't done anything wrong. Nearly everyone experiences the occasional lockup. But after restarting, there are some important steps to take to make sure there are no errors that could cause a repeat lockup in the near future. First, run ScanDisk. (See "Correcting Disk Errors with ScanDisk" in the Saturday Morning session.) Then, if you experience lockups frequently (as in more than once a week), do some troubleshooting, as described in the remainder of the Saturday Morning session.

■ ■

Turning off the computer's power is not a very graceful way to restart, and it can result in file system errors. It's better to use the Start/Shutdown command to restart.

If a program locks up, you can sometimes make things work long enough to do a proper restart by pressing Ctrl+Alt+Delete. This opens a dialog box listing all the running programs. The one that locked up might say *(Not responding)* next to it. Choose it and click on End Task. Wait about 10 seconds, and a dialog box appears saying the program is not responding and asking you to shut it down.

After you shut down the errant program, your system might appear to work normally again, but don't trust this. Restart (Start/Shutdown/Restart) before doing anything else.

■ ■

Certain Programs Not Working

Does your system perform just fine except for a certain program that doesn't work? Several things can cause such a problem, including the following:

- There are errors on your hard disk (which can be corrected with ScanDisk, as you learn on Saturday morning).
- A file the program needs was deleted or has an error.
- Another program you recently installed overwrote a file this program needs to run.
- The link or shortcut you used to start the program does not point to the correct location.

You learn how to fix all these problems in tomorrow morning's session.

Choppy Sound or Video

Many programs these days, especially games, include music and video clips. These can be great when they work. But systems that lack the latest hardware sometimes have problems playing sound and video.

If you experience problems (such as choppiness or stuttering) playing simple sounds, such as Windows event sounds (like the "ding" that signals an error message), there is probably a device conflict between your sound card and some other device on your system. Check out Sunday Afternoon's session on troubleshooting devices for help.

If you have sound or video problems only with certain programs, and those programs tend to be video-intensive (such as a game with lots of live-action video clips in it), you might not have sufficient hardware. An older video card can be the culprit if video or animation plays back with jerks and stops. If only the sound is jerky, suspect the sound card. A slow CD-ROM drive can also cause video playback performance to be poor.

When working on a system with poor quality video or animation, the first thing I do is check the system requirements on the box the program came in, and then compare them to the system summary (which you printed earlier in this session). This can help identify the hardware component that might need to be upgraded.

What's Your Solution?

By this point, you should know the specs of your system, and you should be able to articulate what your general unhappiness is with it. The next step, obviously, is *what do I do about it?*

Repair the Problems

Before you can start tuning up your PC's performance, it needs to be in good working order. That means if you have any problems—with hardware, Windows, or individual applications—you need to fix them.

You can fix some problems simply by running a utility program. Windows comes with several utilities you can use to repair problems with your system. (Windows 95 has some; Windows 98 has more.) I run one of these utilities—ScanDisk—right away when troubleshooting a system, before I do any other troubleshooting.

Other problems are trickier. You might need to reinstall a program, or update a driver, or work around a device conflict. I walk you through all these fixes tomorrow morning. Some of them can include the following:

- Repairing the Windows Registry
- Downloading a patch or an update from a manufacturer's Web site
- Reinstalling or removing a program
- Changing which programs load at startup
- Checking system files

- Manually assigning resources to a device to avoid a conflict with another device
- Locating and replacing missing files
- Setting properties for running DOS-based programs under Windows

Reformat and Reload Everything

If you are unable to fix your problems after going through the Saturday Morning session in this book, and you are fairly sure the problem is with your software rather than your hardware, you might want to go for the last-ditch effort: wipe it all out and start over.

Reloading Windows on a clean hard disk wipes out even the most troublesome problems. I've seen it work when nothing else did. However, this is not an easy fix, and it takes a long time. Figure on at least four hours, from start to finish—more if you have lots of programs, because they all need to be reinstalled.

Obviously, reconstructing a system from scratch is nobody's idea of a fun way to spend an evening, but if you are out of ideas and ready to try it, see the Saturday Evening session. This procedure can include the following:

- Backing up important files
- Making a boot disk and starting the PC with it
- Repartitioning the drive (if necessary) and reformatting it
- Reinstalling Windows
- Reinstalling drivers for each piece of hardware that Windows does not automatically recognize
- Reinstalling all your programs
- Restoring the backup of your data files

In some cases, you can bypass some of this by simply reinstalling Windows in a different location—that way you can leave your data files on the hard disk and still get the benefit of a clean Windows installation. I tell you more about that in the Saturday Evening session.

NOTE In very few cases, I have seen problems continue after a complete reformatting and reloading of Windows. In one case, the hard disk was incorrectly partitioned. (I'll tell you about drive partitioning on Saturday Evening). In the other, the hardware was incompatible with a prerelease beta version of Windows.

Improve the Performance

After everything is in working order, you can focus on improving your computer's performance—tune it up, if you will. There are two ways to do this. One is to run various software utilities and tweak various Windows settings to optimize Windows' performance. The other is to buy and install new hardware.

Generally speaking, the following things can improve your system's performance:

○ Using the latest and best driver files for each of your hardware devices

○ Defragmenting your hard disk using a Disk Defragmenter utility (which comes with Windows)

○ Downloading the latest updates and patches to your software from the manufacturers' Web sites

○ Setting your video display mode to a setting appropriate for your monitor

○ Using a large enough swap file

○ Loading only the programs you need at startup

○ Converting to a 32-bit file system (Windows 98 only)

○ Removing unwanted programs from your system

⚙ Organizing your Start menu and desktop shortcuts so you can easily find the programs you want to run

Buy and Install Upgrades

I won't kid you—the tweaks and performance enhancements that I tell you about on Saturday afternoon are not going to turn your old clunker into a turbo-charged performance machine. At best, they might make your system run 10 to 15 percent better. To really see a big difference in an old PC, you need some new parts.

I wrote a whole book about upgrading PCs, called *Upgrade Your PC in a Weekend,* and you might want to check it out if you are serious about replacing several components in your PC. However, if you think one or two small upgrades can suffice, the information presented on Sunday in this book will walk you through selecting and installing the components. On Sunday morning, I help you decide what you need to buy, and on Sunday afternoon, I walk you through the installation and troubleshooting.

Here are some of the most effective upgrades you can perform:

⚙ Adding more memory, if your motherboard can support it. More memory means faster Windows operation when working with multiple programs at once.

⚙ Replacing the motherboard and/or processor dramatically speeds up your system overall. This is a somewhat complicated upgrade, however, so you might find it worthwhile to pay an expert to install the parts.

⚙ Adding a second hard disk can relieve file overcrowding, giving you room to install more programs and to create more data files.

⚙ Adding a CD-ROM drive (or a drive that reads both CD-ROMs and DVD) allows you to install and use software that comes in those formats.

⚙ Adding a writable CD-ROM drive enables you to create your own CDs.

✿ Adding a scanner lets you import photos and printed text into your computer.

✿ Adding a printer (or replacing your current one) enables you to create printed output (or improve the quality of your existing output).

✿ Replacing your monitor with a newer, larger one can reduce eyestrain and make your computer more enjoyable to work with.

I talk a lot more about selecting upgrade components on Sunday morning. As you might have noticed, there are two main types of upgrades: those that improve the performance of your system (like memory or a faster processor), and those that add new capabilities to it (like a scanner or a DVD drive). I generally favor any upgrade that adds new capabilities, because such components can always be pulled out and reused in a future computer that you might buy. However, I generally do not favor performance-enhancing upgrades, except in unbalanced systems.

What do I mean by unbalanced? Think of a pipe with water flowing through it, with various diameters at different points. Water can flow through the pipe only as quickly as the narrowest part of it allows. If one part of the pipe is a lot narrower than the rest, the whole system suffers. Computer data is a lot like that, flowing through your PC from input to output. The ideal computer system is well-balanced, with all the components approximately the same age and quality, so that none of them slow down the performance of the others.

If your computer has one or two obvious weak areas, such as too little memory or a too small hard disk, upgrading might be just the fix you need. (I deal with upgrades on Sunday.) However, most computer systems are fairly well balanced, such that upgrading one part is not going to significantly improve the system. And building a new computer one part at a time can actually cost a lot more money than selling your old machine and buying a whole new one! Keep that in mind as you formulate your action plan for your PC tune-up.

Take a Break

You're all done for the night! Now you know what components you have, what problems you want to fix, and what the possible solutions might entail. You're ready to start bright and early tomorrow morning on the first step: fixing all of the obvious problems that prevent your system from running normally. Your PC will be a lot more healthy and happy as a result of tomorrow morning's session, and you'll be a lot more satisfied with its performance.

Fixing Problems

- ✿ Preparing to Repair
- ✿ Correcting Disk Errors with ScanDisk
- ✿ Preventing Computer Viruses
- ✿ Fixing Startup Problems
- ✿ Fixing Windows Errors
- ✿ Fixing a Specific Device or Program

There's a joke circulating on the Internet to the effect that if Windows were a car, you would have to take it in for repairs every week. Actually, that's probably closer to the truth than we would like to believe! Many minor problems can crop up in Windows, and if left unchecked, some of them can turn into major problems. Fortunately, many of the most common problems are very easy to fix. In this morning's session, I show you how to solve the most common computer problems yourself, in many cases saving you an expensive trip to a computer repair shop.

In this session, I ask you to be intrepid, to try things you might not have tried before. It's true—some of the things, if done improperly, can mess up your system. But if you are having problems, it's messed up somewhat already, right? If you don't fix it yourself, you have to hire someone to fix it; so even if you do screw things up and have to hire an expert, you are usually no worse off than you would be if you didn't try.

Preparing to Repair

Before you dive into the system corrections and changes I suggest in the rest of this session, take a few minutes to prepare for the worst. What will happen, for example, if you make a mistake and wipe out some important data files? Or if you mess up your Windows configuration files to the point where Windows won't start anymore? Both of these are very real possibilities, but you can recover from a situation like that if you have the right backups. So do yourself a favor and take some precautionary steps before you attempt any fixes.

Backing Up Important Files

Imagine what would happen if you lost everything on your hard disk. You could reinstall most of your programs from the original CDs they came on, and anything that you have downloaded from the Internet could probably be downloaded again. But your data files would be irrevocably lost.

Therefore, you probably don't need to back up every single file on your hard disk. Backing up your data files is sufficient.

Copying Data Files to a Removable Disk

To back up your data files, you can copy them to a removable disk (a floppy or a Zip disk, for instance), and then store that disk in a safe place. This works great if you don't have a lot of data to back up. In addition, because this method stores the files in their original format, you can simply copy the files back to your hard disk to restore them when needed; you don't have to run any special utility program.

 NOTE If you are on a network, you can copy backups to another computer on the network. This can be quicker and more convenient than working with multiple removable disks. To copy to a network drive, display the target location with Network Neighborhood (on the desktop) and drag the files from your My Computer or Windows Explorer window to that pane.

To copy files to a removable disk, use Windows Explorer or the My Computer window. Select the files you want to back up and drag them to the drive icon where you want to put them, as shown in Figure 2.1.

Drag the selected files as a group to the
icon for the drive you want to back up to   Select the files

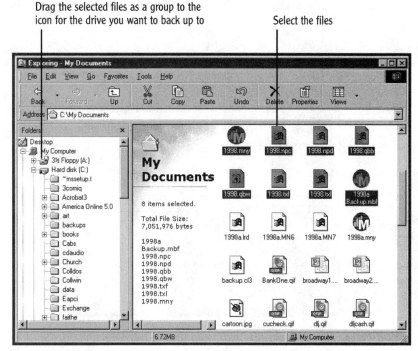

Figure 2.1

Back up important
files by copying
them to a
removable disk.

You also can right-click a selected group of files and choose Send To from
the shortcut menu. The submenu that appears lists the removable drives
on your system; pick the one you want, as in Figure 2.2.

Backing Up Files with Microsoft Backup

If you have lots of data to back up, you might prefer to use Microsoft
Backup (or some other backup program) to back it up to disk. Backup
programs can compress your data so it fits on fewer disks, which can be
a real boon if floppy disks are your only available medium on which to
back up. Backup programs also can remember lists of files and folders
you backed up in the past, so you don't have to manually select the files
to back up each time you do it.

Right-click on
the selected files

Choose Send To and select the
drive to copy the files to

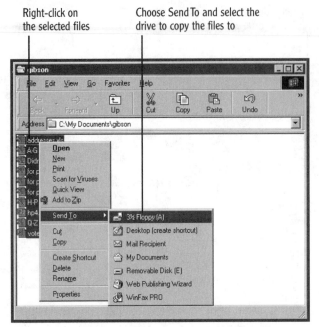

Figure 2.2

Right-click
on selected files
and choose where
to send a copy of
them.

 NOTE There are many brands of backup programs you can buy. Most come with suites of utilities, such as the Norton Utilities. If you use one of these third-party backup programs, follow the directions that come with it. However, Microsoft Backup is free, and you already have it, so there is really no need to go out and buy a separate backup program.

Microsoft Backup comes free with Windows, but it is not installed by default. The following steps explain how to install it:

1. Choose Start/Settings/Control Panel.
2. Double-click on Add/Remove Programs.
3. Click on the Windows Setup tab.
4. Double-click on System Tools. A list of system tools appears.
5. If a check mark does not appear next to Backup, click on the check box to place one there (see Figure 2.3).

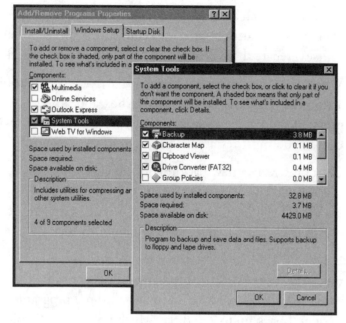

Figure 2.3

Install Backup from the list of Windows components.

6. Click on OK. You return to the Add/Remove Programs Properties dialog box.

7. Click on OK again to close the dialog box.

8. If prompted, insert the Windows CD and click on OK.

9. A prompt appears that you must restart your computer. Click on Yes.

To run Microsoft Backup, choose Start/Programs/Accessories/System Tools/Backup. The first time you run it, Windows checks for backup devices. These are devices, such as tape backup units, that are specifically designed for doing backups. If Windows doesn't find any backup devices, a message appears to that effect, offering to run the New Hardware Wizard to configure one. If you don't have such a device, click on No. The Backup program opens, and you can proceed to one of the next sections.

You can back up to any drive, a floppy, a hard disk, a network hard disk, a removable hard disk, and so on. If you have a high-capacity removable media drive, such as a Zip or Jaz drive, I recommend using that. (You need enough blank cartridges for it to contain the files you want to back up, of course. Prepare these beforehand, deleting any existing files from them.)

When you start Microsoft Backup, a dialog box prompts you for an action (see Figure 2.4). This dialog box appears each time you start the program, and only appears at startup; if you close it (by clicking on Close), you must restart the program to see it again.

Click on Create a new backup job and click on OK. Or, if the dialog box has been closed or does not appear, open the Tools menu and choose Backup Wizard. Either way, the Backup Wizard starts. You can use it to do a complete backup of your entire system or to back up selected files.

Personally, I never back up the whole system because it would waste my time and disks. Most of my hard disk is consumed by programs that I own the CDs for, and I could reinstall those programs easily if I had to. Besides, I back up to Zip disks, which hold 100MB apiece. My hard disk holds 6G, so I would need 60 Zip disks to back up the whole thing. They cost about $10 apiece, and I sure don't have $600 to spare for them! So I back up only my data files. I keep all the data files in a common folder (organized in subfolders within it), and I back up only that folder.

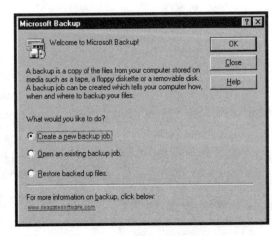

Figure 2.4

Start a new backup job, open an existing one, or restore from here.

Here's how to back up certain files:

1. From the Backup Wizard's first screen, choose Back up selected files, folders and drives and click on Next.

2. An Explorer-like window appears, in which you can select the files you want (see Figure 2.5). Do any of the following to select files:

   ❂ To select an entire drive, place a check mark beside it.

   ❂ To open a list of folders, click a plus sign. (A plus sign means there are subfolders beneath that one.)

   ❂ To select a folder or file, place a check mark next to it.

3. Click on Next.

4. On the What to Back Up screen, leave All selected files selected and click on Next.

NOTE   The other option in step 4, New and changed files, is useful when running another back-up in the future. It backs up only the files that changed since the previous backup. (That's called an *incremental backup*.)

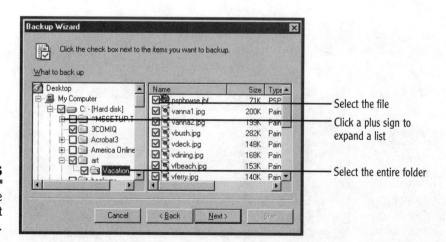

Figure 2.5

Choose the files you want to back up.

5. Enter a destination and name for the backup file (see Figure 2.6).
Click on Browse to browse for a location if needed. Then click
on Next.

For example, in Figure 2.6, I chose my floppy drive (A). You can
use the file name MyBackup.qic, or you can specify a different
name for the backup file, such as the current date or your name.

6. On the How to Back Up screen, select or deselect the following
check boxes as desired and click on Next.

☼ **Compare original and backup files to verify data was successfully backed up.** This option checks each file after backup
to make sure it was backed up correctly. It makes the backup
take longer, but can be worthwhile if you are backing up
extremely important files.

☼ **Compress the backup data to save space**. This option compresses each backed-up file so that the backup fits on fewer
disks. It also makes the backup slower to restore, however (if
and when you need to do that).

7. Type a name for this backup job. (For example, you might use
Complete and today's date.)

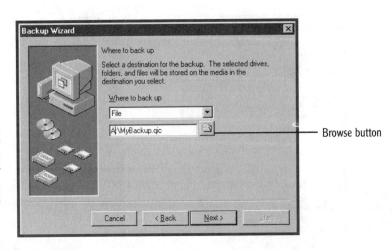

Figure 2.6

Select a name and
destination for
the backup file.
All backed up
files are stored in
that location.

8. Click on Start.

9. Wait for the backup to finish. A Backup Progress window appears as the backup is happening.

   When prompted, insert blank media (your disk) in the drive you are using and click on OK to continue.

10. When the backup has finished, click on OK to close the message box that reports this.

11. Click on OK to close the Backup Progress window.

12. Exit from Microsoft Backup.

Restoring Files with Microsoft Backup

Hard disks are fairly reliable in terms of storage. When you save something to a hard disk, it usually stays there intact. However, the following exceptions might occur:

- Disk errors can corrupt individual files, and the damage can spread to other files if you do not run ScanDisk to fix it.

- Physical trauma to the hard disk while it is operating (such as the PC falling off a table or being kicked) can damage areas of the disk, resulting in whatever data was in that spot becoming unreadable.

- Computer viruses can wipe out the file allocation table (FAT), so that although your data is still on the hard disk, you can't access it. Some viruses can even erase the hard disk itself.

- A mechanical failure in the hard disk mechanism can cause the hard disk not to read or write at all, so you can't access your data even though it's still there.

Any of the above situations would make you very glad you had a backup of your important data! Should you ever need to restore the files from your backup, follow these steps:

1. Correct whatever problems with your system caused you to lose the data in the first place.

2. Insert the first disk of the backup set in your drive.

3. Start Microsoft Backup and choose Restore backed up files from the dialog box that appears. Click on OK to begin.

4. Choose the restore destination (that is, where the backed up files are currently stored) and click on Next.

5. A list of backup sets on the disk appears. If there is more than one, select the one you want; then click on OK.

6. If you see a message about the set continuing on another disk, asking whether you want to continue logging, click on Yes.

7. If you see a message to insert the next disk in the set, do so.

8. On the Restore Wizard screen that appears, select the file(s) you want to restore, just as you selected files to include in the backup initially.

9. Click on Next.

10. On the Where to Restore screen, choose Original Location or Alternate Location. If you choose the latter, specify a location when prompted. Then click on Next.

11. On the How to Restore screen, choose what to do if a file of the same name already exists in that location. Then click on Next.

12. Click on Start.

13. If you see a Required Media box, click on OK.

14. As prompted, insert disks and click on OK. If you see any warnings or errors during the restore, click on OK to move past them and continue with the restore operation.

15. At the Operation Completed dialog box, click on OK.

16. Click on OK to close the Restore Progress dialog box.

17. Exit from Microsoft Backup.

Creating an Emergency Startup Disk

A startup disk (also called a *boot disk*) is a disk that contains the necessary files to start your computer should something ever go wrong with your hard disk that prevents it from starting up. It's a smart idea to always have a startup disk available in case of problems.

When you create a startup disk in Windows, several important disk utilities are also copied to that disk, so if you ever need to check, format, or partition a drive when Windows won't start, you can do so. You can see these utilities in action in the Saturday Evening session.

To create a startup disk, follow these steps:

1. Choose Start/Settings/Control Panel.
2. Double-click on Add/Remove Programs.
3. Click the Startup Disk tab.
4. Click on Create Disk.
5. Place a blank disk (or one that contains nothing you want to keep) in your floppy drive.
6. Click on OK.
7. Wait for the needed files to be copied to the disk.

   If prompted, insert the Windows CD in your CD-ROM drive and click on OK to continue.
8. When the disk is finished, click on OK to close the Add/Remove Programs Properties dialog box.

Store your startup disk in a safe, handy location. You might need it later in the weekend, depending on what fixes you decide to attempt.

Showing All Files

By default, Windows hides certain files from its file listings. It hides files that are marked as hidden, because these are files you should normally not change or delete. It also hides files with certain extensions, such as .dll, .vxd, and others, that also should normally not be touched. However, in your tune-up process, you need access to some of these files, so do the following to turn on their display:

1. Double-click on the My Computer icon on the desktop.
2. Choose View/Folder Options.

3. Click on the View tab.

4. Under the Hidden files folder, click on Show all files.

5. Click on OK.

Showing File Extensions

Another default you might want to change: Windows hides the file extensions for certain file types. An extension is a period and a three-letter code at the end of a file name. It indicates the file type. For example, Microsoft Word files have a .doc extension (short for document). When tuning up your system, you might want to see the file extensions, however. To turn them on, do this:

1. Perform steps 1–3 of the preceding procedure.

2. Deselect the Hide file extensions for known file types check box.

3. Click on OK.

Acquiring and Installing TweakUI

TweakUI (shown in Figure 2.7) is an extra utility program that gives you additional control over Windows. It allows you to adjust certain settings that are not normally customizable—or at least not easily. I refer to its use later in this session, so you might want to install it now in preparation for that.

NOTE   If you have Windows 95, rather than Windows 98, just forget about TweakUI. It isn't necessary—it's just a nice little extra. There was a version of TweakUI released for Windows 95, but you would be hard-pressed to find it available for download anymore. And you shouldn't use the Windows 98 version with Windows 95 because of possible incompatibilities.

TweakUI comes on the Windows 98 CD-ROM; You can find it in the tools\reskit\powertoy folder. (It does *not* come on the Windows 98 Second

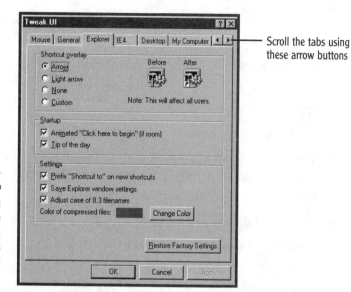

Scroll the tabs using
these arrow buttons

Figure 2.7

TweakUI gives you
the ability to
change certain
Windows settings
that you otherwise
could not.

Edition CD.) If you have the original Windows 98 on CD, you can skip
to "Installing TweakUI" later in this session. If not, follow the steps in the
next section to download a copy of it from the Internet.

♦♦

Microsoft does not support TweakUI, so if you screw up your system using it, you can't
get help from Microsoft's technical support staff. Also, Microsoft has not officially
approved TweakUI for use with Windows 98 Second Edition—that's why it's not on the
CD for that product. However, I have yet to find any problems running TweakUI on Windows 98 Second Edition.

♦♦

Downloading TweakUI from the Internet

If TweakUI is not on your Windows 98 CD, you can download it from
the Internet by following these steps:

1. Start your Internet connection, and using your Web browser, go to
   www.winsite.com/ws_search.html.

2. In the Search for box, type **tweakui98** and click on Search.

3. Select the hyperlink for Tweakui98.exe. A description of the program appears.

4. Click the TweakUI98.exe hyperlink. A File Download dialog box appears, as in Figure 2.8.

5. Click on OK. A Save As dialog box appears.

6. Choose the drive and folder where you want to save the file. I normally save downloads in a folder called C:\Temp, but you can save yours anywhere. Then click on Save.

7. Wait for the file to download.

8. Using My Computer or Windows Explorer, display the folder in which you saved the file.

9. Double-click on the downloaded file. The WinZip Self Extractor dialog box appears.

10. Click on Unzip.

11. When you see a message that the files were unzipped successfully, click on OK.

12. Click on Close to close the WinZip Self Extractor window. The TweakUI files are now in the folder where you downloaded the file.

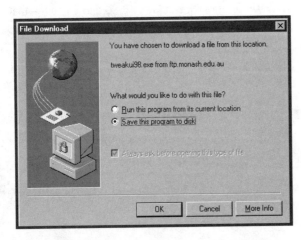

Figure 2.8

Choose to save the file to your hard disk.

Installing TweakUI

Now that TweakUI is available to you (either from the CD or from your download), you can install it in Windows. Do the following:

1. Locate the file tweakui.inf in the file listing and right-click on it. A shortcut menu appears (see Figure 2.9).

2. Select Install from the shortcut menu that appears.

3. When the Help window opens, read the information in it, and then close it. TweakUI is now installed.

Now you're ready to use it! If you're an advanced Windows user, you can experiment with TweakUI now by choosing it from the Windows Control Panel. Beginners should wait until I cover using TweakUI for individual changes later in this book.

CAUTION Beginners should not experiment with TweakUI unassisted. If used improperly, some of these settings can screw up your Windows installation.

Figure 2.9

Right-click on tweakui.inf and choose Install to install the program.

Correcting Disk Errors with ScanDisk

Important, important, important! That's what ScanDisk is. It's the single most useful Windows utility you learn about in this entire book. Running ScanDisk can often do wonders to fix problems, such as random Windows lockups. Whenever I am troubleshooting a PC, I run ScanDisk *first*.

When Windows appears to be malfunctioning, it's often because of a disk error. There are two kinds of disk errors: physical and logical. ScanDisk corrects both kinds.

A physical error on a disk is a "bad spot" from which data cannot be read. Physical errors are usually caused by physical trauma to the computer, such as falling off a table while it is running.

A logical error on a disk is due to a problem with the disk's "table of contents," called the File Allocation Table (FAT). Logical errors are often caused by shutting off the computer's power while it is running, or by a program locking up and failing to close its files properly. Logical errors can snowball if not corrected: One program might lock up because of an existing error and in turn generate even more errors.

Of the two types, logical errors are far more common. You can run two types of checks with ScanDisk: Standard and Thorough. Standard checks only for logical errors and takes only a few minutes; Thorough checks for both and takes a lot longer to run, up to several hours.

NOTE Most people do not run the Thorough check in ScanDisk unless they suspect a physical problem. If you recently knocked the hardware off a table, for example, you might want to run a Thorough check. You might also suspect physical problems if you see an error message including the words "data error reading" or "data error writing."

To run ScanDisk, follow these steps:

1. Choose Start/Programs/Accessories/System Tools/ScanDisk. The ScanDisk program starts and a list of drives appears (see Figure 2.10).

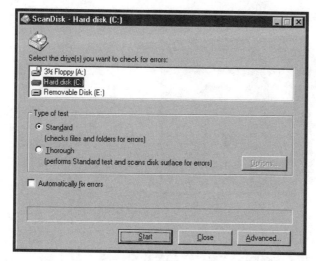

Figure 2.10

Select the drive to check for errors.

2. Click on the drive you want to check. If you want to check more than one drive, hold down the Ctrl key while you click on more than one drive on the list.

3. Click on Thorough to run the full test or leave Standard selected to check only for logical errors.

4. Select the Automatically fix errors check box to avoid having to deal with the errors it finds (especially if you're a beginner).

5. Click on Start.

6. Wait for the checking to finish. A Standard test takes less than five minutes; a Thorough test can take several hours.

   A message box reports ScanDisk's findings when it is finished, as in Figure 2.11.

7. Click on Close to close the message box. Then click on Close in the ScanDisk window to close the program.

After running ScanDisk, restart your PC and try again to reproduce the error or problem you had. Perhaps ScanDisk fixed it! If so, rejoice. If not, keep reading.

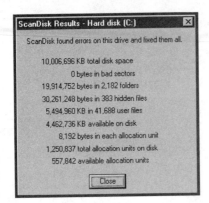

Figure 2.11

ScanDisk reports
its findings.

Preventing Computer Viruses

A few years ago, I used to tell clients who were worried about computer viruses that they were being paranoid. However, today that is no longer the case. Virus infections are becoming more and more common on average people's PCs, primarily because of the Internet. The capability to exchange files and messages with the whole world also brings the capability for viruses to spread freely.

About Viruses

A *virus* is a malicious computer code that attaches itself to your existing programs. From that point, it can infect other files, cause damage to your system, do something embarrassing to you (such as send a pornography link from you to everyone in your address book), or any combination of those things. A *Trojan horse* is a variant of a virus; it's a program that appears to do something useful, but in fact infects your system with a virus.

Your computer can get a virus in only two ways: by booting from an infected floppy or by running a program that contains the virus. You can't get a virus from reading a text-based e-mail message or from opening a document. And a virus can attach itself only to the boot area of a disk or to a program; it can't attach to a document.

These days, however, your computer might run a program without you knowing about it. For example, suppose you visit a Web page online that has a game to play. You are running a program, and that program can contain a virus. Or suppose you open a document that contains word processor macros. Those macros are programs and can contain viruses. As you can imagine, being vigilant about running programs is not enough protection. (Plus, it can make you truly paranoid, afraid to run anything, such that you can't enjoy your computer anymore.)

Antivirus Programs to the Rescue

The solution: Buy and use a good virus protection program. There are many good ones on the market; my favorites are McAfee Antivirus and Norton Antivirus. Both of these offer free trials for download from the Internet (www.mcafee.com and www.symantec.com, respectively). For registered users, they also offer downloadable updates, so you can always have the latest virus information.

A good antivirus program protects your system in several ways:

- It lets you scan the entire system for viruses, checking all files, any time you want.
- It schedules automatic full scans at specified intervals (such as monthly).
- It provides behind-the-scenes virus protection, scanning every file you open.
- It regularly offers to check the Internet for the latest update to itself.
- It offers to create a special boot disk you can use to start your computer if it won't start normally due to a virus infection.

Figure 2.12 shows McAfee Antivirus, for example.

When you install an antivirus program, it checks your system for viruses and offers to remove them if needed. It also lets you create a special start-up disk you can use to start your system if you think your PC has become

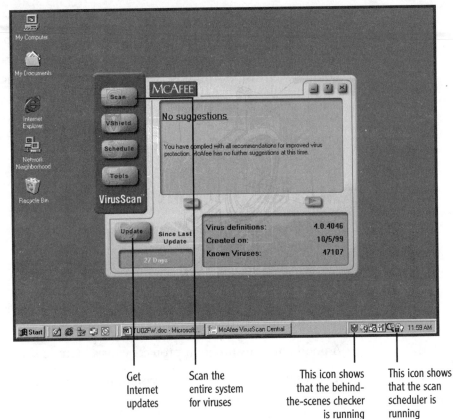

Figure 2.12

McAfee Antivirus, a
full-featured
antivirus program.

Get
Internet
updates

Scan the
entire system
for viruses

This icon shows
that the behind-
the-scenes checker
is running

This icon shows
that the scan
scheduler is
running

infected. Do both of these things right away, and update your startup disk every time you download an update to your antivirus program from the manufacturer's Web site.

Virus Security in Internet Explorer

You can also minimize your exposure to virus risk on the Internet by tweaking the security settings in Internet Explorer (or whatever Web browser you use—Netscape Navigator perhaps). I show you how to do it in Internet Explorer here; if you use Netscape Navigator, see the Help system in that program.

When browsing the Web, you must decide how secure you want to be and balance that with how many of the newest whiz-bang features you want to take advantage of. The highest security levels in Internet Explorer let you explore completely anonymously, with no fear of anything. However, these very high security settings also prevent you from, for example, online ordering, viewing multimedia content, and playing Java-based games.

In Internet Explorer, choose Tools/Internet Options. Then click on the Security tab (see Figure 2.13). On the Security tab, you can find several content zones defined: Internet, Local intranet, Trusted sites, and Restricted sites. You can set a security level for each zone individually and specify which sites are part of that zone. (Click on Sites to manage the list for a particular zone.) Any sites that are not on the list for the Local intranet, Trusted sites, or Restricted sites are automatically assumed to be in the general Internet zone.

Each zone has a slider bar you can drag to control the security level. The default for the Internet zone is Medium, which offers a good compromise

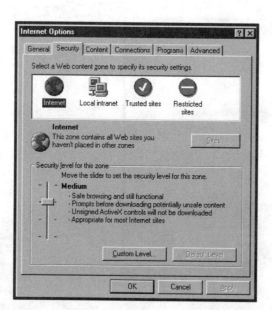

Figure 2.13

Manage the security settings for each zone.

between safety and capability. It lets you do almost anything that the page offers, but it informs you of potential security risks before they happen.

You can also customize the security level for a zone by clicking on Custom Level. This opens an exhaustive list of security settings (see Figure 2.14) you can change for the zone to specify how you want various types of content to be handled.

NOTE *Cookies* are bits of information that a Web page leaves behind on your hard disk to identify you in the future if you return to that page. Most people find them convenient. For example, some cookies log in to a site automatically and display customized information for you. However, some people think cookies are an invasion of their privacy.

To set your security so that you receive a prompt each time a Web page wants to transfer a cookie to your PC, from the dialog box in Figure 2.14, click on Prompt under Allow cookies that are stored on your computer.

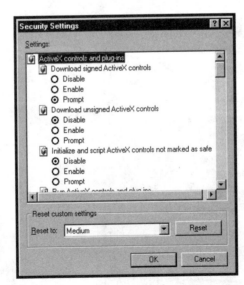

Figure 2.14

You can customize the security level for a zone here.

If You Have a Virus . . .

If your antivirus program tells you that it found a virus, follow its prompts to allow it to remove the virus and restart your PC. Each antivirus program works a little differently, but all are self-explanatory in their prompts.

If your PC simply doesn't work, and you suspect a virus, boot from the emergency floppy disk you made when you installed the antivirus program. (You did make one, didn't you?) Then follow its prompts to check for and remove viruses.

If you don't have such a disk, find a friend or coworker who has an antivirus program installed and ask him or her to make you a virus-removal disk you can use. Most antivirus programs include a command to do so. Make sure your friend downloaded the most recent update for his program before making the disk for you, to ensure that it can detect all the latest viruses.

Take a Break

Stop for a moment, while you decide where to go next. If ScanDisk fixed your problem in the previous section and you have no more problems, you can take the rest of the morning off and pick up at the Saturday Afternoon session. However, if you are still experiencing difficulties with your PC, you can consult at least one of the following sections.

PC problems fall into one of four categories:

- ✿ **Startup problems**. Problems that occur before or during Windows startup.
- ✿ **Windows problems**. Problems that occur with Windows itself, not associated with one specific program.
- ✿ **Device problems**. Problems with a specific piece of hardware, such as a scanner or printer.
- ✿ **Program problems**. Problems with one specific program's operation.

Don't be intimidated by the number of pages remaining in this morning's session. You don't have to read them all! Decide which of the above problem categories best fits your situation, and then jump to that section in the remainder of this session. If you have more than one problem, tackle each in the order listed in the preceding list.

Fixing Startup Problems

Startup programs can be frustrating to troubleshoot because there is no easy utility program to help you fix the problem. In the following sections, I break down the most common gripes and explain how to fix them. (It might not be as bad as you think!)

If Windows Doesn't Start at All . . .

Windows used to start up correctly, but it doesn't anymore. Think back: What was the last thing you did before it stopped working? Did you install some new software? Delete some files? Add a new hardware device? If so, you probably accidentally did something that is causing the problem now. If not, perhaps a file system error corrupted a file that Windows needs to operate, or perhaps one of your hardware devices failed.

Bear with me: "Doesn't start" is a very broad topic, and I need to ask you to narrow down your problem in the following sections.

Blank Screen

The hardest problems to troubleshoot are those in which you don't see anything at all onscreen. Here are some hints:

- **Blank screen, no fan.** The computer is not getting power. Is it plugged in? Is the wall outlet working? If so, perhaps your computer's power supply has gone bad.

- **Blank screen, fan sounds but no disk activity.** A hardware problem exists. This can happen if the hard or floppy disk is not hooked up right (wrong cabling or settings) or if the video card is not functioning or is not firmly seated in its slot on the motherboard.

- **Blank screen, multiple beeps.** The memory is not installed right, or there's a problem with your memory or motherboard.

- **Blank screen, single beep, disk activity.** The computer is starting normally, but the monitor isn't displaying anything. Is the monitor turned on? Plugged in? Connected to the computer?

These are all hardware problems. You can attempt to solve them yourself, or you might consider calling in a techie friend or a computer repairperson. If you want to fix things yourself, check out my book *Upgrade Your PC in a Weekend*, especially the Sunday Afternoon session on troubleshooting.

Error Message on Black Screen

When you first start the computer, some BIOS information (that is, basic input/output system information) appears onscreen. It tells you what video card you have, what processor you have, and how much memory. This is normal. Then Windows usually starts.

If you see an error message instead of Windows starting, however, here are some hints:

- `Floppy disk fail` message. Your floppy drive is bad or is not hooked up right.

- `Hard disk fail` message. Your hard disk is bad or is not hooked up right.

- `Boot failure` message. Your hard disk can't start Windows. It might be going bad, or you might have a computer virus. (More on viruses later.) If you think you might have a virus, see "If You Have a Virus..." earlier in this session.

Lockups During Startup

Suppose you are starting Windows, everything looks fine, and then all of a sudden your PC freezes up and just sits there. What's the deal? Well, one of the programs or files that Windows loads at startup probably is corrupted and is causing everything to come tumbling down when it loads.

If your machine is locked up, turn off the power, wait a few seconds, and turn it back on again. Do you get the same problem again? Or this time do you see a Startup menu on a black screen offering to start in Safe mode? If you have the opportunity to start in Safe mode, do so. (Then skip the next paragraph, while the rest of the readers catch up with you.)

If it locks up every time, you need to call up the Startup menu yourself. To do so, restart the computer, and watch the screen carefully for the message `Starting Windows 98`. It occurs approximately at the same time as the beep you hear. When you see it, press the F8 key as fast as you can. If you see the Windows 98 blue clouds startup screen, you missed it; try again. The Startup menu appears. Choose Safe Mode from it.

TIP If you have Windows 98, you can hold down the Ctrl key as you boot rather than pressing F8 at the right moment.

When you start Windows in Safe Mode, you start it up minus all the special device drivers and programs. This is a troubleshooting mode, not for regular operation. In Safe Mode, you can correct whatever is causing the problem. You can tell that you're in Safe Mode because the words `Safe Mode` appear in each corner of the screen, as in Figure 2.15.

Because not all the drivers are loaded in Safe Mode, you cannot do certain things there. For example, you cannot use your CD-ROM drives because the drivers for them are not loaded. However, you can run Scan-Disk, and the System File Checker, and some of the other critical Windows utilities that you learn about later in this section.

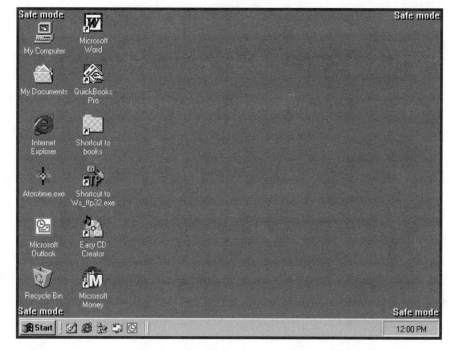

Figure 2.15

Safe Mode enables
Windows to start
when it otherwise
would not.

Safe Mode is all very well and good, but it doesn't help you determine which (of the many) Windows setup routines is causing your problem. To determine that, you can try stepping through the system startup one step at a time. To do so, follow these steps:

1. Restart your computer. When you see `Starting Windows 98`, press F8 as fast as you can. The Startup menu appears.

2. Choose Step by Step Confirmation. Every step in the Windows startup will be confirmed. Press Y to let each step happen.

3. If Windows locks up at a certain point, make a note of what driver, file, or question you just answered Y to onscreen—that's what's causing your problem.

4. Now restart again and repeat steps 1 and 2, but press N when you come to the line that caused the lockup. If Windows starts normally, you now know what the problem is.

You often can tell what a driver does by looking at the path to it reported onscreen. For example, if you see something like this, it's probably a file that came with Windows:

```
C:\windows\vnetsup.vxd
```

If the problem is a certain Windows driver loading, perhaps that driver file has become corrupted. Try recopying it from the Windows 98 CD (see "Checking System Files" later in this session).

On the other hand, if its path includes a folder for a particular device you added, like this, that device is probably the problem:

```
C:\pagescan\drivers\rundrivr.vxd
```

If the problem is a driver for a device you recently added to your system, perhaps it conflicts with one of the other devices on your system. If the new device came with software that runs it (for example, a scanning program or a CD writer program), try uninstalling that program, as described in "Uninstalling an Application" later in this session. Then restart to see if that took care of the problem. If so, visit the device manufacturer's Web site to see if an updated version of the software is available. (See "Updating a Device Driver.")

Registry Errors at Startup

The Windows Registry is a configuration file that contains all your settings for Windows, including information about each program and how it is installed. If the Registry becomes damaged or corrupted, Windows might not start at all, or it might start but have serious operational problems.

Sometimes, when there is a Registry error, your system detects it at startup and runs a program called the Registry Checker automatically before starting Windows. If that happens, just follow the prompts to repair the Registry and let the PC restart itself.

Other, less serious Registry problems might not be detected at startup, but can still cause Windows to malfunction as you use it. See "Repairing the Windows Registry" later in this session for details.

Missing File Error Messages at Startup

There are two types of missing file error messages that occur at Windows startup: those that prevent Windows from starting and those that don't.

Essential Missing Files

If the missing file prevents Windows from loading, you need to fix the problem right away. Do the following:

1. Write down the complete path and name of the missing file, as reported onscreen. It probably looks something like this:

   `C:\windows\system\vnetsup.vxd`

2. Restart the computer, and at the `Starting Windows 98` message, press F8 quickly.

3. At the Startup menu, choose Command Prompt Only. A command prompt appears.

4. Type **CD \{path}** and press Enter, where {path} is the path to the missing file. For example:

   `CD \windows\system`

NOTE Case is not significant when typing at the command prompt; CD and cd are the same thing.

5. Type **DIR {file}** and press Enter, where {file} is the name of the missing file. For example:

   `DIR vnetsup.vxd`

6. A list of files with that name in that folder appear. Does the missing file appear on the list? It does in Figure 2.16.

If the missing file does not appear, find someone who has the same version of Windows as you on his own PC. Copy the needed file from his PC onto a floppy, and then copy it from the floppy to your own PC in the folder specified.

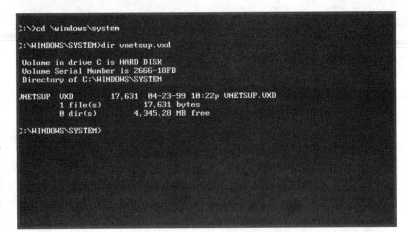

```
C:\>cd \windows\system

C:\WINDOWS\SYSTEM>dir vnetsup.vxd

 Volume in drive C is HARD DISK
 Volume Serial Number is 2666-18FB
 Directory of C:\WINDOWS\SYSTEM

VNETSUP  VXD      17,631  04-23-99 10:22p VNETSUP.VXD
         1 file(s)        17,631 bytes
         0 dir(s)      4,345.28 MB free

C:\WINDOWS\SYSTEM>
```

Figure 2.16

Use the command
prompt to see
whether a missing
file is actually
missing or not.

NOTE   If you don't have access to another computer running your version of Windows, try rein-stalling Windows to see if that fixes the problem. For more information, see "Installing Windows" in the Saturday Evening session.

Here's how to copy the file to your computer:

1. On the working PC, locate the file you want in Windows Explorer or My Computer.

2. Place a floppy disk in the drive.

3. Right-click the file and choose Send To/3 1/2 Floppy; wait for the file to be copied there.

4. Start the non-working PC and display a command prompt, as you learned in steps 2 and 3 of the preceding procedure.

5. Type **COPY A:\{file} C:\{path}** and press Enter, where {file} is the name of the file being copied and {path} is the path where it goes. For example, you might type:

   COPY a:\vnetsup.vxd C:\windows\system

6. Restart your PC and cross your fingers that the copied file allows your system to start!

At the minimum, you should not get the same missing file error message again. You might get a different missing file message! If so, repeat the procedure to replace the other missing file(s).

If you get a missing file error message for a file that is not really missing at all, perhaps the file is corrupted. Replacing it, as you learned in the preceding steps, might help.

If you continue to get missing file error messages that prevent you from starting the PC, and the files are not really missing, you should reinstall Windows. See "Installing Windows" in the Saturday Evening session.

Non-Essential Missing Files

If you see a message that a file is missing, you might be able to press Enter to continue loading Windows. If this happens, the missing file is not a critical one. You can ignore that message and not do any harm to your system, or you can attempt a fix.

You might be able to tell from looking at the file name and path whether the file is needed or not. For example, suppose the missing file is reported as this:

```
C:\pagescan\scanauto.dll
```

You know that PageScan was a program that ran your old scanner, which you have not had hooked up in several months. From that, you can deduce that the missing file is the driver for the scanner. That file is *supposed* to be missing—the error is that Windows still tries to load it. See "Controlling Which Programs Load at Startup" later in this session to prevent Windows from trying to load that file.

On the other hand, if you still use that device on your system, you want to restore the missing file. There might already be a copy on your system. Do the following to find out:

1. Press Enter to bypass the error message and continue loading Windows.

2. After Windows loads, choose Start/Find/Files or Folders.

3. Open the Look in drop-down list and choose your hard disk (usually C).

4. Type the missing file's name in the Named box.

5. Make sure the Search subfolders check box is marked. (This check box is called Include subfolders in some Windows versions.)

6. Click on Find Now. It searches for that file on your system. A list of found files appears, as in Figure 2.17.

If you find a copy of the missing file on your hard disk, do the following:

1. If more than one version of the file appears, as it does in Figure 2.17, look at the Modified column to determine which is the most recent copy. For example, in Figure 2.17, I would select the first file listed, dated 9/5/99.

2. Copy that file to the folder in which Windows is expecting the file. To do this, right-click the file and choose Copy from the shortcut menu. Then display the destination folder and choose Edit/Paste.

3. Restart Windows (Start/Shut Down/Restart) to see if the error message still appears.

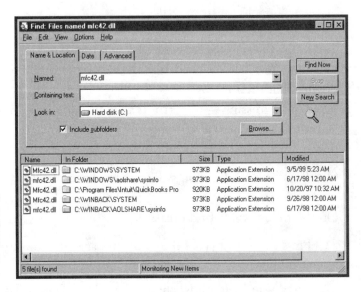

Figure 2.17

Windows found several copies of the needed file in various locations on my hard disk.

If you don't find a copy, you need to reinstall the drivers for that device. Dig up the disks that came with the device and run its Setup or Install program. If the program is on a CD-ROM, you might be able to start the program simply by inserting the CD-ROM in your drive. If not, use My Computer to browse its contents and double-click on the Setup.exe file. See "Reinstalling Device Drivers" in the Saturday Evening session for more information.

Controlling Which Programs Load at Startup

Lots of programs load when Windows starts up, and you might not even be aware that they have started. For example, if you have an antivirus program, it loads at startup. If you have a fax device, a rewritable CD-ROM drive, a scanner, or other special hardware, each of these devices might also load its own behind-the-scenes program at startup.

In most cases, you can leave these automatically started programs enabled. Do not attempt to disable an automatically started program unless you have a reason. Such reasons might include the following:

- You no longer have the device that the program works with, so you no longer want the program to load at startup. (Have you tried uninstalling the program normally? See "Uninstalling Unwanted Programs" in Saturday Afternoon's session.)
- You uninstalled the software, but Windows still tries to load it at startup and you get an error message.
- You are trying to run some new program, but it won't run, and you suspect that it conflicts with one of the automatically started programs. (Antivirus programs are particularly notorious in this regard for causing problems with other programs' operations.)

In the following sections, I show you how to disable a program running in the background and how to prevent it from starting automatically in the future.

Finding Out What Programs Are Loaded

Just what all is really running? To find out, press Ctrl+Alt+Delete right after you start Windows. The Close Program dialog box appears, listing all the running programs. You might be surprised at the long list! Each open window and each running program is represented there. When you are done looking, click on Close to cancel. (It's not a good idea to close a running program from here unless it is malfunctioning and can't be closed normally.)

Don't worry if you don't recognize the cryptic names of the running programs; you don't need to know what every one of them does. Displaying this list is just an exercise to give you an idea of the kinds of programs that load and run automatically on your PC.

Disabling Programs in the System Tray

Some programs that load at startup place icons for themselves in your system tray, so you can control them. The system tray is the area to the left of the clock in the lower-right corner of your screen. You can right-click on any of these icons to see a shortcut menu of commands that let you work with the running program.

Perhaps you just need to disable the program temporarily. You might be able to do so from the system tray. Some of these programs include a Close or Exit command on this shortcut menu, as shown in Figure 2.18, so you can unload the program when needed. (For example, some installation programs for other software require that you disable your antivirus program before running them.) However, the next time you start your PC, the programs reload again.

When you exit certain programs in the system tray, they offer to disable themselves from starting automatically in the future. This is certainly the easiest way to prevent a program from starting, if the program offers that! However, most programs don't offer.

If the program doesn't provide a way for you to disable it, you might need to formally uninstall it to prevent it from loading at startup (assuming that it's important to you that it be disabled; if it doesn't appear to be hurting anything, leave it alone.) See "Uninstalling Unwanted Programs" in the Saturday Afternoon session. Or, you might be able to disable it from the StartUp program group, as discussed in the following section.

Disabling Startup Programs from the StartUp Program Group

Some programs load at startup because shortcuts to them appear in the StartUp program group. To see these shortcuts, choose Start/Programs/StartUp.

If you want to prevent any of the programs listed there from starting automatically, remove them from that folder. To do so, choose Start/Programs/StartUp, and then right-click on the item. A shortcut menu appears; choose Delete from it (see Figure 2.20). Deleting the shortcut from the StartUp program group does *not* delete or disable the program itself; you can run it manually any time you need it. For example, if you very seldom use your fax software, you might remove it from the StartUp group, and then run it from the Start menu to turn it on when needed.

Disabling Startup Programs from win.ini

If a program starts up each time you start Windows, but it doesn't appear in the StartUp program group, perhaps it is loaded from win.ini. win.ini is an initialization file (hence the .ini on the end) that tells Windows what settings to use when it starts. Some programs (especially older ones designed to be compatible with earlier Windows versions) add lines that start themselves to this file. To disable such a program, you remove the reference.

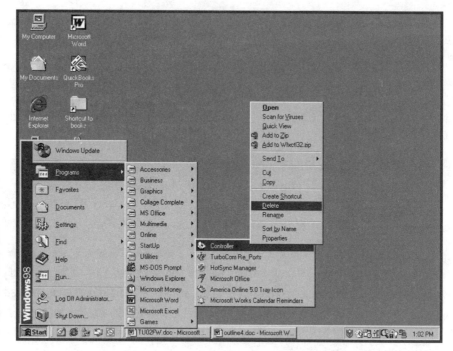

Figure 2.20

To remove a program shortcut from the StartUp program group, right-click on it and choose Delete.

CAUTION

Before you start messing with win.ini and the utilities discussed in the next few sections, try the conventional method of disabling the program first. Try uninstalling it. Try removing it from the StartUp program group. Try disabling it from its own properties. These are all much more graceful methods. Stripping a reference out of win.ini is rather crude, as are the removal methods I tell you about in the next two sections. These crude methods can prevent a particular driver from loading, but unlike traditional uninstalls, they don't clean up after themselves by removing references to the program from your other Windows configuration files.

To edit win.ini, use a utility called Sysedit. It's like Notepad, a simple text editor, except it automatically opens several important Windows startup files. Sysedit is included in the C:\windows folder, but is not directly accessible from the Windows Start menu. Follow these steps:

1. Choose Start/Run. The Run dialog box opens.

2. Type **Sysedit**.

3. Click OK. The System Configuration Editor window appears.

4. Click the win.ini title bar, bringing that window to the front (see Figure 2.21).

5. If you see the program listed on the LOAD= or RUN= line, delete it from there. Leave the LOAD= and RUN= text there. *Be careful not to delete anything else from this file.*

TIP

If you think you might want to add the line back in later, and you don't want to forget the exact wording of it, add a semicolon in front of the line instead of removing it. This is called "remming it out" in techie terms, a designation that comes from the old days of MS-DOS batch files, in which you could disable a line from running by adding REM at its beginning.

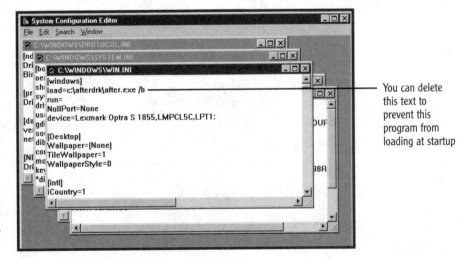

Figure 2.21

Use Sysedit to quickly edit win.ini. Remove startup references to unwanted programs as needed.

You can delete this text to prevent this program from loading at startup

6. Close the System Configuration Editor window, saving your changes.

7. Restart Windows.

You can also disable lines from win.ini using the System Configuration Utility, which you learn about in the following section. That utility only disables entire lines in win.ini; it doesn't let you add lines or remove a portion of a line. In some cases, the LOAD= or RUN= lines have more than one program listed on them, separated by commas, and you will want to remove only one of them. You must do such editing from Sysedit, as you learned about earlier, rather than from the System Configuration Utility.

Disabling Startup Programs in the Registry

Now you're getting into the serious hunting season! If you are trying to track down a pesky unwanted program that loads at startup, and it's not in the StartUp program group or the win.ini file, where is it being called from? Probably the Windows Registry. The Registry is a giant configuration file that Windows processes at startup, telling it what to load, what settings to use, and so on.

Windows comes with a utility program called regedit.exe (found in the C:\windows folder) you can use to edit the Registry, but I don't recommend that beginners (or even intermediates) do this. There is too much potential for error, and for screwing up your system to the point where it won't work anymore. Instead, wherever possible, I prefer to show you how to use the System Configuration Utility, which edits the Registry (as well as other startup files) on your behalf. To learn how to use the System Configuration Utility, follow these steps:

1. Choose Start/Programs/Accessories/System Tools/System Information. The System Information window opens.

2. Choose Tools/System Configuration Utility. The System Configuration Utility dialog box appears.

Here's a shortcut for running the System Configuration Utility: Choose Start/Run, type **msconfig**, and click OK.

3. Click on the Startup tab. A list of all the drivers and programs that load at startup appears (see Figure 2.22).

4. Remove the check mark next to any items that you don't want to execute at startup.

5. Click on OK.

6. Choose File/Close to close the System Information window.

7. Restart the computer to see if your problem is solved.

You also can enable or disable lines from win.ini, system.ini, autoexec.bat, and config.sys from the System Configuration Utility window. Just click on the tab and deselect check boxes for lines you don't want. Remember,

Figure 2.22

Disable certain startup programs or drivers here.

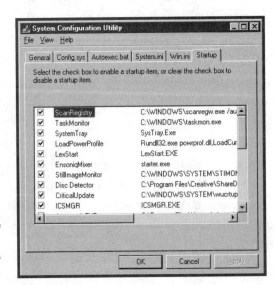

though, this utility merely lets you disable entire lines; if you want to add lines or remove a part of a line, you must use Sysedit, as described in the preceding section.

Correcting a Video Driver Problem

If you start Windows and you see a message that there is a problem with your display, something has probably happened to screw up your video driver. The best thing to do is to reinstall it. If you have the disk that came with your video card, try running its Setup program. If there's no Setup program there, see "Setting Up the Correct Video Drivers" in the Saturday Afternoon session.

Enabling or Disabling the Startup Menu

As you have seen already in this session, you can press F8 quickly at startup, when you see the Starting Windows 98 message, to open a startup menu, allowing you to choose an operational mode for Windows. Some of these special modes can be helpful when troubleshooting problems.

Occasionally, however, a system becomes stuck, so that the Startup menu appears every time you start your PC, whether you press F8 or not. This doesn't hurt anything, but it's annoying.

To control whether the Startup menu appears automatically, you can either use TweakUI or, if you don't have that, change it in the System Configuration Utility or edit the msdos.sys file. I show you all methods here.

If you have TweakUI installed, follow these steps:

1. Choose Start/Settings/Control Panel.
2. Double-click on the TweakUI icon.
3. Click the right-pointing arrow button in the upper-right corner, scrolling through the tabs until the Boot tab comes into view; then select the Boot tab (see Figure 2.23).

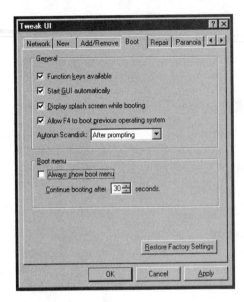

Figure 2.23

The TweakUI
window has more
tabs than can show
at once; scroll
through them with
the right and left
arrow buttons.

4. Select or deselect the Always show boot menu check box. When
   this box is checked, the boot menu always appears; when
   unchecked, it appears only when you press F8 at startup.

5. Click on OK.

6. Restart the computer to test the new setting.

If you have Windows 98, you have the System Configuration Utility at
your disposal, which you learned about earlier in this session. You can use
it to enable or disable the boot menu by doing the following:

1. Choose Start/Programs/Accessories/System Tools/System Information. The System Information window opens.

2. Choose Tools/System Configuration Utility. The System Configuration Utility dialog box appears.

3. On the General tab, click on the Advanced button. The Advanced
   Troubleshooting Settings dialog box opens. See Figure 2.24.

4. Select or deselect the Enable Startup Menu check box to turn the
   boot menu on or off.

5. Click on OK, and then click on OK again to close the dialog boxes.

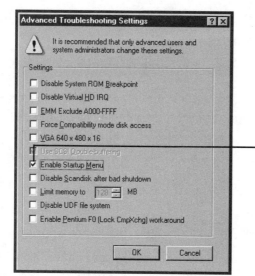

This check box controls the boot menu

Figure 2.24

Turn the boot
menu on or off
from the System
Configuration
Utility's Advanced
Troubleshooting
Settings dialog box.

When you make the change in TweakUI or by using the System Configuration Utility, those programs make the change in a hidden, system file, called msdos.sys, located on your C drive. If you don't have access to TweakUI, you can make this change yourself.

 **CAUTION**   When editing msdos.sys, be very careful not to make any changes to it other than the ones specified here. Otherwise, Windows might not be able to start.

Because msdos.sys is a hidden file, you must set up your Windows display to show hidden files if you have not done so already. Make sure you followed the steps in "Showing All Files" earlier in this session.

The file msdos.sys is also read-only. You can temporarily turn off this attribute, however, to make changes to the file. I show you how in the following steps, as part of the editing procedure:

1. From My Computer, display the contents of your C drive. (Double-click on My Computer, and then double-click on the C drive icon.)

2. Locate the file `msdos.sys` and right-click on it. Then choose Properties from the shortcut menu.

3. Deselect the Read-only check box and click on OK.

TIP Instead of steps 4-8 you can right-click on the file and choose Open with from the short-cut menu. Select Notepad as the program to open it with and click on OK.

4. Choose Start/Programs/Accessories/Notepad. The Notepad program opens.

5. Choose File/Open. The Open dialog box appears.

6. Open the Look in drop-down list and choose your hard disk (C).

7. Open the Files of type drop-down list and choose All files (*.*).

8. Select the file `msdos.sys` and then click on Open.

9. Scroll to the bottom of the file and find the line that starts Boot-Menu=. If you don't see it, add it at the bottom of the file.

10. If you want the Startup menu to appear each time, set the line to BootMenu=1; if you don't want the Startup menu, set it to Boot-Menu=0 (see Figure 2.25).

CAUTION Do not make any other changes to this file. Do not remove extra spaces or extra lines, or the Xs. This file must be at least a certain number of characters in length to work, and those Xs are there to ensure that the file remains above a certain size.

11. Choose File/Exit.

12. When prompted to save your changes, click on Yes.

13. Display the contents of your C drive again in My Computer (see step 1).

14. Right-click on `msdos.sys` and choose Properties.

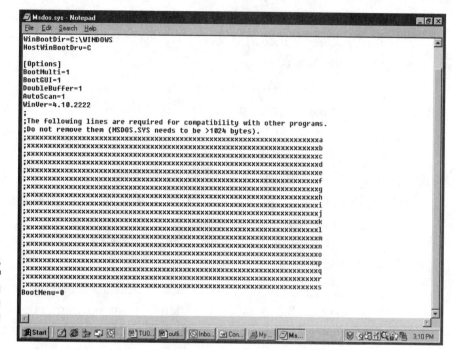

Figure 2.25

Set the BootMenu
to 1 to show the
Startup menu or 0
to not show it.

15. Select the Read-only check box, and then click on OK.

16. Restart the computer to test your new setting.

Fixing Windows Errors

Perhaps Windows starts up okay, but then the problems begin. Programs don't start (more than one program—otherwise suspect the individual program as the problem). Or everything locks up after running a few minutes. Or error messages abound. Windows itself is probably screwed up somehow.

Windows troubleshooting is my least favorite kind. There are several "easy solutions" for fixing Windows problems, each of which takes about 10 minutes. In my experience, however, these fixes often don't solve the problem, leaving me to resort to the more drastic solutions, such as reinstalling Windows. I always try the easy solutions first anyway, though, just in case.

In the following sections, I show you some of the easy fixes. If none of them solve your problem, skip to the "Installing Windows" part of the Saturday Evening session.

Repairing the Windows Registry

As I explained earlier, the Windows Registry is a configuration file critical to Windows operation. It can become corrupted or damaged, either by logical disk errors or by an amateur attempting to edit it and introducing errors.

As I mentioned in the section on startup problems, some serious Registry problems prevent Windows from starting. The Registry Checker kicks in and repairs them in that event and then prompts you to restart your PC.

Other times, however, minor Registry errors overlooked at startup can still cause problems. In addition, errors can be introduced after Windows has already started up. Fortunately, you can run the Registry Checker from within Windows. When the Registry Checker detects a problem, it overwrites the current Registry with the most recent backup it has stored. Therefore, as you can imagine, having a recent backup available is very advantageous. The Registry Checker backs up your Registry every day automatically, but you might also want to back it up after making major system changes (such as installing a new device or program).

The following steps show how to check the Registry from within Windows and how to back it up.

1. Choose Start/Programs/Accessories/System Tools/System Information. The System Information program opens.
2. Choose Tools/Registry Checker. The Registry is checked. If it finds any errors, it restores the most recent backup.

3. If it finds no errors (see Figure 2.26), the Registry Checker asks if you would like to back up the Registry. Choose Yes.

4. At the Backup complete prompt, click on OK.

Figure 2.26

You can back up the Registry now if you want.

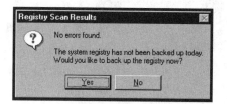

Checking System Files

The Registry keeps track of which files should be employed for what tasks, but for Windows to operate properly, the actual files must be in the right places and must be uncorrupted. If your Registry is okay, check the system files next.

The System File Checker scans the Windows operational files, looking for files listed in the Registry that might be corrupted. If it finds one, it prompts you to reinstall that file from your original Windows disk.

NOTE The System File Checker can also be configured to scan for changed or deleted system files, but usually only computer professionals have the expertise to make such scanning useful. To change what the System File Checker scans for, click on Settings to open its configuration options dialog box.

To run the System File Checker, follow these steps:

1. If the System Information window is not still open from the previous steps, choose Start/Programs/Accessories/System Tools/System Information to open it.

2. Choose Tools/System File Checker. The System File Checker window opens (see Figure 2.27).

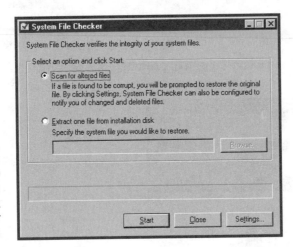

Figure 2.27

Use the System File
Checker to check
the system files for
corruption.

3. Leave the Scan for altered files button selected and click on Start.

4. Wait for the scan to complete. If the scan finds any corrupt files, it prompts you are prompted to replace them; opt to do so.

   When the scan is complete, a message appears to that effect.

5. (Optional) If you are interested in the details of the scan, click on Details. Then click on OK.

6. Click on OK.

7. Click on Close to return to the System Information window.

Replacing a Specific System File

If you get an error message in Windows 98 saying that a particular file is causing a problem, perhaps it has become corrupted. If a general scan with the System File Checker fails to detect and solve the problem (see the preceding steps), you might be able to use the System File Checker to replace that file individually. Here's how:

1. If the System Information window is not still open from the previous steps, choose Start/Programs/Accessories/System Tools/System Information to open it.

2. Choose Tools/System File Checker. The System File Checker window opens (see Figure 2.27).

3. Click on Extract one file from installation disk.

4. Insert the Windows 98 CD-ROM in your drive.

5. Type the name of the file you want to replace. (Or click on Browse, select the file, and click on Open.)

NOTE In step 5, you can select the file from your hard disk (the possibly corrupt copy), or you can type the name. It doesn't matter what source you choose from in step 5, because you are prompted for a path in step 7.

6. Click on Start. An Extract File dialog box appears (see Figure 2.28).

7. Type the path to the CD-ROM (for example, D:\Win98) or click on the topmost Browse button and locate it.

8. Make sure the target location is set in the Save file in box. (If you browsed in step 5, that folder appears here automatically.)

9. Click on OK. You are prompted to back up the existing file.

10. Click on OK again. (If you see a message that the Backup folder does not exist, click on Yes to create it.)

11. Wait for the file replacement to take place. When you see a message that it was successful, click on OK.

12. Close the System Information window when you are finished with it.

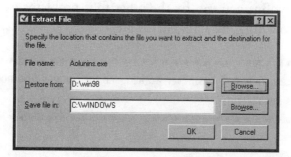

Figure 2.28

Choose the paths for the replacement and the original.

If none of these fixes solve your Windows problem, I'm afraid you'll have to go the more drastic route. You might be able to get away with simply reinstalling Windows (see "Installing Windows" in the Saturday Evening session), but you might end up reformatting your disk and reinstalling everything from scratch. Saturday Evening's session can help you weigh the pros and cons and make a decision.

Fixing a Specific Device

Ah, hardware! I just love buying and installing new gadgets on my system, whether it's the latest rewritable CD drive or a cordless mouse. But when a device doesn't work, frustration can set in.

If the device used to work, but no longer does, what changed? Did you install new software? Other hardware? Did you make changes to Windows settings? Your last action before the device stopped functioning can provide a clue as to what is wrong with it.

There are five reasons why a device might not be working. These are:

- ✿ It's defective.
- ✿ It's not installed correctly.
- ✿ Its drivers are not loaded.
- ✿ It is having a conflict with another device.
- ✿ There is a bug in its software.

Defective devices need to be replaced, of course; I explain how to do that on Sunday. But you can fix the other four problems easily in Windows without touching the actual hardware.

NOTE If the device is new and has never worked, see the Sunday Afternoon session to troubleshoot its installation.

If a bug (that is, an error) in the device's software is causing a problem, visit the manufacturer's Web site. Perhaps an update or patch is available that can correct the problem. See "Downloading from a Manufacturer's Web Site" later in this chapter.

Updating a Device Driver

If a device no longer works after upgrading from Windows 95 to Windows 98, you probably need an updated driver for the device. A *driver* is a file that helps Windows interact with a device. Windows 98 comes with drivers for some of the most popular devices, and most new devices also come with drivers on a disk for use in Windows.

Device drivers can come from any of several sources, including:

- ✿ Windows 98 provides drivers for many of the most common devices on its own CD.

- ✿ Many devices come with a disk containing drivers for various operating systems, including Windows 98.

- ✿ You can employ the Windows Update feature in Windows 98 to search the Microsoft Web site for an updated driver.

- ✿ Many device manufacturers provide updated drivers on their Web sites, free for the downloading.

What to do first? It's a judgment call. If you think you have the needed driver on a disk, continue on to the following steps and try to update the driver. Or, if you are pretty sure you don't have the needed driver, skip ahead to the section "Downloading from a Manufacturer's Web Site."

Ready to update the driver for a device? Then follow these steps:

1. Right-click on the My Computer icon on the desktop and choose Properties from the shortcut menu that appears.

2. Click on the Device Manager tab.

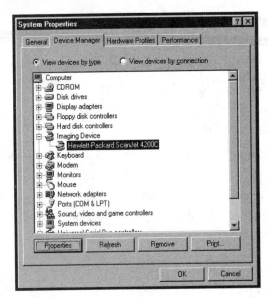

Figure 2.29

Locate the device
in the Device
Manager listing.

3. Locate the device for which you want to update the driver (Click a plus sign to expand a category). (See Figure 2.29).

4. Double-click on the device. Its Properties dialog box appears.

5. Click on the Driver tab.

6. Click on the Update Driver button. An Update Driver Wizard runs.

7. Click on Next.

8. Leave the option Search for a better driver selected and click on Next. A list of sources appears, as in Figure 2.30.

9. Place a check mark next to each location where you want to search. Choose as many as you can, and Windows evaluates the various drivers and chooses the best one. Here are the locations you can choose from:

   ○ If you have a driver on a floppy disk from the manufacturer, choose Floppy disk drives.

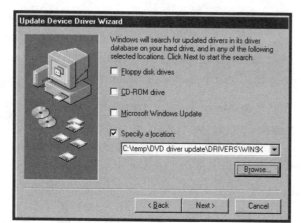

Figure 2.30

Select all the possible sources to search. Windows finds the best driver from these.

⚙ If you have the Windows 98 CD, choose CD-ROM drive.

⚙ If you want to check online at the Microsoft Web site, choose Microsoft Windows Update.

⚙ If you have downloaded a driver from the manufacturer's Web site, choose Specify a location, and then enter the path on your hard disk where you stored the download.

10. Click on Next. Windows searches all the locations you specified.

   If you chose Microsoft Windows Update and you are not currently connected to the Internet, you are prompted to connect.

11. When Windows reports that it is ready to install the driver, click on Next to allow it to do so.

12. If prompted to restart your PC, click on Yes. Your new driver is now installed, and the device should work correctly.

Downloading from a Manufacturer's Web Site

In the following sections, I explain how to get updates from a manufacturer's Web site. This update can be a driver or an updated version of an application. (I refer you back here later in the chapter, when I talk about misbehaving applications.)

For example, when I first got my scanner, the scanning lamp never turned off, no matter how long it was idle. Although this was not a critical problem, I found it annoying. I downloaded a fix from the manufacturer's Web site that corrected the problem.

If you think you might benefit from downloading an update from the device manufacturer's Web site, first you must find out the Web site address. If you're lucky, the address is printed somewhere on the device's documentation. You can also try the obvious address by typing **www.**, the company name, and **.com**, as in www.microsoft.com. Finally, you can search for the company's Web site using a search engine, such as www.yahoo.com. If you can't get the driver from the manufacturer, try the very helpful Web site www.windrivers.com.

NOTE I'm assuming that you know how to start your Internet connection and view a Web page. That's pretty basic stuff. If you need some help with Windows operational basics, check out the book *Learn Windows 98 in a Weekend,* which I wrote with Michael Meadhra.

After you arrive at the manufacturer's home page, where are the downloads? Most sites have an obvious hyperlink, such as Download or Support. Wade your way through until you find the update you want.

For example, suppose I need an updated driver for my scanner. It's a Hewlett-Packard ScanJet 4200C. I find the Hewlett-Packard Web site by taking a guess at the name: www.hp.com. (I am right!) Then I work my way through several layers of pages that narrow down what I'm looking for. Finally, I arrive at the screen shown in Figure 2.31, where links for the available Windows 98 drivers appear. When I get there, I see that there are a variety of *patches* available.

A patch is a program you can run to correct a problem with how the device works. Bingo! One of these patches might just solve the problems I'm having with the device! You might see patches available for your device, or you might see updated drivers or updated software.

To find out what problem a particular patch solves, click More Info

To download a file, click its name

Figure 2.31

Consult manufacturers' Web sites to find available patches to your problems.

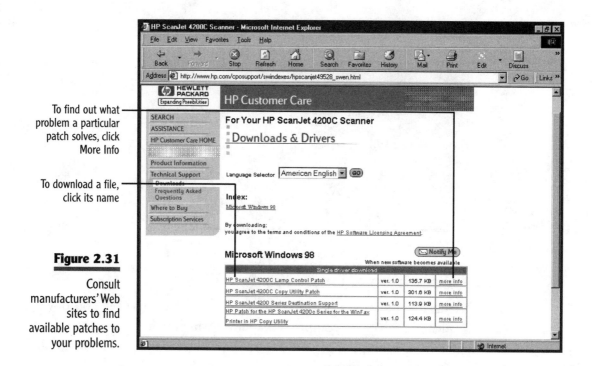

I find a link for downloading the most recent patches for my scanner on its manufacturers' Web site. When I click on a link shown in Figure 2.31, a File Download dialog box appears, asking what I want to do with the file (Figure 2.32). I choose the default (Save this program to disk), click on OK, and a Save As dialog box opens, asking where I want to save it.

You can save the downloaded file anywhere you like, but make sure you remember where you put it! I created a special folder on my hard disk called Temp, in which I place all downloads. That way I never forget where I put one. Select the location (with the Save in drop-down list and by double-clicking on folders) and click on Save. Then wait for the file to be transferred to your PC. You can do other work as it transfers, but do not terminate your Internet connection until it is finished. You can tell that a transfer is still occurring because a bar for it appears in the taskbar.

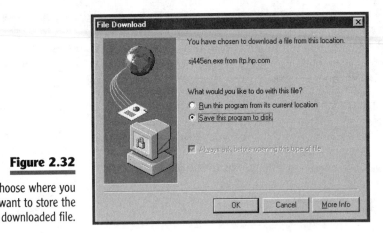

Figure 2.32

Choose where you
want to store the
downloaded file.

Unpacking a Downloaded File

Congratulations, you just downloaded a file! The single file you downloaded is probably a compressed archive, which is like a single package
containing multiple files. When you unpack the package, you make the
individual files available for use.

The next step is to unpack the downloaded file. The procedure for doing
that varies depending on the type of file you downloaded:

❂ **Files with an .exe extension** can be unpacked by double-clicking
on them. Some .exe files are self-extracting archives, which means
that running them simply unpacks one or more files and places
them in the same folder as the downloaded file. Other .exe files are
full-fledged installation programs that update the driver automatically for you.

❂ **Files with a .zip extension** require an unzipping program to decompress them (such as WinZip, available from www.winzip.com). After
you install an unzipping program, use it to unpack the download.
(See the directions that come with that program.) This format is very
common on the Internet in general, but not so common for downloaded drivers, because the manufacturers usually do not assume that
everyone has an unzipping program.

Locate your downloaded file in My Computer and try double-clicking on it. If a setup program starts, work through it. If a dialog box appears indicating that you are unpacking a self-extracting archive, as in Figure 2.33, take note of the folder where it is being unpacked, and then click on Unzip to extract the files.

If unzipped files appear in a new folder, navigate to that folder using My Computer and find a setup program to run. For example, in Figure 2.34, I displayed the new folder and I found a program called SetUp.exe there. That's the one! I double-click on it to run the setup program to install the downloaded patch.

Solving Printer Problems

If your printer isn't working right, your first determination to make is whether the problem lies with the printer itself or with its driver in Windows. An easy way to tell: Haul out the printer's manual, and find out how to run its self-test. Follow the directions given to print a test page. (Usually it involves holding down certain buttons on the printer while

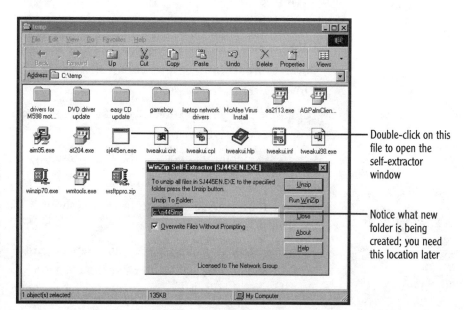

Figure 2.33

When you double-click on some types of .exe files, a self-extractor runs, offering to create a new folder and extract the files into it.

Double-click on this file to open the self-extractor window

Notice what new folder is being created; you need this location later

Figure 2.34

The new folder
created during the
unzipping contains
a SetUp.exe
program I can run
to apply the
downloaded patch.

you turn on the printer's power.) If the test page doesn't look good, your
problem is with the printer itself. Call the technical support phone number listed in the printer's manual for help.

Checking a Printer's Windows Driver

If the test page looks great but you can't print from Windows, make sure
the printer's driver is installed correctly by following these steps:

1. Choose Start/Settings/Printers. The Printers window opens.

    If you don't see your printer listed, skip to "Installing a Printer
    Driver" later in this session.

2. Right-click on your printer's icon and choose Properties. Its
   Properties dialog box opens.

3. On the General tab, click on the Print Test Page button.

    If a test page prints, the printer's drivers are correctly installed.

4. Use the following suggestions to troubleshoot if the test page did
   not print:

    ✿ Check the printer's print queue to make sure it is not paused. To
        do so, click on Cancel to close the Properties dialog box, and
        then double-click on the printer's icon in the Printers window.

From there, open the Printer menu and make sure Pause Printing is not marked. If it is, click on it to toggle off the pause.

✿ If the printout contains garbled characters, click on Cancel to close the Properties dialog box. Then click on the printer's icon and press Delete to remove it. Choose Yes when asked to confirm. Then go to the next section, "Installing a Printer Driver," to reinstall the printer's driver.

✿ If you are having some other kind of problem, call your printer manufacturer's technical support phone number and ask for troubleshooting help.

Installing a Printer Driver

When you run the setup software that comes with a new printer, it usually installs the needed driver correctly. If you don't have setup software for the printer, however, you can use the Add Printer Wizard, as shown in the following steps, to add the printer's driver to your system.

1. Choose Start/Settings/Printers to open the Printers window if it is not already open.

2. Double-click on Add Printer.

3. Click on Next to start the Add Printer Wizard.

4. Choose Local printer and click on Next.

5. Do one of the following:

   ✿ Choose the printer's manufacturer and model from the list provided and click on Next.

   ✿ Insert the disk provided by the manufacturer, and then click on Have Disk, and follow the prompts to select the model.

6. Select the port the printer is connected to from the list of ports that appears. Then click on Next.

7. Type a descriptive name for the printer in the Printer name text box. This description appears in the Print dialog box in applications from which you print.

8. Choose Yes or No to make this printer your default printer or not. Then click on Next.

9. Choose Yes to print a test page. A dialog box appears asking whether it printed okay.

10. Click on Yes if the test page is okay, or No to open a print troubleshooting box, and then follow along with it to try to fix the problem.

11. Click on Finish. If prompted, insert the Windows CD-ROM into your drive and click OK to continue.

The printer's drivers are now installed (or reinstalled, as the case may be.)

Managing Device Conflicts

A device conflict occurs when two devices are trying to claim the same system resource for themselves. There are three basic types of resources that devices use. These include the following:

○ **Interrupt Requests (IRQs)**. These are access paths to the processor. Each device with an IRQ can interrupt the processor's main operations to say "Hey, I need something here!" IRQs are numbered 0 through 15. Generally speaking, each device should have its own IRQ.

○ **Input/Output Range**. These are segments of the computer's memory, and each device should have its own reserved area.

○ **DMA channels**. These are channels, similar to IRQs, that some devices use to communicate with the processor. Sound cards and floppy drives typically use DMA channels; most other devices do not. You probably do not have any DMA channel conflicts, because there are more than enough of them to go around among the devices that use them.

The preceding resources are usually assigned automatically in Windows by the Plug-and-Play feature. Allowing Windows to assign resources is a good idea, in most cases. But some devices can have quirks that require

them to use certain addresses or IRQs; and when two devices want the same resource, a conflict occurs, causing one or both devices to malfunction (or fail to function at all).

Resolving a Device Conflict in Windows

The standard way of resolving device conflicts in Windows is to turn off the Plug-and-Play assignment for a device and to specify an alternative set of resources it should use.

The following steps show how to look for and resolve a device conflict.:

1. Right-click on the My Computer icon on the desktop and choose Properties.
2. Click on the Device Manager tab.
3. Look for a device with a yellow circle and an exclamation point next to it, as in Figure 2.35. This indicates a device conflict.

   If you do not see any devices with the yellow circle, you probably do not have any conflicts and can skip the rest of these steps.

Figure 2.35

Device conflicts show up with a yellow circle and an exclamation point next to one or both of the devices involved in the conflict.

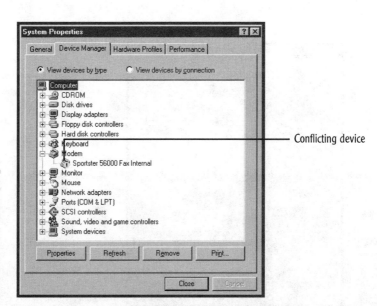

4. Double-click on the device with the conflict. Its Properties dialog box appears.

5. Click on the Resources tab.

6. Check the Conflicting device list. If a conflict is listed, note whether it is an Input/Output Range conflict or an IRQ conflict.

7. Deselect the Use Automatic Settings check box.

8. Open the Setting Based On drop-down list and choose a new configuration. Keep trying different configurations until you find one that reports No Conflicts in the Conflicting Device list (see Figure 2.36).

9. Click on OK to close the dialog box.

10. Click on Close to close the System Properties dialog box.

11. Try using the device; it should work now.

In rare cases, all the configurations on the list (refer to step 8) have a conflict. If you face this situation, you can try changing the Interrupt Request and the Input/Output Range separately. Keep choosing configurations from the Setting Based On list until you find a configuration

Figure 2.36

In this case, Configuration 0002 has no conflicts, so I can use that one.

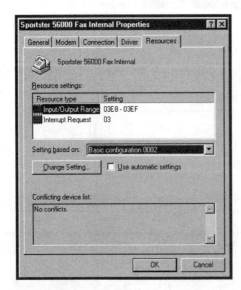

with only one conflict. Make a note of what it is (Interrupt Request or Input/Output Range). Then click on the matching line in the Resource Settings list. Next, click on Change Setting. One of two things can happen: You might see a message that the setting cannot be modified, or you might see a dialog box containing alternate settings. If you see the latter, try a different setting. Repeat this procedure until you find a setting that produces no conflicts.

If Windows tells you that the setting cannot be modified, you have one last remedy to try. In the Conflicting device list, notice the device that is the other half of the conflict. Then try modifying the settings for that device so it no longer conflicts with this one.

Checking for Free IRQs

Your system has 16 interrupt requests, but it's amazing how quickly they all get taken, leaving you with none free. If you are unable to find a configuration that resolves the device conflict (see the preceding section), perhaps your system is simply "full" as far as IRQs are concerned. To check IRQ allocation, do the following:

1. From the Device Manager window (refer to Figure 2.35), double-click on the Computer icon at the top of the tree. The Computer Properties dialog box appears.

2. Make sure the Interrupt Request (IRQ) option button is selected. A list of the IRQs and what devices are using each one appears (see Figure 2.37).

3. Scroll through the list. If no IRQs are free, your system is "full."

4. Click on OK to close the dialog box.

No free IRQs? You have one last thing you can try. Your computer has two COM (serial) ports built-in, COM1 and COM2, and each of them has an Interrupt Request and an Input/Output Range reserved for its use. Notice in Figure 2.37, for example, that IRQ 3 is assigned to COM2.

Now look on the back of your PC for a nine-pin connector with nothing plugged into it. This is a free COM port. On some older systems, one of

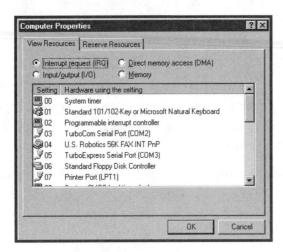

Figure 2.37

Check out the
IRQ assignments
here to see if
any are free.

the COM ports might be 25-pin instead of nine. Look for a label or etching somewhere around a port to confirm what it is; it might say either COM or Serial.

If you aren't using one or both of your COM ports, you can disable one to free up its resources for some other device to use. To do so, you must go into the BIOS setup program—which isn't nearly as scary as it sounds. See the following section to learn about the BIOS, and then see "Disabling a COM Port in the BIOS Setup" to free up a COM port's IRQ.

Understanding the System BIOS

Even if you don't need to free up any more IRQs, you might want to read the following general information about the system BIOS. It's interesting stuff, and you might need to work with the BIOS on Sunday when you install new hardware.

The BIOS setup program is the low-level setup for your computer. (BIOS stands for Basic Input/Output System, by the way.) The BIOS is an automatically executed startup routine that runs tests and allocates resources before Windows loads. This BIOS routine is stored on a ROM (Read-Only Memory) chip mounted on the motherboard. Some people refer to

this as the *ROM-BIOS*, which is its full name. The essential parts of the BIOS program are hard-coded into the chip so they are never lost.

The BIOS settings are permanently stored on the ROM-BIOS chip and can't be changed without a special BIOS-updating utility. Think of the BIOS settings as the house rules. However, sometimes you might want to break one of those rules. For example, the default BIOS might specify that the system has one floppy drive, but your system has two. In that case, you could use the BIOS setup program to enter an override to the BIOS.

When the system starts up, it first reads the original BIOS settings to get the baseline, and then it reads the overrides to make any needed changes. For example, the override message "There are two floppy drives" would override the original BIOS statement "There is one floppy drive."

A special microchip, called a CMOS chip, stores these overrides. (CMOS stands for Complementary Metal-Oxide Semiconductor.) This chip is volatile, like regular memory; in other words, a CMOS chip requires power to sustain its data. But unlike regular memory, the CMOS chip requires only a tiny amount of electricity. The computer's battery provides all the power it needs.

NOTE When your computer battery dies, you lose all the information on the CMOS chip, including the correct date and time and the types of disks installed on the computer. In the absence of CMOS data, the BIOS reverts to its default settings, so the computer might be able to start even when the battery is dead. However, the drives often behave strangely if the default settings do not match the actual system. You'll learn how to change a battery on Sunday afternoon.

On most systems, just after you turn on the computer, you see a message like this:

```
Press F1 to enter Setup
```

This message might show a different key to press (Del and Esc are popular); just do whatever it says to enter the BIOS setup program. Be quick, though, because you can enter setup only as long as that message appears, and the message goes away after a few seconds. If you miss it, just restart the computer (by pressing its Reset button or pressing Ctrl+Alt+Delete) and try again.

After you make it into the BIOS setup program, you see its opening screen. Every BIOS has a different setup program, and even different versions from the same company have different controls. Depending on your system, you might see either a text-based or graphics-based display. Figures 2.38 and 2.39 show examples of each.

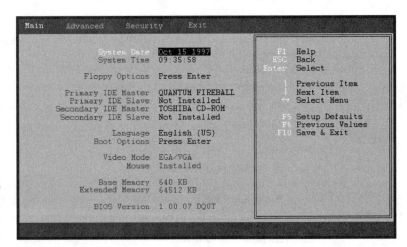

Figure 2.38

Here's a text-based BIOS setup program.

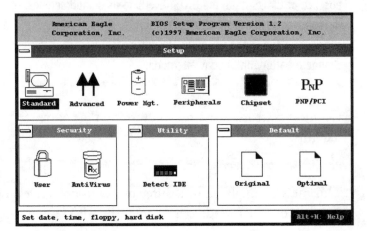

Figure 2.39

This BIOS setup program has a graphical interface.

NOTE There are hundreds of different BIOS setup programs, made by dozens of companies. I show you two examples in this session—one text-based and one graphical. Chances are good that yours will be different, but it should be similar to one or the other.

Somewhere on the screen, the BIOS setup program tells you how to get help. In Figure 2.38, for example, you press F1. (Notice F1 Help in the right column.) In Figure 2.39, you press Alt+H for help. (Notice Alt+H: Help in the lower-right corner.) Press the designated key(s) to display instructions for your program. The instructions in this book are general and do not apply to every situation.

Most BIOS setup programs do not display all their options on the screen at once. For example, in Figure 2.38, the word Main is brighter than the other three words across the top, indicating that the displayed options are the Main options. If you look at the instructions in Figure 2.38, you see a horizontal arrow next to Select Menu. That symbol tells you to press the right or left arrow key to move through the menus. You press the right arrow from the screen shown in Figure 2.38 to open the Advanced menu, for example. Almost all text-based BIOS programs work this way.

In a graphical BIOS setup program like Figure 2.39, you might see a series of icons in boxes, instead of menu names across the top. Each icon represents a menu. Just double-click on an icon to view a menu's options.

Disabling a COM Port in the BIOS Setup

Somewhere in your BIOS setup program, you can find a place to control the COM ports. The exact path to it varies; it might be under Peripheral Configuration.

For example, in the program shown in Figure 2.38, you can display the Advanced menu and then select Peripheral Configuration. Then you select the COM port you want to disable and press Enter. A drop-down menu explains your choices, as shown in Figure 2.40. Choose Disabled from the list and press Enter. Then exit from the BIOS program, saving your changes.

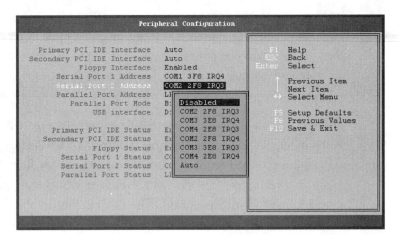

Figure 2.40

Disabling a COM
port in a typical
text-based BIOS
setup program.

CAUTION ◆◆◆◆◆◆◆◆◆◆◆◆◆◆◆◆◆◆◆◆◆◆◆◆◆◆◆◆◆◆◆◆◆◆

Be careful not to disable a COM port that is in use! If you disable the COM port that
your mouse is attached to, for example, the mouse won't work anymore. A PS/2 mouse
(a little round plug) does not use a COM port, so you don't have to worry about accidentally disabling that kind of mouse.

◆◆◆◆◆◆◆◆◆◆◆◆◆◆◆◆◆◆◆◆◆◆◆◆◆◆◆◆◆◆◆◆◆◆

In the sample graphical BIOS setup program (refer to Figure 2.39), you
double-click on the Peripherals icon in the Setup window. A window
appears in which you can set the COM and LPT (parallel) port configuration. From there, you double-click on the line for the COM port you
want and make your selection from the small pop-up box, as shown in
Figure 2.41. Next, press Enter to close the window and exit the BIOS
setup program, saving your changes.

NOTE Some programs use the term Onboard Serial Port rather than COM port. It's the same
thing.

Yes, that's all there is to it! But don't feel like you wasted your time learn-
ing about BIOS setup just for that one little task; you can revisit your
BIOS setup program on Sunday if you decide to install a new drive on
your system.

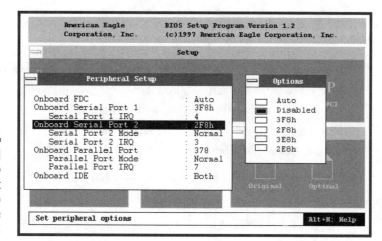

Figure 2.41

In this graphical
BIOS setup
program, you select
which ports to
disable or enable
from a pop-up box.

Fixing a Specific Program

You've been troubleshooting from the top down in this chapter. First, you looked at big scary problems, like the computer not starting at all. Then you narrowed down to individual devices. Now, finally, you're ready to look at problems with individual programs.

When a program doesn't work, you probably experience one of the following symptoms; each has its own fix.

○ Nothing happens at all. This is probably a Windows problem, rather than a problem with the individual application. Restart the PC and then try again. If the problem still occurs, and it happens only with this program, uninstall and reinstall the program, as described later in this session.

○ You see an error message saying there is a missing file. See "Locating a Missing File" later in this session.

○ The program runs, but then locks up. If it's a Windows program, uninstall and reinstall. If it's a DOS-based program, see "Configuring a DOS-Based Program" later in this session.

Locating a Missing File

If a program can't find all the files it needs to run, it gives you an error message reporting which file is missing. The needed file might have been deleted when you uninstalled another program, for example, or you might have deleted it yourself accidentally. When you see such an error message, jot down the name of the missing file. For example, you might see a message like the one in Figure 2.42.

Your mission: To find that file on your hard disk and copy it to the needed location.

You're probably thinking, "Wait a minute, if the file has been deleted, why would it turn up somewhere else on my hard disk?" Actually, it might not. It's a 50/50 chance either way. But some other program might use that same file and have a copy of it in its own folder, so you might get lucky.

Figure 2.42

The program can't start because it can't find one of its files.

CAUTION

Finding a file with the same name as the needed one does not guarantee a fix. Perhaps the name match is a coincidence, and the found file is not exactly the same as the needed file. But again, it's worth a shot. The alternative is to reinstall the program.

Finding the Missing File

To find a file, use Windows' Find feature:

1. Choose Start/Find/Files or Folders. The Find dialog box opens.

2. Enter the file name in the Named list box (see Figure 2.43).

3. Open the Look in drop-down list and select your hard disk (or the drive on which you want to look).

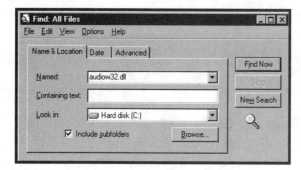

Figure 2.43

Use Find to search for a missing file.

4. Make sure the Include subfolders check box is marked.

5. Click on Find Now and wait for the search to take place. The results appear in a pane below the window, as in Figure 2.44.

Notice in Figure 2.44 that more than one file with the same name was found. Which should you use? It's hard to tell. Usually the one with the date that most closely matches the date of the executable file (the program itself) is the right choice. If you don't know the date of the program itself, try using the one with the latest date.

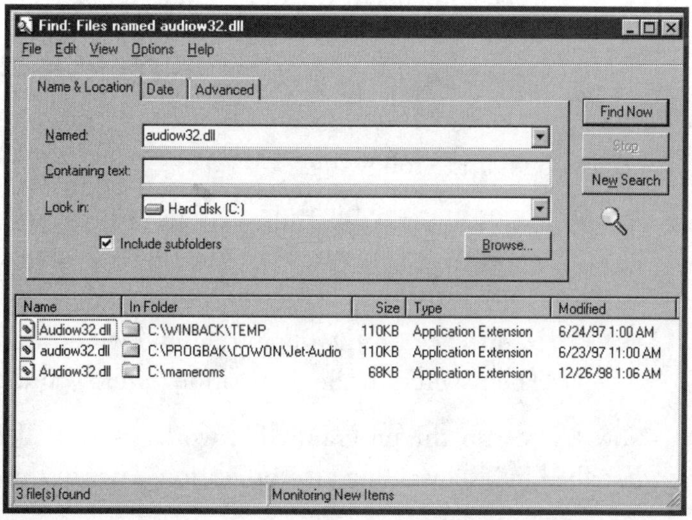

Figure 2.44

The results of the search appear below.

NOTE   You can find out the date on the executable file by locating it on your hard disk, right-clicking on it, and choosing Properties. Information about the file appears, including its date.

If you find a copy of the missing file, just copy it to the needed location and you're all set. See the following section.

Copying the Missing File to the Needed Location

Sometimes the error message reports the needed location for the missing file, such as C:\windows. If so, that's where you want to put the copy if you find one. If no location is reported (as in Figure 2.42), you want to put the file in the same folder as the executable file (that is, the file that ends in .exe, the one that runs the program).

To find out the location of the executable file, right-click on the shortcut, choose Properties, and look in the Target text box (see Figure 2.45).

Now that you know where the file goes, copy it there from the Find window. To do so, follow these steps:

1. Open the contents of the destination in a My Computer window. (To do so, double-click on My Computer, double-click on the drive, double-click on the folder, and keep going until you arrive at the right location.)

2. Do one of the following:

   ✿ Right-drag the file from the Find window to the destination window. When you drop it, a shortcut menu appears; choose Copy Here.

   ✿ Right-click on the file in the Find window and choose Copy. Then switch to the destination window and choose Edit/Paste.

Now try to run the program. If it works—great! If not, reinstall it, as described in "Reinstalling an Application" later in this session.

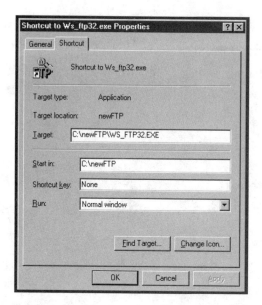

Figure 2.45

This shortcut tells you where to find the executable file that runs the program.

Uninstalling an Application

If you can't make a program work, you might want to uninstall it from your hard disk to free up the space. You also might want to uninstall a program before trying to reinstall it. (This is usually not necessary, but I sometimes try it if reinstalling doesn't work, because uninstalling sometimes removes a corrupted file that reinstalling cannot replace if it already exists.)

Some programs have their own Uninstall utilities. You might find an Uninstall command on the Start menu, in the same folder as the program itself. For example, in Figure 2.46, the HP ScanJet software has an Uninstall listed.

If there is no Uninstall for the program, try uninstalling it from Windows itself with the following procedure:

1. Choose Start/Settings/Control Panel.
2. Double-click on Add/Remove Programs.

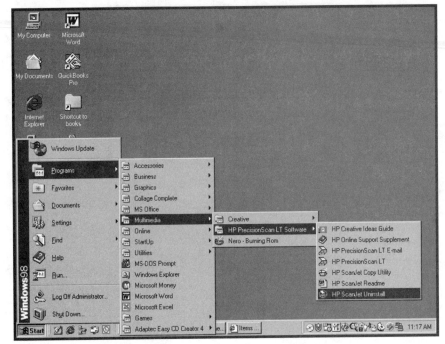

Figure 2.46

If a program
has an Uninstall
utility, use it.

3. On the Install/Uninstall tab, click the program you want to uninstall.

4. Click on Add/Remove.

5. Follow the prompts that appear to uninstall the software. The exact procedure varies depending on the program.

Reinstalling an Application

You can reinstall a program right over the top of an existing installation of it, and things will probably work fine. If a program is malfunctioning, I often reinstall it without first uninstalling. If the program still malfunctions after reinstallation, I go back and try uninstalling before I reinstall.

Many programs on CD launch automatically when you put the CD in the drive. If the program is not installed, the CD launches the Setup program. If the program is already installed, the CD launches the application itself.

If you place the application's CD in the drive and the application starts, close the application. Then do the following:

1. Make sure the setup disk for the application is in the drive.
2. Choose Start/Settings/Control Panel.
3. Double-click on Add/Remove Programs.
4. Click on Install.
5. Click on Next to allow Windows to search the disk drives for a setup program.
6. Click on Finish to run the Setup program.
7. Follow the prompts to set up the application. (It's different for every program.)

Now try the program and see if it works! If not, try uninstalling it and reinstalling again.

If the program still doesn't work and you've tried everything, check the manual that came with it. Perhaps there is a technical support number you can call to get some help.

Configuring a DOS-Based Program

Most programs are Windows-based these days, designed to run specifically under Windows. However, some older programs were written to run under MS-DOS, an older operating system. You can run such programs on a Windows computer in most cases, but they can require some special configuration.

Setting Up a DOS-Based Program

The following steps show how to set up a DOS-based program to run under Windows 98. It's an optimistic procedure, which depends on everything working as it should. Try this first and resort to the procedures later in this session only if this doesn't work.

1. Insert the CD or floppy for the program.

2. Browse the file listing for the program and locate the setup program (usually Setup or Install). Then double-click on it.

3. If the installation program appears in a pinched-looking window,
rather than fullscreen, press Alt+Enter to make it fill the entire
screen.

4. Follow the prompts to complete the installation.

If you are not sure what to pick for an option, stick with the
default.

If the program asks whether it should detect your sound or video,
choose Yes.

If the program asks whether you want it to be set up to be
launched from within Windows, choose Yes.

If the program wants to modify your setup files (Config.sys and
Autoexec.bat), choose No. DOS-based programs assume that you are
running MS-DOS, rather than Windows, and might modify these
startup files in ways that could hamper Windows' performance.

5. When the program is finished, if you see a DOS prompt, type **exit**
and press Enter.

6. If the setup program told you to restart your computer, do so.

7. Browse your disk's file listing and locate the folder where the new
program was installed.

8. Locate the file that runs the new program and double-click on it.
The documentation that came with the program should tell you
what file to use; see the following note for help with this.

NOTE   If you see a file that ends in .pif, use that file to run the program. PIF files are shortcuts
to DOS applications that include special running instructions that help them run better
under Windows. If a DOS program comes with a PIF file, you should use it.

If you see a .bat file, use that. If there are no .pif or .bat files, look for a .com or .exe file
with a name similar to the program name.

9. After you're sure the program works, create a shortcut for it on your desktop.

To create a shortcut, right-drag (that is, drag it with your right mouse button held down) to your desktop and choose Create Shortcut(s) Here from the menu that appears when you drop it.

Troubleshooting DOS Program Operation

If a DOS-based program doesn't work using the preceding setup routine, you probably need to make some changes to its properties.

When you make changes to the properties for a DOS program, Windows creates a separate shortcut (with a PIF extension) to hold those changes. You then use the PIF file to run the program.

What changes should you make? Well, the best place to start is the Windows Help system's MS-DOS Programs Troubleshooter. To locate it, choose Start/Help, click on the Index tab, look up MS-DOS Programs, and then click on Troubleshooting. Next, click on the Click here link and use the controls that appear in the right pane to walk through the troubleshooter (see Figure 2.47).

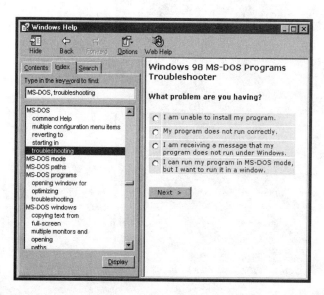

Figure 2.47

Windows Help can offer suggestions for configuring your DOS program to run.

To display the Properties dialog box for the program, right-click on it and choose Properties. Notice that the Properties dialog box for a DOS-based program or PIF file has more tabs than for a regular (Windows) program. Some of the most common changes to make to properties for MS-DOS programs include the following:

- If the program starts with the window squashed (that is, not full screen), you can switch it to full screen by pressing Alt+Enter. But if you set the Usage setting on the Screen tab to Full-screen, as in Figure 2.48, it always starts full screen.

- Some DOS programs have their own shortcut key combinations that you might be accustomed to using. If these key combinations conflict with Windows' own key combinations, the Windows ones take precedence. To make the DOS application's shortcut key combinations dominant, deselect any of the check boxes in the Windows shortcut keys area on the Misc tab (see Figure 2.49).

- If your DOS program locks up every time your screen saver kicks in, deselect the Allow screen saver check box on the Misc tab.

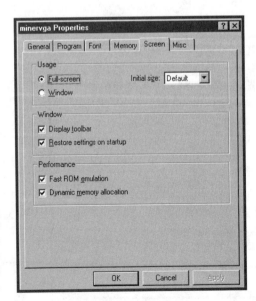

Figure 2.48

The Screen tab controls how the program appears within Windows.

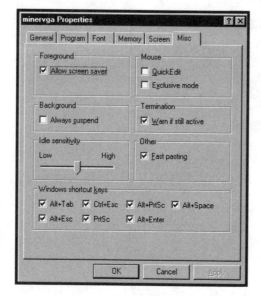

Figure 2.49

The Misc tab controls shortcut keys, screen saver use, and other features.

- Some older programs require you to type switches or parameters after the command to run them at the DOS prompt. To execute those extra instructions every time the program runs, enter the extra text on the Cmd line on the Program tab.

- The Close on exit check box, also on the Program tab, specifies whether the DOS window closes when you exit the program. Usually this is a good thing, but if you are trying to troubleshoot why a program isn't working under Windows, you might want to read any error messages that appear before the program terminates. In such cases, you can deselect this check box so that the DOS window with the error messages remains onscreen until you type **exit**.

- If the program does not run from Windows, and you have tried everything, you might need to run it in MS-DOS mode. This restarts the PC each time you run the program, so that the Windows interface isn't even loaded. When you exit the program, the PC restarts and reloads Windows 98. To set this up, click on Advanced on the Program tab to see the Advanced Program

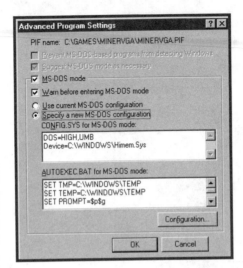

Figure 2.50

Set a program to
run in MS-DOS
mode from the
Advanced Program
Settings dialog box.

Settings dialog box (see Figure 2.50). Click on the MS-DOS mode
check box to turn it on.

○ Some programs running in MS-DOS mode require special addi-
tions or subtractions to the computer's startup files. You can set
these up by clicking on Specify a new MS-DOS configuration in
the Advanced Program Settings dialog box and entering the custom
Autoexec.bat and Config.sys files in the boxes provided. It can be a
little tricky knowing what to put there; beginners might need to
call a techie friend for help at this point.

Take a Break

Whew! What a jam-packed morning you've had. At this point, your computer should be problem free, and ready to tune up. This afternoon, I
show you lots of activities you can perform to improve your system's performance. So go get some lunch and come back ready to go!

SATURDAY AFTERNOON

Enhancing System Performance

- ✿ Improving System Speed
- ✿ Updating Your System
- ✿ Saving Disk Space
- ✿ Improving the Display
- ✿ Making the Computer Easier to Use

ow that your PC is running with no obvious problems, it's time to tune it up to top performance. In this chapter, I show you all kinds of ways to make your PC run better, faster, or more efficiently.

If, after completing this morning's session, your PC is still not running right, don't do this session now. Instead, skip ahead to the Saturday Evening session to take more drastic troubleshooting measures.

Improving System Speed

There's no way around it. The only way to significantly improve a computer's speed is to upgrade its hardware. (I talk about that on Sunday.) However, you can speed up your computer in small ways, garnering perhaps a 10 to 15 percent gain in speed, with some of the following techniques.

Defragmenting the Disk

To understand fragmentation and defragmenting, you need to know something about how files are stored on a hard disk.

The storage system on a hard disk is not sequential. For example, suppose you have a word processing document that takes up 18 clusters (that is, organizational units) on the hard disk. Those clusters are not necessarily adjacent to each other; they might be scattered all over the disk. The File Allocation Table (FAT) keeps a record of which 18 clusters that file uses, and when you open the file, the disk's read/write head hops around gathering up the pieces so they can be assembled into a whole file in your word processor.

When a file is not stored in all-adjacent clusters, it's considered a fragmented file. As you can imagine, hopping all over the disk to pick up the fragments takes time, which is why fragmentation slows down your system's performance.

How does fragmentation happen in the first place? Well, when your hard disk is empty, files are written to it in sequential clusters. Suppose, for example, you save a spreadsheet file that uses five clusters. Then perhaps you install another program. The new files are written right next to your spreadsheet file. Now, you reopen the spreadsheet file and enter more data, and it ends up needing a total of nine clusters. No clusters are available next to the original five, so the additional four clusters' worth of data must go somewhere else. Over time, your file can be split into many different clusters all over the disk.

When you defragment, a special program rearranges the content of your hard disk so that all files are stored in sequential clusters. That way, when you open the files, the disk read/write head reads from a single spot rather than having to hop around, so it can read faster.

Therefore, for best performance, you should defragment your disk regularly (for example, once a month). This procedure can't turn a slow and old system into a powerhouse, but it can result in a modest speedup in activities involving the hard disk.

To run the Disk Defragmenter in Windows, follow these steps:

1. Choose Start/Programs/Accessories/System Tools/Disk Defragmenter.

   The Select Drive dialog box asks which drive you want to defragment (see Figure 3.1). You can defragment only one drive at a time.

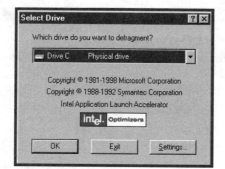

Figure 3.1

Select the drive to
be defragmented.

> **NOTE** You can defragment a floppy disk or other removable disk, but it's probably not worth
> the trouble. Most likely, you will not open files from such disks very often.

---

2. Select your hard disk from the list of drives. Then click on OK.

   If you have more than one hard disk, you need to repeat steps 2
   through 5 for each drive.

> **NOTE** If you are using the Windows 95 version of the Disk Defragmenter, a message box
> appears telling you how defragmented the drive is and suggesting a course of action.
> You don't see this in the Windows 98 version.

---

3. Click on Start (in Windows 95) or OK (in Windows 98) to start
   the defragmentation process.

4. Wait for the drive to be defragmented. To entertain yourself while
   you're waiting, click on Show Details to watch a graphical represen-
   tation of the proceedings, as shown in Figure 3.2.

5. When it finishes, the program asks if you want to quit. Click on
   Yes if all your hard drives are done or No to go back to step 2 and
   choose another drive.

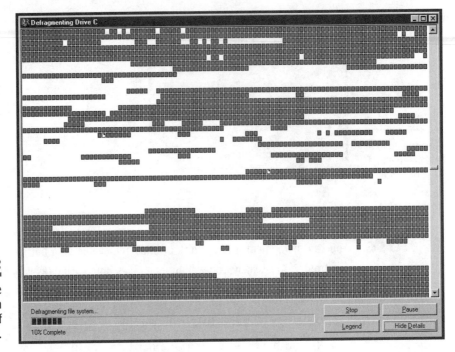

Figure 3.2

You can watch the
defragmentation
take place if
you want.

TIP If Disk Defragmenter displays a message like "Disk Contents Changed, Restarting," even when you haven't touched the computer, programs running in the background might be interfering. Close all other open programs, including any programs in the system tray that you can. (See this morning's session for help with that.) A Microsoft Office utility called Find Fast can also be the culprit in frequent restarts of the defragmenting process. This utility indexes your Office data files so they open more quickly, but it operates in the background and can interfere with the Disk Defragmenter. If the problem continues and you have Microsoft Office installed, open the Control Panel (Start/Settings/Control Panel) and double-click on Find Fast. Choose Index/Pause Indexing. Resume the indexing (by choosing that same command again) when you finish defragmenting or just leave it turned off; it doesn't help your system performance very much anyway.

Setting Cache Size

Caches are blocks of memory set aside to temporarily store data the processor has just used and might need again soon. Using a cache makes your PC run faster, because memory access is much faster than disk access.

• •

NOTE FYI: Have you heard the term *buffer* before? Buffers are related to caches. A buffer is a holding area in memory for data waiting to be processed or sent to an output device. For example, when you print, the print job waits in a print buffer for the printer to print it. Also, when you create a CD-ROM with a writable CD drive, if the PC sends data to the drive faster than it can write it, the excess data waits in the drive's buffer until it can be written.

On MS-DOS systems, it was common to include a line in the CONFIG.SYS file (a start-up file) indicating the number of buffers you wanted (that is, the amount of memory to reserve for buffer use). Windows takes care of buffering automatically, so indicating the desired buffer setting is no longer required (and might actually even degrade system performance).

• •

Both your hard disk and your CD-ROM drive employ buffering systems. You can sometimes slightly improve the performance of a drive by increasing its cache setting. (You can always decrease that setting again later if the larger setting causes problems.)

To check and change drive cache settings, follow these steps:

1. In Windows, right-click on My Computer and choose Properties.
2. Select the Performance tab in the System Properties dialog box that appears.
3. Click on File System. The File System Properties dialog box opens.
4. On the Hard Disk tab (see Figure 3.3), open the Typical role of this computer drop-down list and choose Network server.

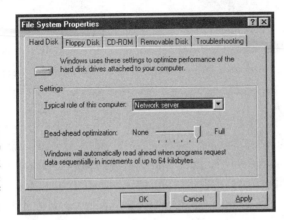

Figure 3.3

Choose Network
server for the
typical role of
the computer.

NOTE   In step 4, it's okay to choose Network server even if your computer is not on a network
and is not a server. This simply sets the drive's cache to the largest value.

5. Make sure the Read-ahead optimization slider is set to Full (all the
   way to the right).

6. Select the CD-ROM tab.

7. Make sure the Supplemental cache size slider is set to Large (all the
   way to the right), as shown in Figure 3.4.

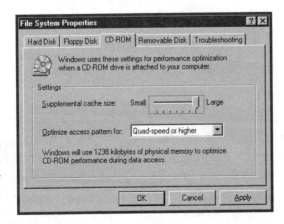

Figure 3.4

Set performance
properties for
the CD-ROM
drive here.

8. Make sure the Optimize access pattern for drop-down list is set to Quad-speed or higher.

9. If you have any removable drives (such as a Zip drive), click the Removable Disk tab. (Skip to step 11 if you do not.)

10. Make sure the Enable write-behind caching on all removable disk drives check box is marked.

11. Click on OK.

12. Click on Close to close the File System Properties dialog box.

13. If you see a message that says you must restart your computer, click on Yes to do so.

Checking for DOS Compatibility Mode

If you have certain DOS-based programs loaded in your startup files when you install Windows 95/98, Windows runs in a special DOS compatibility mode so those programs can continue to function. Perhaps you don't need those programs anymore, but Windows has no way of knowing. DOS compatibility mode can make Windows run much slower than normal.

◆◆

Some viruses cause Windows to operate in DOS-compatibility mode. If you find that your PC is running in DOS-compatibility mode, check your system for viruses, just to be on the safe side.

◆◆

To find out whether your system is running in DOS compatibility mode, follow these steps:

1. Right-click on My Computer and choose Properties. The System Properties dialog box appears.

2. Select the Performance tab. It should say Your system is configured for optimal performance. If it doesn't, you see an

explanation about what is forcing the system to run in DOS compatibility mode.

3. Make a note of the recommended change and change your startup files accordingly. You can use Sysedit, which you learned about in the "Disabling Startup Programs from win.ini" section in the Saturday Morning session, to modify your Config.sys and Autoexec.bat files.

4. Restart the computer.

5. Return to the Performance tab (steps 1 and 2), which should now report that your system is optimally configured. If it doesn't, repeat steps 3 and 4.

Configuring Virtual Memory

Windows requires a tremendous amount of memory to operate. However, not all systems have lots of memory, and the good folks at Microsoft have long known this. So, they came up with an ingenious scheme called virtual memory. *Virtual memory* uses a portion of your hard disk to simulate extra memory (that is, RAM) when more is needed than the system actually contains. Another name for virtual memory is *swap file*.

Here's how it works: Windows sets aside a portion of your hard disk, and whenever it needs more memory than you have, it copies data from memory to the hard disk for temporary storage. Then it uses the freed-up memory space for further processing. When it comes to the operation that requires the data temporarily stored on the hard disk, it swaps that data with some data in real memory, making the data it needs available again. That's where the name "swap file" comes from.

NOTE   As the swap file swaps, your hard disk's light flashes and you can hear its read/write heads moving. Your computer might also seem to bog down temporarily when this occurs. (This activity is sometimes called *churning*.) The less memory your PC has, the more often it happens. That's why adding memory to a computer can often speed up its performance—it decreases the system's reliance on virtual memory.

Early versions of Windows worked better if you changed the default settings for virtual memory, but Windows 95 and 98 use virtual memory very well automatically. Most people should never need to change the virtual memory settings in Windows 95/98.

There are three settings you can control for virtual memory: Minimum, Maximum, and Hard Disk. Beginners (and even intermediates!) should not change the Minimum or Maximum settings. There are some minor improvements to potentially be made with these settings on systems with extremely full hard disks, but non-techies are likely to do more harm than good. If you have a very full hard disk, simply delete some files from it to free up some space.

The Hard Disk setting specifies which of your system's hard disks should be used for virtual memory. The default is your C drive. If you have more than one hard disk, and you are low on disk space on C (perhaps less than 100 megabytes), you might want to change this setting to use that other drive.

To change the drive that the swap file uses, follow these steps:

1. Right-click on My Computer on the desktop and choose Properties. The System Properties dialog box opens.
2. Select the Performance tab.
3. Click on Virtual Memory. The Virtual Memory dialog box opens.
4. Choose the Let me specify my own virtual memory settings option. The controls to do so become available, as in Figure 3.5.
5. Open the Hard disk drop-down list and choose a different hard disk.

♦ ♦

CAUTION Do not set a network drive for your virtual memory. It can be too slow and can actually degrade the performance of your PC. For the same reason, do not use a removable hard disk, such as a Zip drive.

♦ ♦

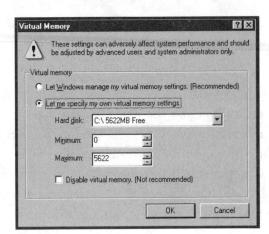

Figure 3.5

You can change the
drive used by
virtual memory if
your default C drive
is full and you have
other, more empty
drives available.

6. Click on OK. A warning appears telling you that you have chosen manual settings.

7. Click on Yes.

8. Click on OK to close the System Properties dialog box.

9. If prompted to restart your PC, click on Yes.

Eliminating Unnecessary Programs from Startup

In this morning's session, to troubleshoot problems, you learned how to control which programs load at startup. This same procedure can also help improve system performance. The fewer programs that load at startup, the more Windows resources are left for other activities. So turn back to the section "Controlling Which Programs Load at Startup" to see if there are any programs loading automatically that don't need to.

Updating Your System

Generally speaking, your system works best when you have the latest versions of everything—of Windows, of each application, of each device

driver, and so on. If your system is more than six months old, you probably do not have the latest versions of everything.

Downloading Updated Drivers and Software

Hardware companies periodically release updates and improvements for their devices' Windows drivers. These updates cannot only fix problems, but in some cases can make the device work better or have additional capabilities. The same goes for software. Depending on the program, you might be able to download a patch that fixes a specific problem or even a whole new version with new features.

You can download and install updates from the company's Web site on the Internet, as you learned in this morning's session, or you can request that the company send you the latest drivers on a disk. (The latter might cost a small amount for postage and handling.) Refer to "Updating a Device Driver" in this morning's session to recall how to download and install driver updates; the same procedure works for software updates too.

Updating Windows with Windows Update

Windows 98 comes with a Windows Update feature that helps you keep your copy of Windows current. It connects you to a special Web site, examines your current system, and recommends downloads to you. Then, with a few clicks of the mouse, you can download and automatically install those updates.

Windows 95 users do not have Windows Update available as part of Windows. However, they can download and install the latest version of Internet Explorer and use the Update feature from within that program.

NOTE To use Windows Update, you must have registered your copy of Windows 98. You might be prompted to register when you attempt to connect to Windows Update; simply fill in the prompts as requested.

To use Windows Update, do the following:

1. From Windows 98, choose Start/Windows Update and select the Product Updates hyperlink. Or, from Internet Explorer, choose Tools/Windows Update.

NOTE If you do not have a Windows Update command on your Tools menu in Internet Explorer, you do not have a recent enough version of that program.

To download a free copy of the latest version of Internet Explorer, go to **www.microsoft.com/windows/ie/default.htm** and select the Download hyperlink. Then follow the directions onscreen.

2. Wait for the utility to analyze your system. When it is finished, a list of recommended updates appears (see Figure 3.6).

3. Place a check mark beside each item listed under Critical Updates.

4. (Optional) Place a check mark beside any other updates you want. Some of these are very useful, such as an update to DirectX technology; others are more specialized, such as support for a specific language.

5. Click on Download. The Download Checklist appears, containing a list of files to be downloaded.

6. Click on Start Download. A license agreement appears (see Figure 3.7).

7. Click on Yes to accept the license agreement.

8. Wait for the downloads to complete and the updates to install themselves.

TIP You can minimize the Internet Explorer window and continue using your PC while the download completes.

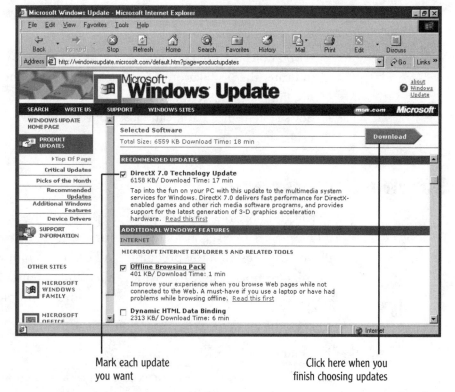

Figure 3.6

The available updates for your system appear. These are based on the current versions of your installed Windows components.

Mark each update you want

Click here when you finish choosing updates

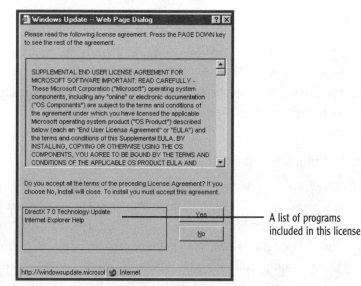

Figure 3.7

This license agreement is for both of the updates I chose to download.

A list of programs included in this license

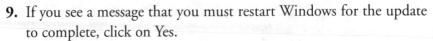

9. If you see a message that you must restart Windows for the update to complete, click on Yes.

If you don't see such a message, you merely see a Web page that indicates the installation was successful. (This is the case when installing an update that does not directly affect any of the Windows system files.) You can close your Web browser or continue using the Internet.

Saving Disk Space

Are you running low on hard disk space? These days, anything less than 100 megabytes free is considered "running low." When your hard disk is full, you can't install more programs, and certain Windows features, such as virtual memory might not work to their full potential. You might also experience problems running certain programs, or problems in printing.

To check the amount of free space on your hard disk, do the following:

1. Double-click on My Computer.
2. Right-click on the icon for your hard disk and choose Properties.
3. Take note of the Free Space amount.
4. Click on OK to close the dialog box.

If you need more hard disk space, you can buy a new hard disk, of course, but that's not the only solution. Before you shell out the money for new hardware, try the following methods of streamlining your hard disk content.

Uninstalling Unwanted Programs

Most people have several programs on their PCs they never use. These programs can be uninstalled to free up disk space (often a considerable amount of it!). For example, suppose your computer came with a whole slew of programs and you have never used any of them. Getting rid of them could potentially save several hundred megabytes of disk space. Or,

suppose you downloaded and installed a game demo, but the demo period has expired. It too could be axed in the interest of disk space.

Deleting the program's files through Windows Explorer or My Computer is *not* the preferred method. True, you are freeing up disk space, but in a rough, ungraceful way. The Windows Registry still retains information about the program being installed, and some other startup files might continue to refer to it. And, unless you are a real tech expert, you probably cannot manually remove all references to the deleted program from your system files.

A much better way is to use the Uninstall feature in Windows through Add/Remove Programs. The exact uninstall routine depends on the program, but they all begin the same way, as shown in the following steps:

1. Choose Start/Settings/Control Panel.
2. Double-click on Add/Remove Programs.
3. On the Install/Uninstall tab, select the program you want to remove (see Figure 3.8).

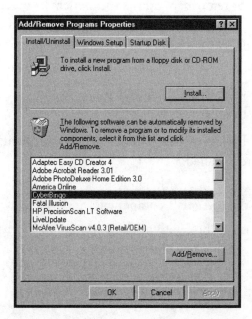

Figure 3.8

Select the program to uninstall, and then click on Add/Remove.

4. Click on Add/Remove.

5. At this point, any of several things can happen. For some programs, an Uninstall utility program runs, and you work through it to remove the program from your system. For other programs, simply clicking on Add/Remove automatically removes the program without further prompting. Just go with the flow of whatever situation you encounter.

6. If prompted to restart your PC, click on Yes. Otherwise, when you finish removing programs, click on OK to close the Add/Remove Programs Properties dialog box.

Removing Windows Components

Windows comes with many helpful accessory programs, such as Word-Pad, Paint, and HyperTerminal. You can change which of these components are installed at any time, adding or removing them as desired. If you are short on disk space on your hard drive, you might want to remove some of these Windows components to save space.

When you add or remove Windows components, you choose a category, and then choose programs within that category. For example, if you want to remove Calculator, you can find it in the Accessories category. (You can browse the categories freely to find the program you want.)

On the category list, each category has one of the following three check box states next to it.

- A cleared check box means none of the components in that category are installed.

- A marked check box with a gray background means that some, but not all, of the category's components are installed.

- A marked check box with a white background means that all the category's components are installed.

Figure 3.9 shows the list of categories, with examples of each of the check box states.

Here's how to remove a Windows component:

1. Choose Start/Settings/Control Panel.
2. Double-click on Add/Remove Programs.
3. Select the Windows Setup tab. After a brief pause, a list of Windows component categories appears (refer to Figure 3.9).
4. To remove an entire category, remove the check mark from the check box next to that category. Then, skip to step 7.

   Or, to remove only certain programs from a category, select the category and click on Details. A list of programs in that category appears, as in Figure 3.10.

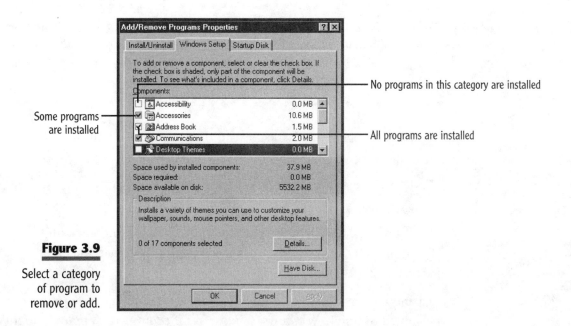

Figure 3.9

Select a category of program to remove or add.

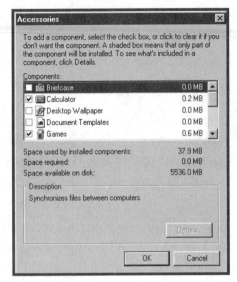

Figure 3.10

The programs
in a category
(Accessories, in
this example).

5. Remove the check marks next to the programs to uninstall.

6. Click on OK to return to the category list.

7. Repeat steps 4 through 6 for other categories if you want.

8. Click on OK.

9. If prompted, insert the Windows 98 CD-ROM and click on OK. (You might not see this prompt, depending on what you are removing.)

Depending on which components you are removing, you might be prompted to restart Windows. Choose Yes if prompted; Windows might not work correctly if you don't restart.

You can use this same procedure, marking check boxes instead of clearing them, to reinstall the Windows components later if you change your mind.

Deleting Unwanted Data Files

You just saw how to remove entire programs, but you can also remove individual files. One way is to select files in Windows Explorer or My Computer, and then press the Delete key. However, you shouldn't do this unless you are sure of the worthlessness of the files you are deleting, because you can really screw up your system if you delete important system files.

Generally speaking, you can safely delete any data files you created yourself. You can distinguish data files from program files by their extensions (that is, the characters following the period in the name). You learned how to turn on the display of file extensions this morning, in the "Showing File Extensions" section. Tables 3.1 and 3.2 list some common extensions.

Tables 3.1 and 3.2 provide only a partial list; there are many other file extensions for both programs and data that you can encounter. *If in doubt about a file, do not delete it.*

TABLE 3.1 DO NOT DELETE FILES WITH THESE EXTENSIONS	
Extensions	**Used for**
.exe, .com, .bat	Programs
.dll, .bin, .dat, .ocx	Helper files for programs
.sys, .ini, .inf	Configuration or system files

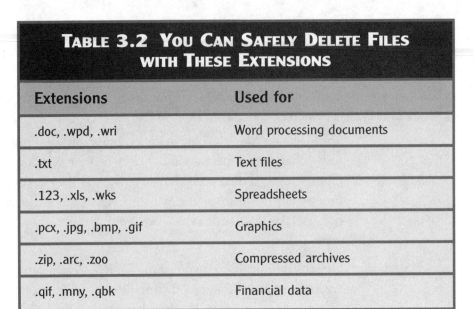

Extensions	Used for
TABLE 3.2 YOU CAN SAFELY DELETE FILES WITH THESE EXTENSIONS	
.doc, .wpd, .wri	Word processing documents
.txt	Text files
.123, .xls, .wks	Spreadsheets
.pcx, .jpg, .bmp, .gif	Graphics
.zip, .arc, .zoo	Compressed archives
.qif, .mny, .qbk	Financial data

CAUTION Not all graphic files are safe to delete to save space. Some programs (notably games) require graphic files to run properly. If you delete the graphic files associated with the program, the program won't work. To be safe, delete only graphics you created yourself or downloaded from the Internet.

The same goes for compressed archives. A few commercial programs (again, notably games) use .zip files as they run; if you delete the .zip files from that program's folder, it might not work. To be safe, delete only compressed archives you downloaded from the Internet yourself.

If you are not sure about the content of a particular data file, try double-clicking on it. If the program that created it is still installed on your PC, the data file might open in that program and you can see what it contains.

TIP You can check out some data files with a feature called Quick View. Right-click on the file and look at its shortcut menu for a Quick View command. If one appears there, choose it, and the file's content appears in a window. Close that window when you are done looking at it. This works for only certain file types (mostly those created in Microsoft programs).

Removing Unnecessary Files with Disk Cleanup

In addition to data files on your hard disk, there are probably many other files that could be deleted too—if you could only locate and identify them. It's tricky for a beginner to do so reliably, and a single mistake can render the system inoperable.

That's where the Disk Cleanup utility comes in handy. It comes with Windows 98; Windows 95 users do not have it available (unless the Windows 95 Plus Pack is installed).

The Disk Cleanup utility looks at the files on your system and suggests files to delete in several categories. These categories include the following:

- **Temp files**. Files that Windows or some other program created temporarily and apparently forgot to delete for some reason. These sometimes, but not always, have a .tmp extension and/or the first character is a tilde (~).

- **Saved Web pages**. For faster operation, your Web browser retains information about Web pages you visit so it can display the pages more quickly if you call for them again. These saved pages can be removed safely from your system to save disk space; if you view that page again later, the Web browser simply re-retrieves it from the Internet.

- **Offline Web pages**. A variant of the previous. You can set up Internet Explorer to completely transfer some Web pages to your hard disk so you don't need to be connected to the Internet to view them. If you did this, you can delete these offline pages to save space.

- **Downloaded program files**. When you visit certain Web pages that contain programs (Java or ActiveX, usually, not that it matters for your purposes here), those programs get downloaded to your PC. You can delete them to save space.

- **Recycle bin**. You are probably already familiar with your PC's Recycle Bin, the place where deleted files go. You can empty this yourself from the desktop, of course, but the Disk Cleanup program can do it also.

To use Disk Cleanup, follow these steps:

1. Choose Start/Programs/Accessories/System Tools/Disk Cleanup. A dialog box appears from which you can select a drive (the default is C).

2. Select the hard drive to clean up from the list (or leave C selected) and click on OK. The program analyzes your hard disk contents, and the dialog box shown in Figure 3.11 appears.

3. Click to place a check mark next to each category of files you want to delete.

   To see a complete list of the files in that category, select the category and click on View Files. (Close the list window when finished with it.)

4. Click on OK. A confirmation message appears.

5. Click on Yes. Disk Cleanup removes the specified files, and the program closes.

NOTE   By default, the Disk Cleanup program runs automatically when space gets low on your hard disk. To turn this automation off, select the Settings tab in the Disk Cleanup dialog box and deselect the check box there.

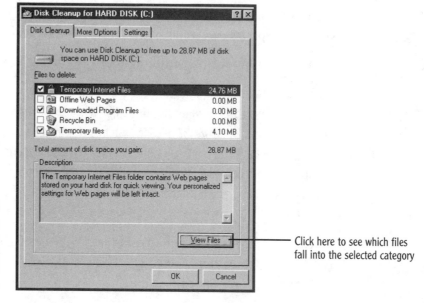

Figure 3.11

The Disk Cleanup program recommends files that can be deleted.

Click here to see which files fall into the selected category

Converting to a 32-Bit File System

This is for Windows 98 users only: if you upgraded your system to Windows 98 and you have a very large, nearly full hard disk, you might get some benefit from converting your file system from 16-bit to 32-bit with a free utility that comes with Windows 98.

NOTE If you convert to a 32-bit file system, you cannot use DriveSpace to increase your disk storage capacity. The two features are incompatible with one another. Read the upcoming section "Compressing a Disk with DriveSpace" before you make a decision about which to use on your system.

What's a 32-bit file system? Well, without getting too techie about it, a 32-bit file system is a filing system that is more efficient and eliminates some of the wasted space on your hard disk so it can store more data than normal. You won't see as dramatic an improvement with the conversion as you do if you use DriveSpace. However, converting to a 32-bit file system is actually good for your system and makes it run better, whereas using DriveSpace slows some aspects of the system down.

Windows 98 supports 32-bit file systems; Windows 95 does not.

NOTE Some later OEM releases of Windows 95 (that is, versions of Windows 95 that came with new PCs) include support for 32-bit file systems; but there is no conversion program included, so you have to completely wipe out and repartition/reformat your hard disk to set it up. (You learn how to do that this evening.) For most people, that's too much trouble. It is easier to upgrade to Windows 98 and use the Drive Converter utility there.

To run the converter, choose Start/Programs/Accessories/System Tools/Drive Converter (FAT32). Then follow the self-explanatory prompts to perform the conversion.

Compressing a Disk

Windows 95/98 comes with a disk compression program called Drive-Space. It approximately doubles the capacity of your current hard disk. The trade-off is that your hard disk might work a bit more slowly, and utility programs, such as Scandisk and Disk Defragmenter, can take at least twice as long to run.

CAUTION Before you use a compression program to alter your drive, you should back up any important files onto another drive. The drive compression process is fairly reliable, but it's not 100 percent safe. Disk problems are known to occur occasionally during compression. Better safe than sorry. Also, be aware that with a compressed drive, it is harder to recover from errors than on a regular, uncompressed drive.

How Disk Compression Works

Here's the techie explanation of how disk compression works. (Feel free to skip this if you want.)

Hard disks store data very reliably, but there is often lots of wasted space between files. DriveSpace removes all the wasted space in the file storage system by storing the files using a different method.

The way it works is kind of tricky. The DriveSpace program essentially fools your system into thinking a file is a disk, and it puts all your files from the hard disk into that big disk-like file. Because it's really a file, it isn't constrained by the inefficient filing system on a real disk, so it can store your hard disk content more efficiently.

Let's say your hard disk is drive C. DriveSpace creates a big file on C and calls it H. The operating system treats this file like an extra hard disk. Then, one by one, the program moves your files from C to H, gradually increasing the size of H until H takes up almost all the space on C. Now this massive file is consuming your C drive, and within that file is drive H and all the programs that used to be on C.

There is one last step: All your programs are expecting to be on C. If they're on a drive called H, they might not work right. So DriveSpace swaps the letters—that is, your original C drive is renamed H, and the new H drive is called C. Now all the programs are happy again, because they think they are still on C. This process is completely automatic; you don't have to worry about swapping anything yourself.

Compressing a Disk with DriveSpace

To compress a disk with DriveSpace, follow these steps:

1. Choose Start/Programs/Accessories/System Tools/DriveSpace. A dialog box appears listing the drives on your system.

2. Click on the drive you want to compress. Figure 3.12 shows the list of drives from the Windows 98 version of DriveSpace; the one for Windows 95 looks a bit different.

3. Open the Drive menu and choose Compress (in Windows 98) or click on Compress (in Windows 95).

4. Follow the self-explanatory onscreen prompts to finish the process.

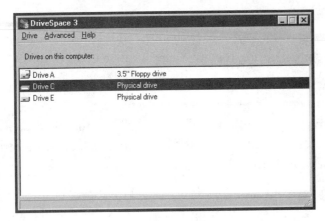

Figure 3.12

Select the drive to be compressed.

If you use Windows 98, or Windows 95 with the Windows 95 Plus Pack, you have an additional program called Compression Agent. (It's on the System Tools submenu along with DriveSpace.) You can use it for greater control over your compressed drive. For example, you can specify some infrequently used files for additional compression or specify some often-used files to leave uncompressed. This utility is mostly for advanced users who love to tweak settings; average users will not find any great benefit from using it.

Take a Break

Time to take a quick breather! Make yourself a snack. How about popcorn? Give yourself at least 10 minutes away from this book, and away from your PC, to refresh and relax.

Improving the Display

The display you see onscreen is limited by the capabilities of your video card and your monitor as a team. In other words, your display looks only as good as the weaker of those two components can make it look.

The following sections take you through the following steps:

- Making sure Windows correctly identified your video card and monitor

- Choosing a color depth and display resolution appropriate for your needs (and your monitor size)

- Setting the refresh rate for optimal viewing

Setting Up the Correct Video Drivers

When you install Windows (or when it is installed at the factory, if it came already installed on a new PC), Windows is supposed to detect your hardware and install the appropriate drivers. That's called Plug and Play. Sometimes it works, sometimes it doesn't. For this reason, it's known in techie circles as Plug and *Pray*.

Sometimes, Windows thinks it detects a piece of hardware, but it is mistaken. Usually, the settings for the device it thinks you have are very similar to the settings for your actual stuff, so the device probably can function, more or less. However, some features might not work just right.

Case in point: your video card. If Windows can't recognize your video card specifically, it detects it as a Standard VGA adapter. That's fine in that it allows it to work, but it limits your display to standard VGA mode, which is 640 X 480 resolution and 16-color depth. (You learn what that means shortly.) To take advantage of higher video resolutions, you need to help Windows recognize your video card as its actual make and model.

Follow these steps to see what Windows currently thinks your video card and monitor are:

1. Right-click on the desktop and choose Properties.
2. Select the Settings tab.
3. Click on Advanced. The properties for your video card appear.

4. Select the Adapter tab and check to see what video card is listed at the top (see Figure 3.13). If the correct video card name does not appear, see "Changing the Video Driver" later in this session.

5. Select the Monitor tab and check to see what monitor is listed at the top (see Figure 3.14). If the correct monitor name does not appear, see "Configuring the Monitor" later in this session.

The following sections cover two procedures. Use the first one, "Updating the Video Driver," if your video card was correctly identified but you want to see if a better driver is available for it. Use the second, "Changing the Video Driver," if Windows has not correctly identified your video card.

NOTE To determine whether Windows identified the video card correctly, you must know the right answer yourself. Most people buy the video card as part of a whole PC, rather than buying and installing it themselves. If you aren't sure what kind of video card you have, now is a good time to look through the documentation that came with your PC to find out. Look for a packing slip or receipt that came with the PC that might list it. If you're feeling intrepid, you can also turn off the PC and remove the cover to try to locate a name and model number of the video card itself.

Updating the Video Driver

You might want to update the video driver if, for some reason, the correct video card name appears but the video display doesn't seem right. For example, one of my clients was having a problem with his video display. Every time he changed to a higher resolution and number of colors (as you learn to do later in this session), it defaulted back to 16 colors and 640×480 resolution (standard VGA) when he restarted his PC. We fixed the problem by reinstalling the video driver from the disk that came with his PC. If that hadn't worked, I would have checked the video card manufacturer's Web site to see whether an updated driver was available.

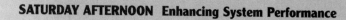

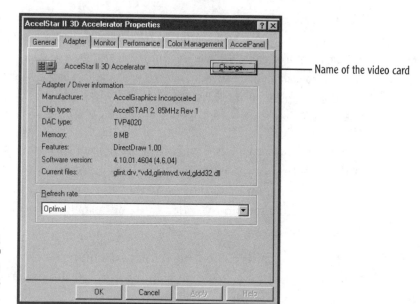

—— Name of the video card

Figure 3.13

Check to see which video card Windows thinks you have.

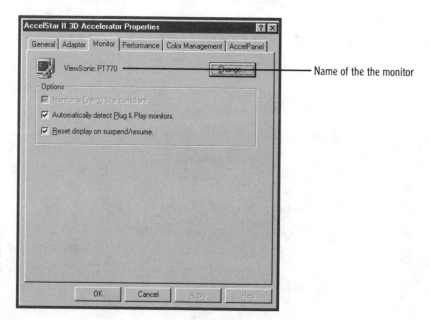

—— Name of the the monitor

Figure 3.14

Check to see which monitor Windows thinks you have.

NOTE To download an updated driver from a manufacturer's Web site, see the "Downloading from a Manufacturer's Web Site" section in this morning's session. The file you download might contain an automated installation program, in which case you do not need the manual procedure that follows.

Some video cards come with their own setup program on disk. Browse the disk that came with yours. If a Setup.exe file is on it, go ahead and run that program instead of using the following steps. The setup program automatically sets up the video card and installs any utility programs that came with it.

Other video cards come with a disk that simply contains the drivers, with no setup utility. In that case, you must install the drivers as explained in the following steps:

NOTE The following steps apply to Windows 98; in Windows 95, the procedure is slightly different.

1. If needed, download an updated driver from the Internet. (See Saturday Morning's session to remember how.) Or, locate and have ready the disk that came with the video card.

2. Right-click on the desktop and choose Properties.

3. Select the Settings tab.

4. Click on Advanced.

5. Select the Adapter tab. (Refer to Figure 3.13.)

6. Click on Change. The Update Device Driver Wizard runs.

7. Click on Next.

8. Choose Search for a better driver, and then choose Next. A list of locations to search appears (see Figure 3.15).

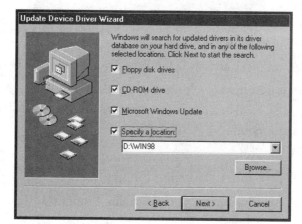

Figure 3.15

Choose where you
want Windows
to search for
the driver.

9. Place a check mark next to each place you want to search for a new driver:

- **Floppy disk drives.** Choose this if you have a floppy disk from the manufacturer.

- **CD-ROM drive.** Choose this if you have a CD-ROM from the manufacturer.

- **Microsoft Windows Update.** Choose this if you want to check for a better driver on Microsoft's Web site. I always mark this option; it doesn't hurt. (You can do this only if you registered your copy of Windows.)

NOTE If you choose Microsoft Windows Update, and your Internet connection is not running, you might be prompted to connect.

- **Specify a location.** Choose this and enter (or browse for) a folder on your hard disk where a driver is stored. (If you downloaded a new driver from the manufacturer's Web site and placed it in a folder, for example, you specify that folder here.)

10. Insert any needed disks into your floppy or CD-ROM drive, depending on what you chose in step 9.

11. Click on Next and wait for Windows to look for better drivers.

12. A message appears telling you whether it found a better driver. Click on Next to install the new driver or leave the old one in place as recommended.

13. Click on Finish.

14. Click on Close to close the Properties dialog box for the video card.

15. Click on Close to close the Display Properties dialog box.

16. If prompted to restart your computer, click on Yes.

Changing the Video Driver

If the video driver shown in the Display Properties dialog box does not match the make and model you think you have, you can try installing a different driver. For example, if Windows thinks your video card is VGA, but you know it's really an AccelStar II 3-D model, you need to change to the correct driver.

If the video card came with a setup program on disk, run that. If it didn't, use the following steps:

1. Perform steps 1 through 7 of the preceding procedure, "Updating the Video Driver." This takes you into the Update Device Driver Wizard.

2. Choose Display a list of all the drivers and choose Next. A list of drivers appears for the card that Windows currently thinks you have.

3. Choose Show all hardware. A list of video card manufacturers appears in the left pane.

4. Do one of the following:

   ✿ If you have a disk that came with your PC or video card that contains Windows 95/98 drivers, insert that disk and click on Have Disk. Next, click on Browse and navigate to the drive and folder that contains the drivers. Click on OK.

   ✿ If you do not have a disk, choose the video card manufacturer and model from the list that Windows provides (see Figure 3.16). Then click on Next.

5. When prompted that Windows is ready to install the new driver, click on Next.

   You might be prompted to insert the Windows CD or the disk that came with the video card; if you see this prompt, insert the requested disk and click on OK.

   If you see a message telling you that a file being installed is older than a file already on your system and asking whether you want to skip that file, click on Yes.

Figure 3.16

Find the correct video card manufacturer and model.

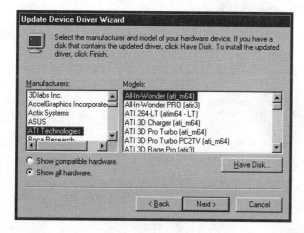

TIP
■■■■■■■■■■■■■■■■■■■■■■■■■■■■■■■■■■■■■■■
If you are prompted in step 5 to insert a disk you don't have, you might be able to work around it. Perhaps the needed file is already on your hard disk from a previous installation and the setup program simply doesn't know where to look.

Click on OK, as if you had inserted the requested disk. A box appears informing you that the file is not in that location and allowing you to browse for it. It also gives you the file's name that it is looking for. Jot down that file's name, and then use the Find feature in Windows (Start/Find/Files or Folders) to see whether a copy of that file is already on your hard disk somewhere. If it is, use Browse to point the installation program to it.

■■■■■■■■■■■■■■■■■■■■■■■■■■■■■■■■■■■■■■■

6. When you see a message that the installation of the new driver is complete, click on Finish.

7. Click on Close to close the Properties dialog box for the video card.

8. Click on Close to close the Display Properties dialog box.

9. If prompted to restart your computer, click on Yes.

Configuring the Monitor

As I mentioned earlier, the overall display quality is limited by the combined capabilities of the monitor and the video card. You just learned how to set up the video card; now it's time to look at the monitor.

Windows probably detected your monitor as a Plug-and-Play Monitor. That's fine, unless your system is capable of higher refresh rates than what is specified by the generic plug-and-play monitor driver. (See "Changing the Display Refresh Rate" later in this session for details about that.) For the best quality image onscreen, if possible, you should set up Windows for the specific monitor you have.

Here's how to set Windows straight about your monitor model:

1. Right-click on the desktop and choose Properties.

2. Select the Settings tab.

3. Click on the Advanced button.

4. Select the Monitor tab. If it shows the correct monitor name, you're done; click on OK and then on OK again. Otherwise, go on to step 5.

5. Click on Change.

6. Click on Next.

7. Choose Display a list of all the drivers.

8. Click on Next.

9. Choose Show all hardware.

10. Select your monitor's manufacturer and model, and then click on Next. (Or, if your monitor came with a disk, click on Have Disk and browse to that disk.)

11. Click on Next. If prompted, insert the Windows CD-ROM and click on OK.

12. Click on Finish.

13. Click on Close.

14. Click on OK to close the Display Properties dialog box.

15. If prompted to restart your PC, click on Yes.

Windows now knows the correct video card and monitor, and the correct drivers are installed for them. Now you can move on to setting the video mode you want to use.

Selecting a Video Mode

Based on the video card and monitor, Windows lets you choose among several video modes. The video mode is made up of two main factors: resolution and color depth. (A third, more minor factor is refresh rate, which I cover in the next section.)

Resolution is the number of individual pixels (dots) that make up the video mode. The higher the numbers, the smaller the dots and the sharper the image (and the smaller the image). Figures 3.17 and 3.18 show the same screen in 640 X 480 and 800 X 600 resolutions, respectively. Common resolutions are 640 X 480, 800 X 600, and 1024 X 768.

Figure 3.17

A Windows screen at 640 X 480 resolution.

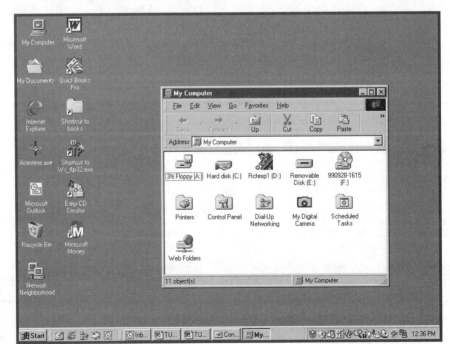

Figure 3.18

A Windows screen at 800 X 600 resolution.

Which resolution is best? It all depends on what you plan to do with your PC and the size of your monitor. As you can see by comparing Figure 3.18 to Figure 3.17, a higher resolution makes everything onscreen look smaller. If you have a large monitor, you can use a very high resolution without straining your eyes to see things. On a small monitor, you might want to stick with a lower resolution. Think, too, about how you use your PC. Someone who works with large spreadsheets might appreciate a higher resolution because it allows her to see more spreadsheet cells on the screen at once. But someone who spends a long time sitting at the computer reading e-mail each day might find that a lower resolution prevents eyestrain because things are easier to see.

Color depth is the number of colors that can be displayed simultaneously onscreen. Standard VGA is 16 colors; most people run Windows in at least 256-color mode. High Color (16-bit) and True Color (24-bit) are higher modes that show more colors. Why is color depth important? If you display photographs or video clips onscreen, they look much better at higher color depths because the colors shown onscreen will be closer to reality. When you use a lower color depth, Windows attempts to simulate the missing colors by blending two or more colors in a cross-hatch pattern. This is called *dithering*. From a distance it looks okay, but when you examine it closely, it looks fuzzy. When you use a higher color depth, Windows has more real colors to work with, so it doesn't have to dither as much.

In general, more color depth is better. However, if you want to use a program (usually a game) that works best at a particular color depth (such as 256 colors), you might want to temporarily set the color depth for a lower setting than the maximum your system is capable of. Such programs usually state in the documentation, onscreen, or in both places that they prefer a certain color depth.

To change the video mode (both resolution and color depth), follow these steps:

1. Right-click on the desktop and choose Properties.
2. Select the Settings tab.

3. Open the Colors drop-down list and choose the color depth you want.

4. Drag the Screen area slider to the resolution you want. For example, in Figure 3.19, it is set for 800 X 600 pixels.

5. Click on OK.

6. Do one of the following:

   ✿ If you are changing only the resolution (not the color depth), a box appears telling you that Windows will now change the display. Click on OK to accept that. Next, a box appears asking whether you want to keep the new setting. Click on Yes.

   ✿ If you are changing the color depth, a box appears suggesting that you restart Windows. Click on Yes. If you do not restart your PC after changing the color depth, the colors might not look quite right, depending on which color depths you are changing and the capabilities of your video card.

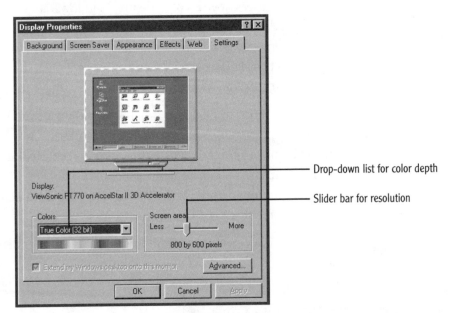

Drop-down list for color depth

Slider bar for resolution

Figure 3.19

Set the resolution (screen area) and color depth (colors).

Changing the Display Refresh Rate

The *refresh rate* is the rate at which the image onscreen is refreshed, or repainted, by the light beams inside the monitor. The higher the refresh rate, the less flicker in the display.

If you have ever seen video footage of a computer system in which the monitor appeared to be scrolling or blinking, that was because of a refresh rate on the monitor that is out of sync with the video recording speed. The human eye doesn't notice it as much, but it is obvious on video. The flicker of a low refresh rate (under 72Hz) can make your eyes tired if you look at such a display for a long time.

Here are your choices for refresh rate:

- ✿ **Adapter default**. This is the default setting for your video card. It is not always the highest possible setting, but it works with every monitor, so it is a safe setting.

- ✿ **Optimal**. This is the highest setting possible given the monitor and video card you told Windows you have. Windows examines the capabilities of both devices and calculates the best setting.

- ✿ **Specific settings**. If this setting is available for your video card and monitor, you can choose a specific setting, measured in Hertz (Hz). Larger numbers are better.

◆◆

CAUTION If the refresh rate you choose exceeds the capabilities of either your monitor or your video card, the screen appears distorted or even scrambled. It can damage your monitor to run at a too-high refresh rate, although this is rare.

◆◆

To set the refresh rate, do the following:

1. Right-click on the desktop and choose Properties.
2. Select the Settings tab.
3. Click on Advanced.

4. Select the Adapter tab.

5. Open the Refresh rate drop-down list and choose the setting you want (see Figure 3.20). If you do not know what to pick, choose Optimal.

6. Click on OK. A message appears that Windows is going to adjust your refresh rate.

7. Click on OK. The refresh rate changes and a message appears asking whether you want to keep the setting.

8. Click on Yes.

9. Click on OK to close the Display Properties dialog box.

After adjusting the refresh rate and video mode, the image you see Onscreen might be slightly off-center, slightly too large (edges cut off), or too small (a blank ring around the outside) for the monitor. On most monitors, you can adjust the image size and positioning with its built-in controls. See the manual that came with your monitor for details. If that's not an option, try a different refresh rate or monitor driver.

Figure 3.20

Set the refresh rate on the Adapter tab of the video card's Properties dialog box.

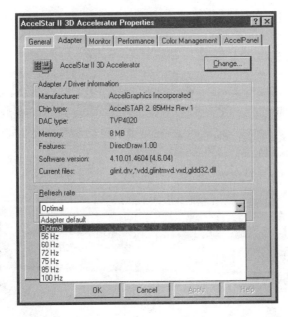

Making the Computer Easier to Use

The following sections explain ways to set up your PC to help you be more efficient. These procedures can make it easier to start the programs you use most frequently and to automate the maintenance tasks you perform regularly (or resolve to perform but never seem to get accomplished on your own!).

Organizing the Start Menu More Efficiently

As you install more and more programs, your Start menu can begin to get very crowded. There might even come a point where the folder and program names don't all fit onscreen at once. (To scroll to see the rest of them when that happens, click the arrow at the bottom of the menu, as shown in Figure 3.21.) Luckily, you can arrange and organize the programs on the Start menu to make things more compact and tidy.

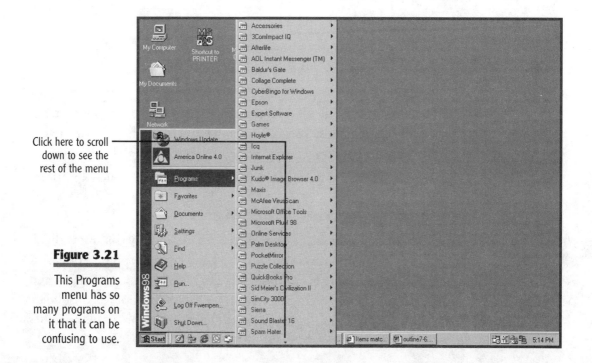

Click here to scroll down to see the rest of the menu

Figure 3.21

This Programs menu has so many programs on it that it can be confusing to use.

The Start menu is actually a folder on your hard disk (C:\Windows\Start Menu), and its contents are determined by the folders and shortcuts stored there. For example, the Start menu contains a folder called Programs (C:\Windows\Start Menu\Programs)—that's the Programs menu you see when you click Start and point to Programs. Within that Programs folder is a folder called Accessories, and within Accessories is a folder called System Tools, and so on. When you create, delete, and rearrange submenus, you are actually working with those folders.

The programs on the Start menu's various submenus are actually shortcuts to those programs, just like the shortcuts on your desktop. Removing a shortcut from the Start menu does nothing to the original file that runs the program.

Rearranging Items on the Start Menu

If you just want to reposition a folder or shortcut on the existing menu system, you can drag it around. You can do so by following these steps:

1. Choose Start/Programs. The Programs menu opens.
2. Point to the item you want to move, but don't click on it yet.
3. Press and hold down the left mouse button. (Do not click—that is, do not release the mouse button yet.)
4. Drag the item to the desired new location on the Start menu or any of its submenus. Point to a submenu to open it. A horizontal line shows where the item is going.
5. Release the mouse button, dropping the item into its new location.

Restructuring the Start Menu

You might decide your entire Start menu organization needs an overhaul. (I do this every six months or so, just for good housekeeping.) For example, perhaps you have a lot of programs installed (as in Figure 3.21) and you need a way of organizing them. Or, perhaps you want to consolidate some of the folders, placing the shortcuts for similar programs together in a single folder.

As I mentioned earlier, the Start menu takes its content from the C:\Windows\Start Menu folder. This is a regular folder you can work with using My Computer or Windows Explorer.

To modify the Start menu's content, follow these steps:

1. Right-click on Start and choose Explore. This opens the folder C:\Windows\Start Menu in Windows Explorer.

2. Double-click on the Programs folder. All the shortcuts and folders from the Programs menu appear (see Figure 3.22).

3. Change the structure of the Programs menu system by doing any of the following:

   ✪ Create new folders (File/New/Folder). These become new sub-menus on the Programs menu.

Programs menu   Current content of Programs menu

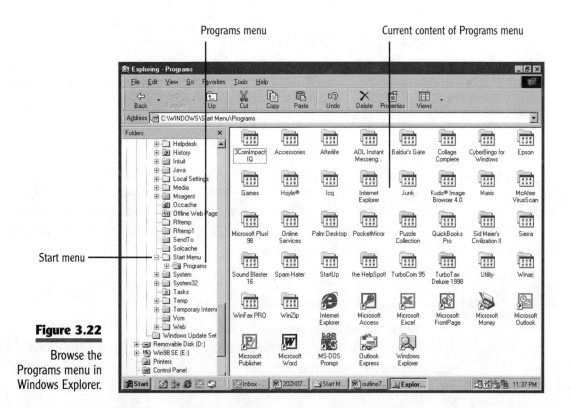

Start menu

Figure 3.22

Browse the
Programs menu in
Windows Explorer.

- Drag folders into the new folders you create, or into any other folders, to make them into submenus.

- Delete any unwanted folders or shortcuts by selecting them and pressing the Delete key.

4. Check your work by opening the Start menu and pointing at various folders to see their content. Close the Start menu by clicking away from it without selecting a command.

5. When you finish editing, close the Windows Explorer window.

If you are not sure how to reorganize things, here are some of my favorite strategies.

Create a few new folders with generic names, such as Games, Utilities, and Business. Then drag the shortcuts for various programs into the appropriate folders and delete all those specific folders for each application.

Sometimes, you might not want to delete the specific folder for an application. For example, if the folder contains the program shortcut and shortcuts to several related utilities, you might want to keep the folder to keep those shortcuts grouped together. If you want to tidy things up without getting rid of the specific folder, drag the whole folder into one of your generic-named new folders. It then becomes a submenu of it. Figure 3.23 shows the menu system from Figure 3.21 all tidied up with categories.

If you have a lot of programs that installed directly on the Programs menu, you can create a folder for them and place their shortcuts there instead. For example, Microsoft Office places shortcuts for all its applications on the Programs menu. You might create a folder called Office and move all those shortcuts into it.

Managing Desktop Shortcuts

As you know, your desktop contains shortcut icons to some of the most common programs and file management windows, such as My Computer, Internet Explorer, and the Recycle Bin. Depending on what programs

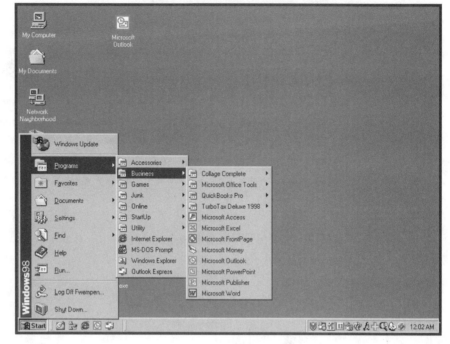

Figure 3.23

The reorganized, streamlined Start menu.

are installed, you might have other shortcuts there too, such as a game, an online service, or a utility program.

Arranging Shortcuts

You can drag shortcuts around on the desktop, placing them anywhere you like. For example, you might want to move the ones you don't use very often to an out-of-the-way corner. For that matter, you could just delete the ones you don't use very often, unless they are system shortcuts that can't be deleted, such as My Computer. To delete a shortcut, click on it and press the Delete key.

Creating Shortcuts

You can create new shortcuts on your desktop too. Desktop shortcuts allow you to bypass the Start menu and start a program more quickly.

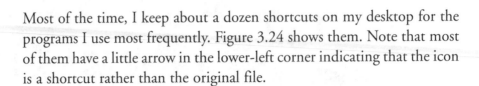

Most of the time, I keep about a dozen shortcuts on my desktop for the programs I use most frequently. Figure 3.24 shows them. Note that most of them have a little arrow in the lower-left corner indicating that the icon is a shortcut rather than the original file.

NOTE The little arrow in the corner is not a foolproof method of distinguishing a shortcut from the original. Some icons on your desktop, especially those placed there by Windows itself, do not have that little arrow and yet are shortcuts all the same.

To create a shortcut for a folder or file, follow these steps:

1. Locate the file or folder in a file listing (such as My Computer or Windows Explorer).

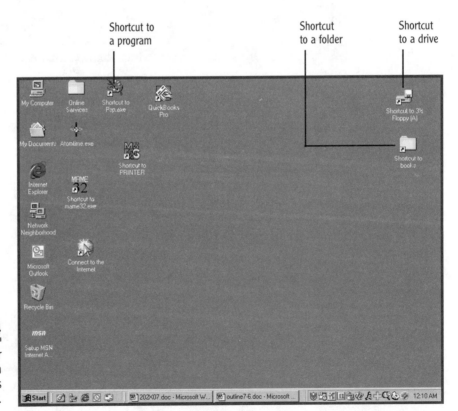

Figure 3.24

The desktop for my home PC, with the many shortcuts I created on it.

2. Right-click on the file or folder and choose Create Shortcut. A shortcut for that item appears in the same location.

3. Drag that shortcut onto the desktop.

To create a shortcut for a drive, do the following:

1. Double-click on My Computer on the desktop.

2. Right-click on the drive and choose Create Shortcut.

A message appears stating that you cannot create a shortcut in this location, asking whether you want to create the shortcut on the desktop.

3. Click on Yes.

Here's an alternate method (possibly quicker): Right-drag the item (file, folder, or drive) onto the desktop from its current location. When you drop it, a menu appears. Choose Create Shortcut(s) Here from that menu. This also works to create shortcuts from programs and folders on the Start menu; simply right-drag them from the Start menu to the desktop.

You can create shortcuts anywhere, not just on the desktop. For example, suppose you have a folder called Projects in which you keep the important files for the projects you are working on. One of the projects is a team effort with a friend in another office, so you agree to store all the files for it on your company's network. You could create a shortcut to that folder and store the shortcut in your own Projects folder. That way you can quickly access that folder when you need it without physically placing a copy of the folder on your hard disk.

Renaming Shortcuts

Some shortcuts have the words "Shortcut" to in their names, which can be cumbersome. You might want to rename the shortcut to remove that. You might want to rename a shortcut for some other reason too. For example, if you are setting up a shortcut for an installation program for a friend who is not very experienced with computers, a file called Shortcut

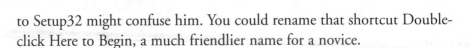

to Setup32 might confuse him. You could rename that shortcut Double-click Here to Begin, a much friendlier name for a novice.

Renaming a shortcut is the same as renaming any other file or folder. Select it, press F2, and then type the new name. (Or, right-click on it and choose Rename from the menu that appears.)

Customizing the Quick Launch Toolbar

The Quick Launch toolbar is a group of small icons that appears to the right of the Start button. It provides easy access to Internet Explorer, Outlook Express, and more (see Figure 3.25). (The exact buttons that appear on it can differ depending on your setup.) The Quick Launch toolbar is present only if you have Windows 98, or Windows 95 plus Internet Explorer 4.0. If you don't have either of those, you can skip this section.

TIP The Show Desktop button, pointed out in Figure 3.25, is very handy. It minimizes all open windows, so you can see your desktop.

You can add buttons to and remove them from the Quick Launch toolbar as desired. For example, you might add a button that starts your dial-up Internet connection.

If you use a certain few programs a lot, you might want to add shortcuts to them to the Quick Launch toolbar rather than placing shortcuts to

Figure 3.25

The Quick Launch toolbar provides quick shortcuts to a few common Windows programs.

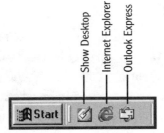

them on your desktop. The advantage is that the Quick Launch toolbar is always visible, whereas the desktop might not be. The drawback: The icons on the Quick Launch toolbar are picture only (no words beneath), so if you place two shortcuts there that have the same icon, you might have a hard time telling them apart.

To add a button to the Quick Launch toolbar, do the following:

1. Select the file, folder, drive, or shortcut you want to place on the Quick Launch toolbar.
2. Drag the item and drop it on the Quick Launch toolbar in the spot where you want it.

To delete a button from the Quick Launch toolbar, right-click on it and choose Delete from its shortcut menu.

Three other toolbars come with Windows; you can display them if you like. However, they take up a lot of space on the taskbar, so you probably do not want them displayed all the time. Right-click on the Quick Launch toolbar, choose Toolbars, and then choose the name of the toolbar you want to toggle on or off. They are as follows:

- **Address**. Provides an Address box into which you can type URLs and other addresses you want to browse, either on the Web, on your local network, or on your own PC.
- **Links**. Provides buttons that link to various Web pages.
- **Desktop**. Provides buttons for the shortcut icons on your desktop, so you don't have to minimize all the windows for access to them.

Experiment with these on your own as desired. (Personally, I don't find them very useful.)

NOTE You also can create more toolbars from existing folders if you want. Right-click on a toolbar and choose Toolbars/New Toolbar. Locate and select the folder you want to make into a toolbar and click on OK. However, I have never had occasion to need to do this, and you probably won't either. I simply add all the shortcuts I want to the Quick Launch toolbar.

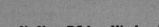

Scheduling Maintenance Tasks

Some of the tools you have learned about so far in this book (most notably ScanDisk and Disk Defragmenter) take a long time to run and yet should be run on a regular schedule. How can you remember to do so and not procrastinate running them when there are other things you would rather be doing with your PC?

If you have Windows 98, or Windows 95 with the Plus Pack, you can use the Task Scheduler to make such programs run when you are not home or when you are sleeping, so that their running does not interfere with your productivity.

Running the Maintenance Wizard

The Maintenance Wizard configures some common utilities (ScanDisk, Disk Cleanup, and Disk Defragmenter) to run automatically. You can set up using either Express or Custom modes. Express is very easy and great for beginners; Custom enables you to specify when and how often each individual program should run.

To use Express scheduling, follow these steps:

1. Choose Start/Programs/Accessories/System Tools/Maintenance Wizard.
2. Choose Express, and then click on Next.
3. Choose when you want the maintenance to run: Nights, Days, or Evenings (see Figure 3.26). Then click on Next.
4. (Optional) To run all the scheduled tasks for the first time right now, mark the When I click Finish, perform each scheduled task for the first time check box.
5. Click on Finish.

If Custom scheduling is what you want, do the following:

1. Choose Start/Programs/Accessories/System Tools/Maintenance Wizard.
2. Choose Custom, and then click on Next.

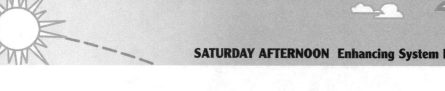

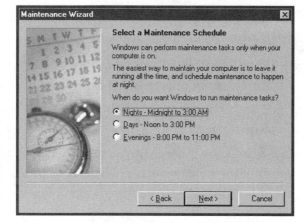

Figure 3.26

With Express setup, your only major decision is when to run the maintenance tasks.

3. Choose when you want the maintenance to run: Nights, Days, Evenings, or Custom. Then click on Next.

4. A list appears of programs start when Windows starts. Deselect the check box next to any of those you want to disable from starting automatically (see Figure 3.27). Then click on Next.

NOTE You probably do not want to disable any programs in step 4, because you already learned other ways to prevent programs from loading at startup in this morning's session.

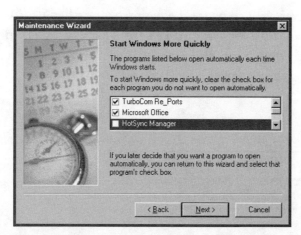

Figure 3.27

Disable any of the automatically started programs you want.

5. To place Disk Defragmenter on the maintenance schedule, choose Yes, defragment my hard disk regularly. Then do any the following:

   ✪ Click on Reschedule to specify when it should run.

   ✪ Click on Settings to change the default settings for the program.

   ✪ Click on Next when you finish configuring the Disk Defragmenter.

6. To place ScanDisk on the maintenance schedule, choose Yes, scan my hard disk for errors regularly. Then set its schedule and settings as you did for Disk Defragmenter in step 5. Click on Next when finished.

7. To place Disk Cleanup on the maintenance schedule, choose Yes, delete unnecessary files regularly. Then configure its settings and click on Next.

8. (Optional) To run all the scheduled tasks for the first time right now, mark the When I click Finish, perform each scheduled task for the first time check box.

9. Click on Finish.

After setting up a maintenance schedule, a Task Scheduler icon appears in the system tray (see Figure 3.28). You can double-click on it to open the Task Scheduler window at any time to modify the settings for the scheduled tasks.

If you ever want to pause the maintenance schedule (for example, if you don't want it to kick in during a large file download), right-click on the Task Scheduler icon and choose Pause Task Scheduler. Unpause it by repeating these steps.

Figure 3.28

The Task Scheduler icon in the system tray indicates maintenance tasks are scheduled.

Task Scheduler

Scheduling Additional Recurring Tasks

You can modify the Task Scheduler to run other programs at regular intervals too. Here's how to set one up:

1. Double-click on the Task Scheduler icon in the system tray (refer to Figure 3.28). The Scheduled Tasks window appears.

2. Double-click on Add Scheduled Task. The Scheduled Task Wizard runs.

3. Click on Next to begin. A list of programs installed on your PC appears, as shown in Figure 3.29.

4. Choose the program you want to schedule, and then click on Next.

5. Type a name for the scheduled task (or leave the default name).

6. Choose an interval at which to schedule (Daily, Weekly, and so on). Then click on Next.

7. Set the controls that appear based on the interval you chose in step 6. For example, if you chose Weekly, you would work with the controls shown in Figure 3.30. Click on Next when finished.

8. (Optional) To set advanced properties for the scheduled item, mark the Open advanced properties for this task when I click Finish check box.

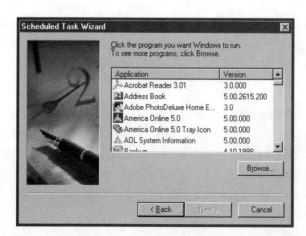

Figure 3.29

Select the program to schedule.

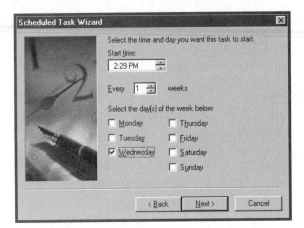

Figure 3.30

Specify details for
the chosen interval.

9. Click on Finish.

10. If you marked the check box in step 8, set any additional properties
for the item in the box that appears on the Settings tab. Then click
on OK to finish.

Take a Break

You can be pretty proud of yourself—you just saved hundreds of dollars
in consultant fees by tuning up your PC on your own. Now that you
know many of the tricks of the computer consulting trade for tuning up
Windows, you might find yourself very popular with family and friends.
I can't count the number of dinner invitations I've received that have
ended with, "Oh, by the way, while you're here, could you take a look at
my PC?"

If your computer is running well at this point, celebrate by taking the
evening off. Go to a movie, talk to your mate, do something fun. But if
you are still having major problems with your computer's performance,
and the fixes and tune-ups you learned about today haven't fixed it, stick
around for this evening's session, in which you learn how to rebuild a
Windows installation from scratch.

Starting Fresh with a Clean Install

- ✿ Partitioning and Formatting a Hard Disk
- ✿ Installing Windows
- ✿ Reinstalling Device Drivers
- ✿ Reestablishing Your Network and Internet Connections
- ✿ Reinstalling Applications

If you are reading this, your computer still isn't working correctly, even after trying everything in the last two sessions. You're probably tired and frustrated right now, wondering if your computer will ever work right again. I can assure you that it will. This is what I love about computers—there is always a fix. No problem is without a solution. It's only a question of how drastic you have to get.

Why Do a Clean Install?

In this session, you learn how to do the most drastic fix possible—a clean install. A clean install wipes out everything on your hard disk—all your data, programs, everything. *It also wipes out all your errors* and any unwanted files taking up space on your hard disk. Then you reload all your programs, recopy your data back to the hard disk, and everything works fine. A clean install is a lot of trouble, obviously, but it can take less time than all those hours of fruitless troubleshooting trying to track down a certain error with limited technical expertise.

Eradication of Tough-to-Troubleshoot Problems

Almost all Windows problems occur because Windows is no longer in its factory-fresh state.

Whenever Windows shuts down abnormally (such as with a power outage), the system files that were in use at the moment are subject to corruption. Further, as you install and remove programs in Windows, some system files are replaced, and others are added or deleted. Each program you install also writes changes to your configuration files and the Windows Registry. All this activity can introduce errors that can cause your PC to malfunction. You learned how to correct some errors in this morning's session, but a utility program cannot correct all errors.

When you do a clean install, you wipe out the entire hard disk and reinstall Windows from its original CD. You then reinstall clean, pristine versions of each of your programs, so that Windows is closer to factory-fresh configuration than ever.

Removal of Unwanted Files

When you install programs, files are copied to your hard disk. When you remove a program, not all of the files associated with that program are removed, however. Some of them are left behind in your Windows folder or other folders. Those are orphan files, because they aren't associated with any installed program. They have no use, but they take up valuable hard disk space. And usually, the Disk Cleanup program you learned about in this afternoon's session doesn't identify them.

When you do a clean install, you wipe out all such orphan files, so that every file on your hard disk is a needed file you purposefully put there. This can save an amazing amount of hard disk space. After you clean out all the junk, you might find you don't need a bigger hard disk after all.

NOTE   There are add-on programs you can buy for Windows, such as Clean Sweep, that aggressively scan your system for orphan files and can recommend many of them to be deleted. However, such programs are far from foolproof, and sometimes they recommend deleting a file you actually still need.

Other add-on programs, such as Norton Uninstaller, monitor each program's installation, making note of which files were added or changed. Then if you need to uninstall the program, you do it through that utility instead of Windows' Add/Remove Programs dialog box, and it does a more thorough job than normal. But again, this is not 100 percent foolproof.

What to Try First

Before resorting to a clean install, make sure you try all the solutions listed in the Saturday Morning session. In particular, do the following:

- ✿ Make sure you download and install all the latest device drivers for your hardware.

- ✿ Make sure you use Windows Update to download all the latest patches and updates for Windows.

- ✿ If the problem occurs only with a certain program, remove and reinstall that program.

- ✿ If a particular device is not functioning, check to make sure the hardware is installed correctly and working properly. A clean install does not fix hardware problems. If you find you need to replace some hardware, see tomorrow's session.

- ✿ Consider whether the problem might be an incompatibility between two devices on your system, particularly if they share resources. For example, if your scanner and printer share the parallel port, and the printer no longer works now that the scanner is installed, a clean install probably cannot help.

How Clean Is Clean?

There are various levels of clean in a clean install. A full clean install wipes out everything on your hard disk and starts with a completely empty, freshly formatted drive. But there are lesser levels too—for example, you can reinstall Windows in a new folder without wiping your whole hard disk clean.

I explain repartitioning and reformatting in the following sections, and you can come to your own conclusion about the level of clean that is right for you.

Do You Need to Repartition Your Hard Disk?

Repartitioning the hard disk is not necessary to correct system problems. The only reason to repartition the hard disk is to allocate the space on the physical drive in a different way.

To decide whether repartitioning is right for you, you need to understand the basics of how a drive works. Here's a synopsis.

The little metal hard disk box mounted inside your computer's case is the *physical drive.* For the physical drive to communicate with your operating system (Windows), it must be partitioned using a partition utility program and formatted using a formatting utility.

When you partition a drive, you can choose to make the entire physical drive one big *logical drive* (that is, to assign a single drive letter to all that space) or to create multiple logical drives. For example, a 3.6 gigabyte drive could be partitioned as one 3.6 gigabyte C drive. Or it could be two one gigabyte drives (C and D) and one 1.6 gigabyte drive (E). Partitions need not be the same size.

Versions of Windows prior to Windows 98 did not allow you to create partitions over two gigabytes, so if you have a computer that came with a large hard disk and Windows 95, the hard disk is probably partitioned into multiple logical drives. If you since upgraded to Windows 98, you can repartition the physical drive into larger chunks if you want—even making the entire physical drive into a single logical drive.

Techie factoid: Windows 95 had several different versions. Besides the original retail version, there were updates that were available only when buying a new PC with Windows 95 installed. The latest of these versions, called OEM Version C, supported large partitions.

Partitioning or repartitioning a drive wipes out all the disk content, so you do not want to do it frequently. Because you are preparing for a clean install, however, now is an excellent time to repartition.

In some older computers, the BIOS program does not recognize hard disks of more than two gigabytes. Such computers did not come with hard disks larger than that, so it was not an issue. However, if you install a new drive on such a computer, any extra space of about two gigabytes is simply ignored. This has nothing to do with partitioning; this is a BIOS limitation. To fix such a problem, you must update the BIOS. You can update some BIOS with software; others require a chip replacement on the motherboard. Contact your PC's manufacturer to find out which kind you have.

Some hard disks come with a program (one brand of which is called *EZ-BIOS*) that can circumvent an older PC's BIOS limitation. You might try the program if your only other alternative is a BIOS update; it might work (or it might not—you won't know until you try).

Do You Need to Reformat Your Hard Disk?

If you repartition, you also need to reformat. If you don't repartition, reformatting is optional.

Formatting a drive wipes everything from it: programs, data, system files, startup files, and so on. It provides a truly clean slate on which to reinstall, guaranteeing that the file(s) that were causing the problem are eradicated.

It also clears out any unwanted files you might have forgotten or not known were there. However, because it wipes out all your data, you must back up whatever you want to keep before you reformat, and backing up can be time-consuming.

Earlier, I told you about the two benefits of a clean install: eradicating problems and cleaning up your disk. If you do not reformat, you miss out on the latter benefit. You can still reinstall Windows without reformatting, and probably fix your system problems, but your hard disk will still contain most of the same folders and files. To get rid of them, you need to delete them yourself.

If any of the following are true for you, I suggest reformatting:

✿ You just repartitioned your drive. In this case, you *must* reformat.

✿ Most of what's on your hard disk is junk you want to get rid of. Reformatting efficiently removes all files in one swoop.

✿ You already tried a clean install in which you did not reformat, and you are still experiencing problems.

✿ You suspect your computer has a virus.

CAUTION

Reformatting removes most types of viruses. However, if you boot from an infected floppy disk, the virus immediately transferrs back to the hard disk. If you suspect virus infection, boot from a write-protected startup disk made on a computer you know is not infected. Refer to the section "Preventing Computer Viruses" on Saturday Morning for more information.

A few virus types hide in the drive's master boot record, which isn't touched by reformatting or even repartitioning. If you suspect such a virus, try to remove it with an antivirus program. If you don't have an antivirus program, you can wipe out the master boot record by repartitioning with the FDISK /MBR command.

Preparing for a Clean Install

Before doing a clean install, you must make sure you have everything you need to reinstall Windows and to set up your PC the way it was before. A few minutes of thought and preparation can save you hours of grief later.

Backing Up Your Important Files

If you decide to reformat, you need to back up every file you want to keep. Remember, your hard disk will be completely empty after reformatting! Even if you are not reformatting, you might still want to back up any critical data files, just to be safe. Refer to "Backing Up Important Files" in the Saturday Morning session for help with this.

You don't need to back up program files. You can reinstall the programs from their installation disks after reinstalling Windows.

Checking Installation Disks

Here's a big, big issue: Check your Windows installation CD. Make sure it does not say "Upgrade" on it. If you have an upgrade edition of Windows, you cannot use it for a clean install. Instead, you must install your older version of Windows, and then use the upgrade CD to install the later version on top of it. Check this now, not later!

You also need the installation disks for all the applications you want to reinstall. Make sure you have them handy. If you can't find one of them, try to borrow it from a friend.

NOTE Even if you are not reformatting your hard disk, you still need to reinstall each Windows program. That's because Windows programs place information in your Windows Registry when they install themselves, and that needed information will not exist in the Registry of the new installation. Generally speaking, you cannot reinstall a Windows program from the old copy on your hard disk; it usually requires the installation disk.

If you can't find the installation disk for a critical program you need, you might want to reconsider doing a clean install. Maybe you can live with your system problems after all, at least until you can get an installation disk for that program.

Making Notes about System Settings

Make sure you back up any configuration information you might need to set up your PC the way you want it again. These can include the telephone number of your Internet connection to dial, stored passwords for logging on to a network, favorite Web site addresses, and so on. Make sure you have this information written down somewhere so you can reenter it.

NOTE If your ISP sent you a startup kit when you signed up for your Internet service, see if you can locate the paperwork for it. That paperwork should contain your Internet connection phone number and settings.

Here are some tips:

- To see the settings for your current dial-up Internet connection, double-click on Dial-Up Networking from the My Computer window. Then right-click on your Internet connection and choose Properties. Make notes of all the settings on all the tabs in this dialog box. On the Server Types tab, click on the TCP/IP settings button and make sure you write down all the settings on all these tabs too.

- To save your Favorites list in Internet Explorer, choose File/Import and Export to run a wizard that walks you through the process of exporting them to a file. Then back up that file. After you reinstall Windows, use this same wizard to import the list again.

- Make a printout of your system settings, as you learned to do in the "What Have You Got?" section of Friday's session. This can come in handy after you reinstall Windows if you are uncertain about what makes and models of hardware you have.

✿ Make a printout of all the e-mail addresses and other contact information you stored in your contact management program or e-mail program. Then export your data from that program to a data file on a floppy disk. You can restore the backed up data after reinstalling your program, but the printout adds an extra measure of security in case you are unable to import your data later for any reason.

Testing Your Startup Disk

You learned how to make a startup disk in the "Creating an Emergency Startup Disk" session in Saturday Morning's session. If you didn't do it then, do it now.

Next, test the startup disk by doing the following:

1. Insert the disk in your floppy drive.

2. If your computer is currently off, turn it on.

    If the computer is already on, choose Start/Shut Down. Click on Restart, and then click on OK.

3. Wait for the computer to start.

    The computer should start itself from the floppy disk.

 NOTE If Windows starts up even though you have your startup disk in the drive, perhaps your BIOS program needs to be configured to boot first from the floppy, and then from the hard drive. See the information following these steps for more information.

4. When prompted, choose 1 to start the computer with CD-ROM support and press Enter.

When the A:\> prompt appears onscreen, the startup process has completed successfully.

If Windows insists on starting, even though you have your startup disk in the floppy drive, your BIOS configuration probably needs to be changed.

See the section "Understanding the System BIOS" in Saturday Morning's session if you did not read that material this morning. It's important that you understand the BIOS before fiddling with it. That section also explains how to enter, move around in, and exit a BIOS setup program.

Somewhere in the BIOS setup program, you can find a setting that controls the order of devices that are used for startup. It might be referred to as the *boot sequence*. You want to set this so that A is checked first for startup files, and then C. Next, save your changes and try booting again from the floppy disk.

What Next?

The section you should read next depends on what you have decided to do. Use the following to determine what steps to take next:

- If you decided to repartition, see the next section, "Partitioning a Hard Disk."

- If you plan to format but not repartition, skip to "Formatting a Hard Disk."

- If you are neither partitioning nor formatting, go to "Preparing to Install Without Reformatting."

Partitioning a Hard Disk

This is your last chance to back out! After you repartition, everything on your hard disk is gone. Are you sure that's what you want? If so, keep reading.

Each hard disk has a primary partition. That's your C drive. Depending on how your PC is currently configured, you might also have an extended partition (which is all the space on the hard disk besides the primary partition), and that extended partition can have one or more logical drives on it. For example, perhaps you have a six gigabyte hard disk. Let's say the primary partition (your C drive) is two gigabytes. The extended partition is four gigabytes. The extended partition has two logical drives (D and E), each of which are two gigabytes.

In addition to the primary and extended partitions (which are known as DOS partitions), you might also have one or more non-DOS partitions. These typically are small (only a few megabytes in size) and are used for some special system function, such as on a laptop to back up data in the event of a critically low battery. If you have a laptop and it has a small non-DOS partition, you might want to leave that partition intact, rather than delete it.

 NOTE •

Sometimes the presence of a small non-DOS partition with a strange name can indicate that your PC has been infected with a boot-sector virus.

• •

Perhaps you are not happy with the way your drive is currently divided up. Maybe you want one giant primary partition (that is, one big C drive). If that's the case, you need to delete the existing partitions and create new ones.

Follow these steps to delete the existing partitions and create new ones:

1. Boot from your startup floppy disk, if you haven't already. If you still need to do that, see "Testing Your Startup Disk" earlier in this session. You should see the A:\> prompt onscreen.

2. Type **fdisk** and press Enter.

3. If you see a message about enabling large hard disk support, type **Y**. The Fixed Disk Setup Program runs, as shown in Figure 4.1.

4. Type 4 and press Enter. A list of the current partitions appears. Figure 4.2 shows an example that contains a primary DOS partition, an extended DOS partition, and two non-DOS partitions. You might not have all these types.

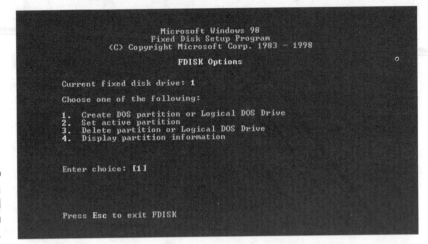

Figure 4.1

Use this program to examine and change partition data for the drive.

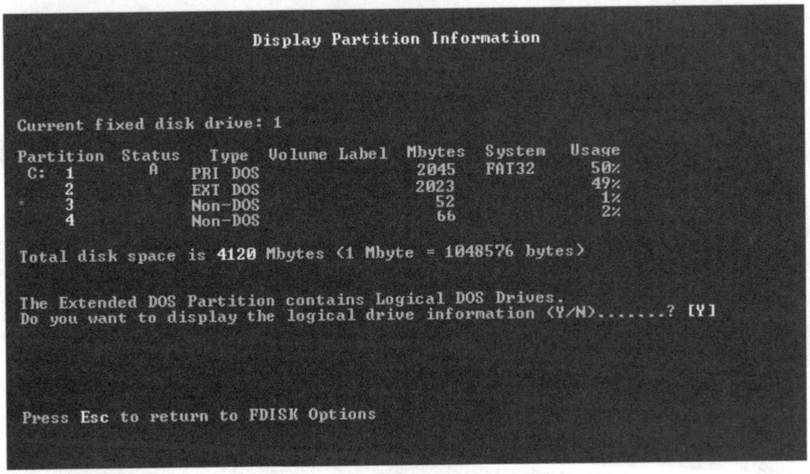

Figure 4.2

This screen shows what partitions are currently defined.

5. If you see a note asking whether you want to display the logical drive information (refer to Figure 4.2), press Enter to accept the default Y next to that command. Then review the list of logical drives on the extended partition.

6. Press Esc to return to the main menu (refer to Figure 4.1).

Now, you must delete the partitions, one by one, as described in the following steps. You start by deleting any non-DOS partitions you want to get rid of, then any logical drives on the extended partition, then the extended partition, and finally the primary partition.

7. Type **3** and press Enter. A menu of deletion options appears.

8. Delete each of the partitions, returning to step 7 after each deletion. Do the following to delete the partitions:

   ✿ If you have a non-DOS partition you want to delete, type **4** and press Enter. A list of non-DOS partitions appears. Locate a non-DOS partition on the list, type its number, and press Enter. When asked whether you want to continue, type **Y** and press Enter. Press Esc to return to the main menu and return to step 7.

   ✿ If you have an extended DOS partition with one or more logical drives on it, type **3** and press Enter. The list of logical drives on the extended partition appears. Type the drive letter to delete and press Enter. It asks for the volume label. Type whatever text you see in the Volume Label column for that drive (if it's blank, don't type anything) and press Enter. Then type **Y** to confirm and press Enter. Press Esc to return to the main menu. (If you just deleted the last logical drive on that partition, you must press Esc twice to return to the main menu.) Return to step 7.

   ✿ After you delete all the logical drives on the extended partition, remove the extended partition itself. Type **2** and press Enter. When prompted, type **Y** and press Enter to continue. Press Esc to return to the main menu. Return to step 7.

   ✿ Finally, delete the primary partition. Type **1** and press Enter. Type the partition number and press Enter. Type the volume label (leave it blank if there isn't one listed) and press Enter. Type **Y** to confirm. Press Esc to continue. Now that there are no more partitions, go on to step 9.

9. Now, you create a new partition. At the main menu, type **1** (Create DOS partition or Logical DOS Drive) and press Enter. The Create DOS Partition or Logical DOS Drive menu appears.

10. Type 1 (Create Primary DOS Partition) and press Enter. Wait while the drive integrity is verified.

11. You are asked whether you want to use the maximum available size for the primary DOS partition. To create a single, large C drive, press Enter to accept the default (**Y**).

In these steps, for simplicity, I assume you want to create a single primary partition of the maximum size (step 11). If you want to split the drive into multiple drive letters, type **N** and press Enter in step 11, and then enter the size to use. You can then create an extended DOS partition that uses the remainder of the disk space.

12. You see a message telling you that you must restart your system. Press Esc to exit FDISK.

13. Press Ctrl+Alt+Delete to restart your PC. Do not remove the floppy disk from the drive; you need it to restart the PC.

14. Restart the PC using the startup disk. When prompted, choose to start the computer with CD-ROM support.

Congratulations, you just did something that many people consider very intimidating—you repartitioned your hard drive. A freshly partitioned drive is not usable, however, until you format it, which you learn how to do in the following section.

Formatting a Hard Disk

Formatting a drive makes it ready to receive files and folders you want to store there. It also wipes out any existing files and folders on the drive, so you should reformat only after you remove everything from the drive that you want to keep. After you partition a drive, you must format it to make it usable.

To format a drive, use the FORMAT command at the command prompt, as described in the following steps.

1. Restart your PC using the startup disk (unless you just did so at the end of the preceding steps). A message appears like this:

   ```
   The diagnostic tools were successfully loaded to drive D.
   ```

   Make a note of which drive letter appears in this message.

2. Type the letter that was in the message, followed by a colon, and press Enter. For example, type **D:** and press Enter.

NOTE The startup disk has more utilities on it than can normally fit on a single floppy. They are stored there in compressed format. When you start the PC using the startup disk, it creates a virtual disk out of part of your system's memory (also called a *RAM disk*) and decompresses some of the utilities onto it. It assigns the next available drive letter to that RAM disk after accounting for your hard disk(s). So if you have a single hard disk C, the RAM disk is D. Make a note of the onscreen message to see what drive letter your RAM disk uses.

3. Type **format c:** and press Enter. A warning appears that all data will be lost.

4. Type **Y** and press Enter to confirm. The drive formatting process begins.

5. Wait for the drive to be formatted. It can take several minutes. (Larger drives take longer.)

6. When you see a prompt for a volume label, enter one (up to 11 characters) and press Enter or, if you don't want one, just press Enter.

NOTE The volume label is the name that appears under the drive's icon in Windows. It is not critical; you can skip entering one if you want by simply pressing Enter.

Now your drive is clean and reformatted and ready to receive a new Windows installation. Skip to the section "Installing Windows" later in this session.

Preparing to Install Without Reformatting

If you decide not to reformat, your path is different. Windows is still on your hard disk, along with all your old configuration files and settings—one or more of which might be the cause of your problems. You need to delete or disable certain old files so they can't cause problems in the new installation.

There are three key areas you need to disable or delete before a clean install:

✪ The entire C:\Windows folder. This contains all the Windows files from the old installation.

✪ The entire C:\Program Files folder. This contains the files from the old installation of your programs.

✪ The files in the root folder (C). This contains configuration files used to start your PC.

NOTE The root folder is not a folder named root. It's called the root folder because it's the top-level folder on the disk—the folder in which all other folders reside. If your disk were an office building, the root folder would be the lobby, the entrance point.

You can either delete these folders and files or you can rename them so your system cannot find them anymore, effectively disabling them. For the folders, I recommend renaming, that way, if you need a particular file from one of those old folders as you are setting up your new Windows installation, it is there. You can always delete the old folders later, when you are sure you don't need anything from them. For the files in the root folder, I recommend deleting. I show you how to do that shortly.

Preparing the Disk Space

To reinstall Windows and all your applications in new folders, you need quite a bit of free disk space (perhaps as much as 500 megabytes, depending on the number and size of the applications). If you are short on disk space, you can reclaim some by doing some or all of the following in Windows:

- Go through the section "Saving Disk Space" in the Saturday Afternoon session again, to see if you can save any space in the ways listed there.
- Use Add/Remove Programs (from the Control Panel) to uninstall all your applications in Windows. This helps shrink the size of the C:\Program Files folder. See "Uninstalling Unwanted Programs" in Saturday Afternoon's session.
- Use Add/Remove Programs to remove all optional Windows components. This shrinks the size of the C:\Windows folder. See "Removing Windows Components" in the Saturday Afternoon session.

Don't worry about removing programs you might need; in a few minutes, this whole Windows installation will be disabled anyway.

Renaming Folders

Now you are ready to disable the old folders. Take a deep breath.

First, start your PC using the startup disk. See "Testing Your Startup Disk" earlier in this session if you still need to do that. You should see the A:\> prompt onscreen. Next, follow these steps to rename the folders:

1. Type **c:** and press Enter.
2. Type **ren windows winback** and press Enter. (Capitalization is not important.)
3. Type **ren progra~1 progbak** and press Enter.

Why use progra~1 in step 3 instead of program files? Well, when working at the command prompt, file and folder names are limited to the old MS-DOS naming convention of eight characters. Longer names are truncated with a ~ sign and a number. The truncated name for the program files folder is progra~1.

Cleaning Out the Root Folder

Next, you should get rid of all the files in your root folder. This step is not essential—and it's fairly scary for a beginner to do—but it ensures that none of your old Windows settings carry over to the new installation. In other words, it makes things more like they would be if you reformatted.

Many of the files in your root folder have hidden, system, and/or read-only attributes. Those attributes prevent casual users from seeing and deleting the files. Before you can delete the files, you must remove those attributes.

The following steps take you through clearing the file attributes and deleting the files:

1. If you are still at the A:\> prompt, type **C:** and press Enter. The prompt should now read C:\>.

2. Type **attrib *.* -r -h -s** and press Enter.

 NOTE In case you're interested, the command in step 2 means "use the attributes command (attrib) on all files (*.*) to turn off read-only (-r), turn off hidden (-h), and turn off system (-s)."

3. Type **del *.*** and press Enter. A warning appears.

4. Type Y.

Take a Break

Congratulations on your progress so far. You're ready to install Windows. But before you tackle this task, take a few minutes to stretch and relax. Call that computer whiz friend of yours, and start out by saying "You'll never guess what I just did!" It's fun to share the moment with someone who actually knows what you mean by FDISK and RAM drive. Hey,

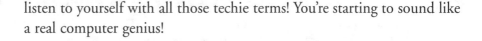

listen to yourself with all those techie terms! You're starting to sound like a real computer genius!

Installing Windows

You're practically home free now! It's time to reinstall Windows.

Start by booting your system from your startup disk, if you haven't done so already. (No need to restart if you've already done it.) Make sure you started up with CD-ROM support, because you need access to the Windows CD-ROM.

You can install Windows in either of the following two ways:

⚙ You can install it from your Windows CD-ROM. (This is the normal way to do it.)

⚙ You can copy the Windows installation files from the Windows CD to your hard disk and run the setup program from there. This takes up approximately 130 megabytes of space on your hard disk, but you will seldom (if ever) have to reinsert the Windows CD-ROM when you add or remove Windows components in the future. If you have a large hard disk with plenty of space, I suggest this.

I cover each method in its own section in the upcoming sections.

Running Windows Setup from the CD

If you decide to run Windows setup from the Windows CD, do the following:

1. Start your PC using your Windows startup floppy disk and choose to enable CD-ROM support.

2. Insert the Windows CD in your CD-ROM drive.

3. Type the letter of your CD-ROM drive and a colon at the prompt (for example, **E:**)and press Enter.

TIP

■■

Because you booted from the startup disk, your CD-ROM drive letter is probably not the same as it once was. Look onscreen for a message like this:

```
MSCDEX Version 2.25
Copyright (C) Microsoft Corp. 1986-1995 All rights reserved
      Drive E: = Driver MSCD001 unit 0
```

That message tells you your CD-ROM letter (E in this example).

■■

4. Type **setup** and press Enter.

5. Skip to the section "Completing Windows Setup" later in this session.

Running Windows Setup from Your Hard Disk

If you want to run Windows setup from your hard disk, you must create a folder on your hard disk for the setup files and then copy them there.

You can name the folder anything you like, but I normally name it C:\Cabs. Cab is short for cabinet file. Most of the setup files for Windows have a .cab extension. (Yes, I know, this is a real geek thing!) The following steps use that name, but feel free to substitute something else if you prefer, like C:\Winsetup. Also, in the following steps, I assume your CD-ROM drive letter is E. If it's not, substitute the correct drive letter wherever you see E.

Follow these steps to copy the setup files to your hard disk and to start Windows Setup.

1. Start your PC from your startup disk, if you have not done so already.

2. Make sure you know what your CD-ROM drive letter is. (See the tip in the preceding section.) Also, make sure you know which version of Windows you have: Windows 95 or Windows 98.

3. Insert the Windows CD in your CD-ROM drive.

4. Type **C:** and press Enter. The prompt now shows `C:\>`.

5. Type **md cabs** and press Enter.

6. Type **cd cabs** and press Enter. The prompt now shows `C:\CABS>`.

7. If you have Windows 95, type **copy e:\win95*.***, or if you have Windows 98, type **copy e:\win98*.***. Then press Enter.

8. Wait for the files to copy to your hard disk. It might take a few minutes.

9. When the prompt returns (`C:\CABS>`), type **setup** and press Enter.

10. Go to the next section, "Completing Windows Setup."

Completing Windows Setup

The following steps pick up right after you type **setup** and press Enter. To finish the Windows setup, do the following:

NOTE These steps are for Windows 98, but Windows 95 is very similar. Some of the steps might come in a slightly different order, but the basic procedures are the same. You don't need to follow these steps closely anyway; just follow along with the onscreen prompts.

1. A message appears that Setup is going to check your system. Press Enter.

2. Wait for the test to complete. When you see a message that the drives had no errors, type **x** to exit.

3. At the Windows 98 Setup window, click on Continue.

4. At the License Agreement screen, select I accept the Agreement. Click on Next.

5. Enter your Windows product key. This is the number on the back of your CD-ROM jewel case or your Windows license agreement card, depending on the version of Windows you have. Click on Next.

6. At the Select Directory screen, choose C:\WINDOWS and click on Next. If you receive a warning that you will have to reinstall your programs, choose Yes or OK to move past it.

7. At the Setup Options screen, leave Typical selected and click on Next.

8. At the User Information screen, enter your name and company name and click on Next.

9. At the Windows Components screen, leave Install the most common components selected and click on Next.

10. At the Identification screen, if you need to set up a particular computer name and workgroup for your network, enter them in the boxes provided. Otherwise, leave the defaults in place. Then click on Next.

11. At the Establishing Your Location screen, choose your country or region and click on Next.

12. At the Startup Disk screen, click on Next.

13. At the Insert Disk prompt, click on Cancel. (You don't need to create a startup disk because you already have one.)

14. At the Remove the disk. . . prompt, click on OK.

15. At the Start Copying Files screen, click on Next.

16. Wait for the files to copy to your hard disk. It takes about 20 to 30 minutes.

17. When you see a message that Setup is ready to restart your computer, remove your setup disk from your floppy drive and then click on OK.

18. If you see a Restart Now button, click on it. If you don't, the PC restarts by itself after a 15-second pause.

19. Wait for Windows to restart and begin detecting your hardware.

20. When prompted, specify the date and time, and choose your time zone. Click on Close to go on.

The rest of the setup process is different for each PC, depending on the hardware installed. Just follow the prompts. You might be prompted to complete a wizard (that is, a series of configuration dialog boxes) for a certain device, to restart, and/or to insert a disk for a device. When Setup is finished, it restarts your PC one last time, and when Windows reloads, it's ready to use.

Well, almost ready to use. Some of your devices might not be working yet, because Windows did not have the needed drivers to set them up automatically. See "Reinstalling Device Drivers" later in this session for help setting them up.

After all your devices are working again, you want to begin reinstalling your software. See "Reinstalling Applications" later in this session for details.

Avoiding Reregistering Windows after Reinstalling

When you reinstall Windows, it has no way of knowing that you aren't a brand-new user. Consequently, it pesters you to register your copy of Windows and might not let you use certain features (such as Windows Update) until you complete the registration process again.

There's a workaround, but it's somewhat techie. You create a registration file, and then merge it with your Windows Registry, tricking Windows into thinking you registered. Follow these steps:

1. Start Windows Notepad by choosing Start/Programs/Accessories/Notepad.

2. Type the following text, each on a single line:

```
REGEDIT4
[HKEY_LOCAL_MACHINE\SOFTWARE\Microsoft\Windows\CurrentVersion]
"RegDone"="1"
[HKEY_LOCAL_MACHINE\SOFTEARE\Microsoft\Windows\CurrentVersion\
➡ Welcome\RegWiz]
"@"="1"
```

3. Save the file as Register.reg in your C:\My Documents folder and close Notepad.

4. Double-click on My Documents on the desktop, opening the My Documents folder.

5. Double-click on Register.reg.

6. At the confirmation dialog box, choose Yes.

7. Click on OK. Now Windows thinks you have registered.

Reinstalling Device Drivers

You already know quite a bit about device drivers from your work earlier today.

First, let's get that video driver configured, if it isn't already. Turn back to "Improving the Display" in the Saturday Afternoon session and install the correct video and monitor drivers for your system.

Next, visit your Device Manager (by right-clicking on My Computer, choosing Properties, and selecting the Device Manager tab), and see which devices didn't get set up automatically during Windows Setup. Errant devices have yellow-circle exclamation points next to them. Refer to "Fixing a Specific Device" in Saturday Morning's session for details.

Test all your devices to make sure they work. Some devices might require you to run their own setup software before they can work. (Such devices might include a scanner, rewritable CD-ROM drive, or sound card.)

Reestablishing Your Network Connection

If you are on a network, you need to set up your PC for network access again. The following sections outline the steps for doing so.

Installing the Network Card Driver

Your first step is getting Windows to recognize the network card. If the card supports Plug and Play, Windows might do this automatically during setup. You probably will be prompted for a setup disk for it; use the one that came with the network card. Refer to "Fixing a Specific Device" on Saturday Morning for details.

Installing Network Drivers

Next, you must install the necessary drivers in Windows to enable network support. In most cases, that consists of the following:

○ Client for Microsoft Networks

○ Client for NetWare Networks

○ IPX/SPX-Compatible Protocol

○ NetBEUI

In addition, if you plan to use dial-up networking (such as Internet connection through a modem) or to share an Internet connection with another PC, you want TCP/IP.

To check to see if any or all of these are already installed, go to the Control Panel and double-click on the Network icon, or right-click Network Neighborhood (if you have that icon on your desktop) and choose Properties. On the Configuration tab of the Network dialog box, look for the listed drivers (see Figure 4.3).

If any of the following are not installed, install them:

○ **Client for Microsoft Networks**. Click on Add, click on Client, and then click on Add again. A list of client manufacturers appears. Select Microsoft in the left pane, and then double-click on Client for Microsoft Networks in the right pane (see Figure 4.4).

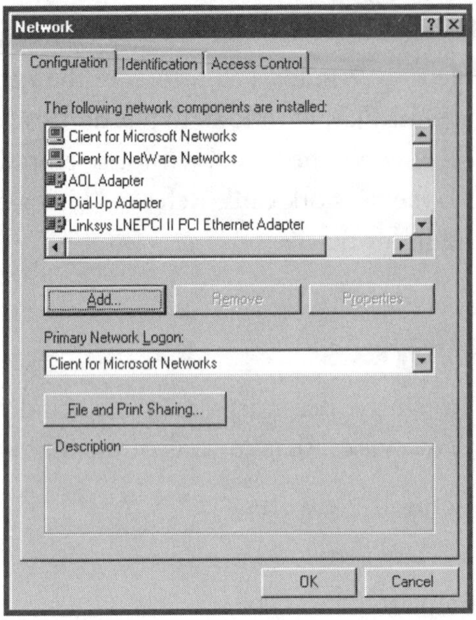

Figure 4.3

You must have the necessary Windows network drivers installed to use the network.

○ **Client for NetWare Networks**. This is the same as installing the Client for Microsoft Networks, except you choose a different item from the right pane. (As you can see in Figure 4.4, both are considered Microsoft clients.)

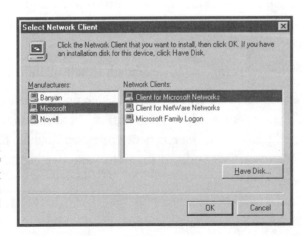

Figure 4.4

Client for Microsoft Networks is a client found under Microsoft.

- **IPX/SPX-Compatible Protocol**. Click on Add, click on Protocol, and then click on Add again. A list of protocols appears. Choose Microsoft as the manufacturer and double-click on IPX/SPX-Compatible Protocol on the list.

- **NetBEUI**. Same as IPX/SPX-Compatible Protocol except you choose NetBEUI instead. NetBEUI is also a protocol, and it is also under Microsoft.

- **TCP/IP**. Same as IPX/SPX and NetBEUI.

You probably will be prompted to restart your computer at least once during all this. Whenever you see such a prompt, choose Yes or OK. After you restart with all the needed drivers in place, go on to the next section.

Setting Up Network Access Control

If you want other people on the network to be able to access your files and/or your printer, you must set up access control for the drives and printers you want to share. By default, none of your system is shared. To make your files and printers accessible to others, follow these steps:

1. Open the Control Panel and double-click on the Network icon.
2. On the Configuration tab, open the Primary Network Logon drop-down list and choose Client for Microsoft Networks or Client for NetWare Networks, depending on what kind of network you are connected to.

 NOTE If you have a home-based, peer-to-peer network (that is, a network without a server), choose Client for Microsoft Networks in step 2.

3. Select the Identification tab.
4. Type the name you want to give your PC in the Computer name box.

If you are on a network at work, ask your system administrator what name to use. If you are configuring your own home network, make up a name that is unique from the other computers.

CAUTION   If you are on a network at your workplace, check with your system administrator to make sure it's okay for you to be modifying your network settings. Some administrators prefer to perform all the network configuration themselves to ensure it is done correctly.

5. Type the name of your workgroup in the Workgroup box.

    If you are on a network at work, your system administrator can give you a name to use. If you are setting up a home network, you can use anything you like here, but the name should be the same for all PCs on your network. The name is case-sensitive.

6. Enter a description of your PC in the Computer Description box (see Figure 4.5).

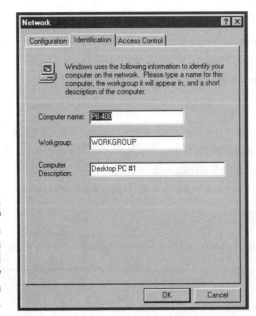

Figure 4.5

Enter the information your PC will provide to identify itself to others on the network.

7. Select the Access Control tab.

8. Make sure Shared-level Access Control is selected.

9. Click on OK. If prompted, insert your Windows CD and click on OK.

10. When prompted to restart your PC, choose Yes.

11. When your PC restarts, a Logon window appears requiring a username and password.

    If you are on a network at work, enter the username and password that was given to you by the system administrator. If you are on a home network, you can make up a user name and password (or you can leave the password box blank to not use one). Click on OK. Do not click on Cancel, or you cannot log on to the network.

Sharing a Drive or Printer

The final step in configuring networking is to share a drive or printer. If you don't do this, other computers on the network cannot use this computer's resources.

To set up sharing, do the following:

1. In the Control Panel, double-click on the Network icon.

2. Select the Configuration tab.

3. Click on File and Print Sharing. The File and Print Sharing window opens.

4. Select both check boxes to enable both file and printer sharing (see Figure 4.6). Click on OK.

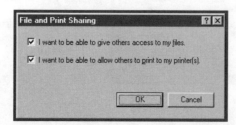

Figure 4.6

Choose to share files and printers.

5. When asked if you want to restart your computer, choose Yes.

To share the files on a drive with other computers on the network, follow these steps:

1. Double-click on My Computer on the desktop.

2. To share an entire drive, right-click on the drive and choose the Sharing command.

Or, to share only a single folder, double-click on the drive containing the folder, and then right-click on the folder and choose the Sharing command.

3. Select the Shared As option button.

4. Type a name by which this drive or folder should be known on the network in the Share Name box.

5. Choose an Access Type: Read-Only (can read but not change), Full (can both read and change), or Depends on Password (see Figure 4.7).

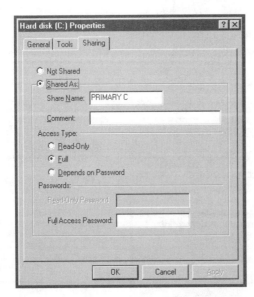

Figure 4.7

Choose how you want to share the files on this disk (or in this folder).

6. Type passwords, if desired, in the Passwords section.

   Depending on what you choose in step 5, different boxes in this section are available. For example, if you choose Read-Only in step 5, the Read Only Password box is available.

7. Click on OK.

8. Repeat these steps for each drive or individual folder you want to share.

To share a printer, the procedure is somewhat the same:

1. Open the My Computer window and double-click on the Printers icon.

2. Right-click on the printer you want to share and choose Sharing from the shortcut menu.

3. On the Sharing tab that appears, select the Shared As option button.

4. Enter a name by which the printer should be known in the Share Name box.

5. (Optional) If you want to assign a password to use the printer, enter it in the Password box.

6. Click on OK.

To access files on another computer, use the Network Neighborhood icon on your desktop, or when browsing for files in an application, choose Network Neighborhood from the list of drives.

Reestablishing Your Internet Connection

If you use a modem to connect to the Internet, you need to set up a Dial-Up Networking connection for it. You also need to make sure Windows recognizes your modem correctly.

Checking the Modem

Most modems these days are Plug and Play—in other words, Windows detects and configures them automatically. To make sure your modem is installed and working correctly, do the following:

1. From the Control Panel, double-click on Modems. The Modems Properties dialog box opens.

2. Make sure your modem is listed on the General tab, as shown in Figure 4.8.

   If it is not, click on Add and work through the Add Hardware Wizard to set it up. If that doesn't work, try installing the software that came with the modem, or run through the device troubleshooting sections from Saturday Morning.

3. Select the Diagnostics tab.

4. Select the modem's COM port.

5. Click on More Info.

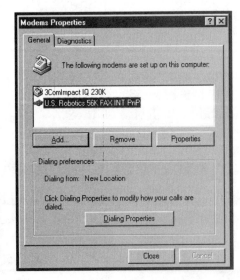

Figure 4.8

Check to see whether Windows sees your modem.

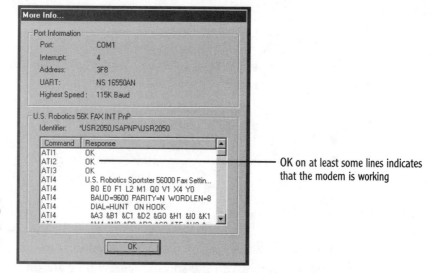

OK on at least some lines indicates
that the modem is working

Figure 4.9

This modem is
functioning
properly.

Windows checks the modem by sending it certain commands and noting the responses. If the modem is working correctly, results appear in a More Info box, as shown in Figure 4.9. If an error message appears instead, there is a problem with the modem.

6. Click on OK, and then click on OK again.

If you run into any problems or error messages in the preceding procedure, something is wrong with the modem. Perhaps it is not installed correctly, or perhaps it has a resource conflict with another device. See "Managing Device Conflicts" in the Saturday Morning session for troubleshooting help.

Running the Internet Connection Wizard

The Internet Connection Wizard (ICW) automates the process of setting up your PC for Internet connectivity. I assume that you already have an Internet account, and you just want to set it up again on your PC. You can also use ICW to choose a new Internet provider, but that's material for a different book.

To set up your existing Internet connection, you need the following information handy:

- The telephone number for your modem to dial.
- Your username (such as jdoe200).
- Your password (which might be case-sensitive).
- The incoming and outgoing mail servers to use. These are probably something like pop.mysite.net for the incoming and smtp.mysite.net for the outgoing.
- The IP address and/or DNS server address to use, if your provider requires that you use specific ones. These are four sets of numbers separated by periods, such as 198.70.33.50.

You plug this information into the blanks provided as you work through the wizard; just follow these steps:

1. Start the Internet Connection Wizard.

   The first time you run Internet Explorer after installing Windows, the ICW runs automatically. You might also have an icon for it on your desktop. If not, you can access it from the Start menu (Start/Programs/Accessories/Internet Tools/Internet Connection Wizard).

2. On the first screen of the ICW, choose I want to set up my Internet connection manually, or I want to connect through a local area network (LAN). Click on Next.

3. When asked how you connect to the Internet, choose I connect through a phone line and a modem. Click on Next.

4. Continue working through the wizard and filling in the information provided. Most of the fields are self-explanatory.

NOTE If you need to specify a certain IP or DNS address to use, click on Advanced on the Step 1 of 3 screen. An Advanced Connection Properties dialog box opens. Select the Addresses tab and enter the IP address and/or the Primary and Secondary DNS server addresses, as shown in Figure 4.10.

5. When the wizard finishes, the Dial-up Connection dialog box appears. Click on Connect to try out the connection.

Reinstalling Applications

Now that all your hardware is working smoothly with Windows, you can reinstall your software. This is fairly easy, but time-consuming. Some programs, such as Microsoft Office, take up to 30 minutes or more to install and require you to reboot after the installation.

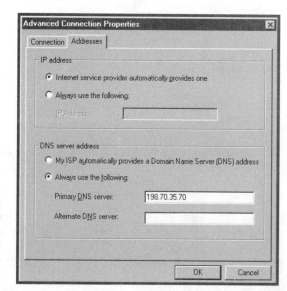

Figure 4.10

If your ISP requires specific IP or DNS addresses, enter them here.

See "Reinstalling an Application" in the Saturday Morning session for details on installing a program.

TIP

Test each application after installing it, before going on to the next program. Nothing too involved—just start the program, move around in it a bit, and then exit it. That way, if there is a conflict or a problem, you find out right away, and know which program is causing it. It's much easier to troubleshoot a problem if you can pinpoint which program is the culprit.

Take a Break

Surely you're tired after this long, productive day. Now your computer is running smoothly at last, and you're ready to get a good night's sleep. Tomorrow, I tell you about hardware upgrades and help you select and purchase the add-on components that are right for your system.

Planning System Upgrades

- ✿ Upgrades That Enhance Performance
- ✿ Upgrades That Add New Capabilities
- ✿ Name-Brand or Generic Parts?
- ✿ Making Your Buying Decision
- ✿ Where to Buy Upgrades

Your current system now runs at peak performance, but is that enough? Even after tuning up your PC, you might find it lacking in some way. Perhaps it's still slower than you'd like, the display is still fuzzy, or you still can't do something with it that you want to accomplish. If so, it's time to think about upgrading one or more of its components.

There are two kinds of upgrades: those that enhance performance, such as memory upgrades, and those that add new capabilities, such as the addition of a scanner or digital camera. In the following sections, I explain your options for each type of upgrade and help you make some decisions.

Upgrades That Enhance Performance

On Friday evening, I told you about how data flowing through a computer is like water flowing through a pipe. Just as water can flow no faster than the narrowest part of the pipe allows, data can be processed no faster in your PC than your weakest component allows. Here are some of the upgrades that can improve the data flow and storage capacity and, hence, the computer's overall performance.

A Faster Processor

If your computer runs slowly overall, a new processor can potentially improve its performance.

However, upgrading the processor is not as straightforward as you might think. The motherboard and the processor work as a team, and most motherboards work with only a short list of processors. (See the motherboard's manual, or the computer's manual, to find out which processors work with yours.) That means if you want to replace the processor, you must often get a new motherboard as well. Then the upgrade process starts to get messy and complicated, and it's best to turn it over to a professional computer technician.

Here's something else to think about: A computer that uses an old processor is probably an old computer in general, with other old components. The hard disk is probably small, and the memory insufficient for today's programs. It is much cheaper to buy a whole new computer than to upgrade individual parts on it. If your computer is more than three years old, it is seldom a good value to upgrade it. Buy a new one and donate your old one to charity for a tax deduction.

NOTE If you are serious about putting a new motherboard and processor into your current PC, check out my book *Upgrade Your PC in a Weekend,* also published by Prima Publishing. It contains specific step-by-step instructions for doing that.

There are two kinds of processors you can buy: replacement processors and upgrade processors.

Replacement processors are "regular" processors, the same type you would buy if you were creating a whole new system. Your system is a good candidate for a replacement processor if your motherboard's manual indicates that it can accept a faster processor than what you currently have installed. If you buy a replacement processor, make *sure* your motherboard can work with it before you plunk down the cash. Contact the PC's manufacturer if you don't have a motherboard manual.

Upgrade processors are designed to work with a variety of motherboards and to replace a variety of existing processors. These typically double or even triple the speed (in MHz) of your current system. For example, you might be able to find an upgrade processor that increases your 90 MHz Pentium system to 233 MHz, or increases your 166 MHz Pentium to 333 MHz. Popular manufacturers of these upgrade processors include Kingston and Visiontek.

NOTE Visit the manufacturer's Web site for the upgrade processor before you buy it. You might find information there that confirms whether the upgrade works with your system.

Upgrading a processor can be tricky. You might need to set jumpers on the motherboard or do other setup. This is one of those upgrades you might want to pay an expert to perform for you.

More Memory

Lack of adequate memory is one of the most common reasons a computer runs more slowly than it should, especially in Windows. As I explained earlier, when you don't have enough real memory in your computer, Windows relies heavily on virtual memory. This virtual memory is slow and inefficient, and it's probably why your computer runs so slowly, especially if the slowness occurs after you have been using the computer for a while and you hear whirring sounds (thrashing) coming from your hard disk when the system slows down.

The most important part of memory shopping is making sure you know what kind of memory your system needs before you make the purchase. Several types of memory (RAM) are available.

Memory Types

Most memory sold these days comes in two varieties: SIMMs (Single Inline Memory Modules) and DIMMs (Dual Inline Memory Modules). Some motherboards can accept either kind, but most require one or the other. Generally speaking, the newer the system, the more likely it uses DIMMs.

SIMMs are found in 486 and some Pentium systems. SIMMs come in 72-pin or 30-pin sizes, as shown in Figure 5.1. The pins are the little metal strips along the bottom. The 72-pin size is the most common, and it comes in three varieties. These are the following:

- ✪ **True parity memory.** This memory is for systems that require parity memory. Many older 486 systems require true parity. Look for a 36 in the specifications for parity memory, as in 16 × 36-60ns. (I'll explain the rest of that spec later.)

- ✪ **Fast page mode (FPM) memory.** FPM is generic memory. It works in just about any system that requires non-parity memory and doesn't mention anything about EDO. Look for a 32 in the specifications for this, as in 16 × 32-60ns.

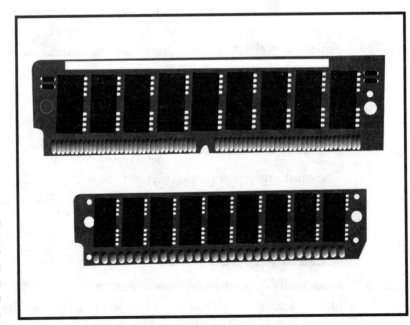

Figure 5.1

SIMMS are a common memory type; they come in 72-pin (upper) and 30-pin (lower) models.

✿ **Extended data out (EDO) memory.** EDO is a newer, better kind of non-parity memory. Many of the Pentium-class systems use it.

The second type of SIMM is the 30-pin SIMM. This type of memory is older, and you might not find it in high denominations. A recent check at my favorite memory vendor's Web site showed that only 4MB pieces were in stock. Thirty-pin SIMMs are available in only one variety: true parity.

Most of the systems currently being sold today use 168-pin dual inline memory modules (DIMMs). One variety, called S-DRAM DIMM, is the latest rage because it is faster and better than a SIMM. You can find DIMM slots in Pentium II and Pentium III systems.

◆◆◆◆◆◆◆◆◆◆◆◆◆◆◆◆◆◆◆◆◆◆◆◆◆◆◆◆◆◆◆◆◆◆◆◆◆◆◆

Memory for Macintosh computers also comes in the form of 168-pin DIMMs. If you are buying S-DRAM DIMMs, make sure you are buying the type for IBM-compatible PCs.

◆◆◆◆◆◆◆◆◆◆◆◆◆◆◆◆◆◆◆◆◆◆◆◆◆◆◆◆◆◆◆◆◆◆◆◆◆◆◆

You can buy memory modules in various denominations, ranging from 256K (that's one-quarter of a megabyte) to 128MB and higher. You need to make sure when choosing a denomination that your motherboard supports it and that you are not mixing denominations in a memory bank. Each DIMM slot is a bank unto itself, so you don't have to worry with DIMMs; but most SIMM slots work in pairs, and you must have the same denomination in each slot of the pair. (More about this later in this session.)

RAM also comes in different speeds, measured in nanoseconds (ns). A lower number is faster, and faster is better. Most RAM you buy today is 60ns, but you can sometimes buy 70 or even 80ns at a discount. You must buy RAM that is at least as fast as your system requires. Using a faster speed of RAM than your system specifies doesn't help, but it usually doesn't hurt either. So, for example, if your system needs 70ns RAM, you could probably use 70ns or 60ns equally well. (A few older systems require a specific RAM speed, and say so in their documentation.) But if it needs 60ns, it can't work right with anything slower. You should not mix speeds in the same computer. If you already have 70ns RAM, you should buy more 70ns RAM to go with it or replace all the RAM.

Determining the Memory You Need

If you don't know what kind of memory your computer uses, that's actually a good thing—it means you're not a total computer geek, and you have better things to do than remember such trivia.

To determine what kind of memory to buy, you need to know two things:

○ What open memory slots you have on your motherboard

○ What type, speed, and denomination your motherboard accepts

What Memory Slots Are Free?

You should add RAM into the empty memory slots on your motherboard—if you have any empties, that is. If you don't, you have to take out some of the RAM that's already there and replace it with RAM of a higher denomination. For example, suppose you have four slots, and each one already has a 4MB SIMM in it. If you want more memory, you must remove at least two of the SIMMs (because they usually work in pairs) and replace them with 8MB or 16MB SIMMs. (This advice assumes your motherboard can accept higher denomination SIMMs; I address that shortly.)

Therefore, before you buy RAM, take a look at your motherboard and find out whether you have any open memory slots. If so, which ones are they and what size? Look on the motherboard for a small circuit board propped up at a 45-degree (for SIMMs) or 90-degree (for DIMMs) angle to the motherboard. You might find one, two, four, or eight of these, all lined up in a row. Altogether there should be at least four slots for RAM (or at least two for a system that uses DIMMs), and ideally, some are empty to allow for adding more RAM. Figure 5.2 shows some SIMM slots on a motherboard, with one SIMM installed.

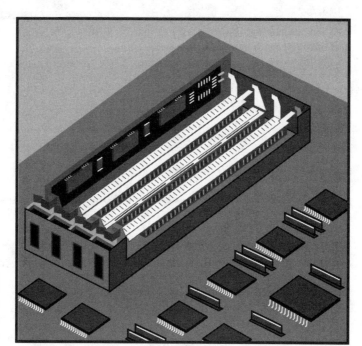

Figure 5.2

Here's what SIMMs look like on a motherboard.

What RAM Can Your PC Accept?

Look in the manual that came with your computer or your motherboard. You should find a paragraph or a chart that shows what RAM configurations your system accepts. For example, Figure 5.3 shows a specification for a Pentium-class system with four 72-pin SIMM slots (two banks of two slots each) and two 168-pin DIMM slots.

From Figure 5.3, you can tell that the system has a great deal of flexibility; it can take either FPM or EDO SIMMs, and either S-DRAM or EDO DIMMs. It does not specify a speed, so assume 60ns. It also tells you that it can't handle two DIMMs and four SIMMs at the same time.

If you have a 486 system, the memory specifications can be even more complicated. For example, the chart in Figure 5.4 is for a motherboard with two 72-pin SIMM slots and four 30-pin SIMM slots. (The chart in Figure 5.4 is an abbreviated version; the real chart went all the way up to

Figure 5.3

Some computer manuals might provide general guidance for memory, like this.

```
                          Memory:

Up to 256MB in two banks using four SIMMs of 8, 16, 32, or 64
with support for FPM and EDO DRAM and two DIMMs of 8, 16, 32,
or 64MB with support for S-DRAM and EDO DRAM.

SIMM 3,4 and DIMM1 cannot be used at the same time.

When using S-DRAM, JP6 must be set to 3.3V position (A).
```

64MB.) Your motherboard's chart might be different from this one; I use this example only to teach you how to read a chart.

NOTE

In Figure 5.4, they use M to mean megabyte; in this book, I use MB. It's the same thing; just two different naming conventions.

Here's how to read the chart. Let's say you know the system in Figure 5.4 has 8MB of RAM currently: two SIMMs in the 72-pin slots and four empty 30-pin slots. From Figure 5.4, you can see that the motherboard has six slots altogether. Each of the two 72-pin slots constitutes one individual bank, named 0/2 and 1/3, respectively. (See the x 1 next to each entry in the corresponding columns.) The four 30-pin slots form a single bank collectively. (See the x4 next to each entry in that column.)

If there are currently SIMMs in both 72-pin slots, and the system has 8MB in total, you can conclude that each module is a 4MB SIMM. Only one of the 8M rows in the table (the third row) shows something in each of the 0/2 and 1/3 banks and nothing in bank 2. That row lists 4MB X 1 in each of those two columns. So that's the current configuration. From the information at the top of the chart, you also can conclude that the RAM in the system is at least 80ns in speed, which is what the

DRAM Installation

DRAM Access Time: 80ns, page mode

DRAM Type: 256KB/1MB/4MB/16MB SIMM Module (30 pin)

　　　　　　　1MB/2MB/4MB/8MB/16MB/32MB SIMM Module (72 pin)

Memory Size	Bank 2 (30 pin)	Bank 0/2 (72 pin)	Bank 1/3 (72 pin)
8M	1M x 4	4M x 1	---
8M	1M x 4	---	4M x 1
8M	---	4M x 1	4M x 1
8M	---	8M x 1	---
8M	---	---	8M x 1
9M	256K x 4	4M x 1	4M x 1
9M	1M x 4	4M x 1	1M x 1
9M	1M x 4	1M x 1	4M x 1
10M	1M x 4	4M x 1	2M x 1
12M	1M x 4	4M x 1	4M x 1
12M	4M x 4	---	8M x 1
12M	---	4M x 1	8M x 1
12M	---	8M x 1	4M x 1
16M	4M x 4	---	---
16M	---	16M x 1	---
16M	---	---	16M x 1
17M	256K x 4	16M x 1	---
17M	256K x 4	---	16M x 1
17M	4M x 4	1M x 1	---
17M	4M x 4	---	1M x 1
18M	256K x 4	1M x 1	16M x 1
18M	256K x 4	16M x 1	1M x 1
19M	256K x 4	16M x 1	2M x 1
20M	1M x 4	16M x 1	---
20M	1M x 4	---	16M x 1
20M	4M x 4	4M x 1	---
20M	4M x 4	---	4M x 1
21M	256K x 4	4M x 1	16M x 1
21M	256K x 4	16M x 1	4M x 1
24M	1M x 4	4M x 1	16M x 1
24M	1M x 4	16M x 1	4M x 1
32M	4M x 4	16M x 1	---
32M	4M x 4	---	16M x 1
32M	---	16M x 1	16M x 1
32M	---	32M x 1	---
32M	---	---	32M x 1

Figure 5.4

Excerpt from a memory configuration chart for a 486 computer.

system requires, and that it is page mode, which is short for Fast Page Mode (FPM).

Suppose you want to upgrade this PC to 16MB of RAM. What are your options? Well, looking at the table in Figure 5.4, you can see three possible configurations for 16MB: You can put a single 16MB SIMM in either of the two 72-pin banks (bank 0/2 and bank 1/3), or you can fill up bank 2 (the four 30-pin SIMM slots) with four 4MB SIMMs. Either way, you cannot reuse your existing 4MB SIMMs.

What if you bought a 16MB SIMM for one of the 72-pin slots and reused a 4MB SIMM in the other for a total of 20MB of RAM? According to the chart, the only possible configurations for 20MB are one 16MB 72-pin SIMM and four 1MB 30-pin SIMMs. For some reason, this particular motherboard doesn't let you have different denominations of SIMMs in banks 0/2 and 1/3 unless bank 2 is also full. Good thing you checked.

Well then, what if you put some SIMMs in bank 2? Check out the 21MB line on the chart. You could put 256KB SIMMs in bank 2, and then use one of the old 4MB SIMMs in banks 1/3 or 0/2 along with the new 16MB SIMM that you plan to buy. Look at the 24MB line too; you would also put 1MB SIMMs in bank 2 for a total of 24MB. Is this a good idea? Only if you happen to have old 30-pin SIMMs lying around already. Don't buy them just for this purpose. (They're hard to find these days anyway, because the newer systems don't use them.)

Memory is so cheap these days that I would recommend upgrading this PC to 32MB by buying a second 16MB SIMM. As you can see on the 32MB line of the chart, you can have 16MB in both banks 0/2 and 1/3 for a total of 32.

Pretty complicated, eh? Figuring out what memory to buy is the hardest part of adding memory to a computer. If you can survive this, installing the memory (which you learn this afternoon) is a piece of cake.

Brand Name Versus Generic

Memory either works or it doesn't. There's no performance difference between brands, which is why I usually buy generic memory. It's cheaper, and if it doesn't work, I can send it back for replacement.

Memory seldom goes bad after the first 48 hours or so of use (referred to as the *burn in period*). If a SIMM or DIMM works initially, it probably will continue to work until long after your computer is obsolete. So a one-year or even lifetime warranty on memory is not a big selling point.

New Hard Disk

Most people don't pay any attention to their hard disks until they become full. Then, suddenly, the hard disk is a big issue.

Hard disks are distinguished from one another in several ways: the interface they use, their capacity, and how quickly they can read and write data. The following sections look at each of these factors individually.

Choosing an Interface

Your current hard disk is probably an IDE of some variety. These drives offer decent performance at a very good price, and they run on almost any computer. Your computer probably has built-in support for four IDE devices, so you can probably add another IDE drive without buying anything extra except the new drive. The most common types of IDE-compatible drives are EIDE (the E stands for enhanced) and ATA-2. There is also a new IDE type, UltraDMA (UDMA) IDE, which offers improved performance over other types of IDE drives.

You can also get SCSI (Small Computer Systems Interface) hard disks. These hook up to SCSI interface cards, so if you don't already have a SCSI interface card in your system, you need to buy one if you want to use a SCSI hard disk. SCSI hard disks are usually more expensive than

IDE drives. Many computer experts consider SCSI hard disks superior, and they do perform better under some conditions. Personally, I have never been able to tell much difference.

Choosing a Drive Capacity

When choosing a new hard disk capacity, always overestimate. Decide how much space you think you want for all the programs you can ever imagine buying, and then triple that amount. For example, I bought a 6.4 gigabyte drive in the new computer I got earlier this year. It seemed huge at the time, but it's more than half-full already. You don't want to have to buy another hard disk a year from now, so buy the largest capacity drive you can possibly afford. You can buy anything from 1.2 gigabytes to more than 30 gigabytes these days (and maybe more by the time you read this) so let your wallet be your guide.

NOTE In addition to capacity, you also need to consider the physical size of the drive. Most hard disks are called half height or third height. This designation refers to the portion of an old-style full-height drive bay that they consume. (In the old days of computing, hard disk technology was so primitive that hard disks had to be very large in physical size. To get an idea of how tall a full-height drive was, picture two CD-ROM drives stacked.) Some ultra-high–capacity drives, such as Quantum's Bigfoot drive, have larger than average physical dimensions. If you have limited space inside your computer's case for your upgrade, ask about the dimension of a drive before you buy it.

Choosing a Minimum Drive Performance

Hard disks have two critical measurements. These are:

✪ **Average access time.** This is the time it takes for the drive head to reach and read the average bit of data. It's measured in milliseconds (ms). The lower the number, the faster the drive. A decent speed is 10ms.

✪ **Data transfer rate**. This measurement refers to how quickly data moves from the hard disk to memory. The higher the number, the faster the rate. Look for a data transfer rate of 11 to 16 megabytes per seconds.

Most advertisements for hard disks give these two measurements. If this information is missing, call the supplier or manufacturer and ask.

Selecting the Drive You Want

Of course, all the factors are important, but here is how I select a hard disk.

First, I eliminate all the drives that have the wrong interface. If I'm shopping for IDE, I ignore SCSI drives. Then I look at the available drives in the capacity I want.

From that narrowed list, I check to see which drives have the best data transfer rates and average access times. Of the drives with the best performance measurements, I go with the cheapest one, provided it is a brand I have heard of before. Popular brands include Maxtor, Western Digital, Seagate, Quantum, and JTS.

A Larger or Better Monitor

When shopping for a monitor, appearance is (almost) everything. You're going to be looking at that monitor for hours on end—how does the picture look to you? If the monitor has a great picture, everything else is probably okay. The features that make up a good monitor feed into this central goal.

Screen Size

Size refers to the diameter of the screen. Monitors come in sizes ranging from 14 inches (the standard no-frills model) to 21 inches and up. If you are not sure what size you have, it is probably 15 inches because that is what is sold with most computer systems. (Systems purchased in the last year, however, might have 17-inch monitors, because this size has become more popular recently.) The size is measured diagonally, just like on a television.

Large monitors (17 inches and larger) make a lot of sense for people who sit at their computers all day and want to avoid eyestrain. Be warned, however, that a big monitor is not necessarily a crisp one, and you can get a worse headache from looking at a big fuzzy picture than a small sharp one.

Large monitors are also good for people who need to run their video display at a very high resolution so they can fit lots of information on the screen at once. A very high resolution makes everything on the screen tiny and hard to read unless you have a big monitor.

When you see the size listed, you might see two different numbers. For example, you might see 17-inch (15.9-inch viewable). This differential is because, like television manufacturers, monitor makers try to wring every last centimeter out of the system for advertising purposes. Most monitors advertised as 17-inch actually do have a 17-inch piece of glass in them, but the plastic frame around the edges covers part of it, so that area is not viewable. When comparing two monitors of the same alleged size, you should also compare the viewable areas; one 17-inch monitor might have a 15.4-inch viewable area, whereas another might have a 16.2-inch viewable area. That's more than half an inch difference—which makes a big difference in real estate onscreen.

Maximum Resolution

A monitor's maximum resolution refers to the maximum number of separate dots it can display horizontally and vertically. Many small monitors can display up to 1024×768—that is, 1024 dots across and 768 dots down. If you combine the monitor with a video card that has enough memory to handle that resolution, you have a well-matched set. Larger monitors display much higher resolutions; the better quality the monitor,

the higher its maximum resolution. Almost all monitors can display an infinite number of colors. The color limitation is a function of the video card and its memory.

Monitor Technology

Your video display is made up of tiny dots. The *dot pitch* is the measurement of how close together the dots lie. A dot pitch of .28 is considered the minimum adequate amount. Lower dot pitch is better; I have a monitor with a .25 dot pitch that I use most of the time. You can sometimes find inexpensive monitors in large sizes, such as 19-inch and above, but they usually have a higher dot pitch (like .31 or .32), making their picture less crisp.

The most common kind of monitor is called *dot trio shadow mask*. With this technology, three colored guns (red, green, and blue) shine light through a grille of round holes to form the picture. These monitors deliver clean edges and sharp diagonals, which is important for showing text onscreen.

Another kind of monitor has an *aperture grille* rather than dots. (Trinitron monitors fall into this category.) These monitors use an array of stretched wires to create images. Their performance is measured in stripe pitch, rather than dot pitch. Look for a stripe pitch of .25mm or less. These monitors have superior brightness and contrast, but their poorer diagonals make them less well-suited for displaying text.

NOTE Monitors with aperture grilles have two faint horizontal lines running across them, at approximately one-third and two-thirds of the way down the screen. These never go away; they're caused by the wires that run across the back of the monitor glass. You get used to them eventually, but they are noticeable, especially on a white background, if you look for them. Some people decide not to get an aperture grille monitor because they find these lines so annoying.

A third kind of monitor is a *slot mask*. NEC invented this hybrid that combines the attributes of a shadow mask and a aperture grille. It uses a .25mm mask with elliptically shaped phosphors.

The final kind of monitor, LCD, is mostly found on laptop computers. Some manufacturers are beginning to use LCD in larger desktop monitors with stunning results. These monitors can be nearly flat, and the displays are beautiful. Unfortunately, desktop monitors of this type sell for more than $1,000, so they are out of the reach of most people. The technology is continuing to become cheaper, however, so a flat-screen LCD panel of 17 inches might become standard equipment for new PCs.

Interlacing and Refresh Rate

To understand these two factors, you need to know a bit about how monitors work. The screen is made up of tiny dots that contain particles that glow when a light hits them. A light gun (or a set of three guns: blue, red, and green) moves very quickly over the monitor, dot by dot, making each dot glow with the appropriate color. Without being refreshed by the light gun, the particles in each dot fade quickly, so the light gun must refresh each particle hundreds of times per second. The rate at which the particles are refreshed with the light gun is the *refresh rate*. You have probably seen some monitors that are hard to look at because the display appears to flicker; the flicker is a result of a low refresh rate. Because each particle begins to lose its charge before the gun returns to it, the display appears to flash on and off. A higher refresh rate means each particle is refreshed more frequently, so there is little or no flicker.

TIP   *Convergence* refers to how well the three guns—red, blue, and green—inside the monitor align to paint the color onto each dot. If one of the guns is misaligned, the colors are not true. The best way to check convergence is to display a pure white screen. Open a Windows-based word processor and start a new document; it displays a nice expanse of whiteness. Do you see a blue, green, or red tint to the white? If so, the monitor has convergence problems.

On some cheaper monitors, the light gun simply can't keep up; to compensate, the manufacturers use a scheme called *interlacing* to keep the display readable. With interlacing, the light gun scans alternate horizontal lines, rather than every line, on each pass, so the gun can make twice the number of passes in a given amount of time. Because the horizontal lines are so close together, your eye can't pick up on the fact that every other line is not refreshed. However, your eye probably does notice a faint flicker or a fuzz on an interlaced display.

Non-interlaced monitors are the standard these days, so there is no reason you should settle for an interlaced model.

The best monitors are ones capable of non-interlaced operation and a high refresh rate. Look for a monitor with a maximum refresh rate of at least 85KHz. My monitor supports up to 120KHz, and I am very happy with it. (Of course, your video card has to support the same high resolution or you cannot take advantage of it.)

 NOTE Alhough your monitor supports a high refresh rate, your software might not automatically use the highest refresh rate. Turn back to Saturday Morning to set an optimal refresh rate for your system, if needed.

Other Monitor Features

Some extras are nice in a monitor, but not necessary. Here are some examples:

- ✪ **Speakers**. Some monitors have speakers built in, eliminating the need for desktop speakers.
- ✪ **USB connectors**. Some of the very newest monitors have an extra cable that lets you hook up to the main USB port and relay it to a pair of unpowered USB ports on the front of the monitor. Such a monitor is an investment in the future, when presumably many devices will run on USB connections.

✪ **Calibration controls**. Some monitors provide built-in calibration setup programs that let you match printer output to screen image color precisely.

✪ **Other adjustment controls**. Look for easy-to-use brightness, contrast, and image position controls located on the front of the monitor.

✪ **Clean back**. For corporate reception areas, it is nice to have a plain back on a monitor, with no unsightly cables sticking out. On such monitors, the cables come out the bottom instead.

✪ **Cable length**. If you are going to put the computer case on the floor and your monitor on a table, a 6-foot cord between them works better than the shorter 3-foot cord that comes on some bargain monitors.

✪ **Footprint**. If space from back-to-front is an issue on your desk, look for a monitor with a shorter depth. In general, most monitors are the same depth as they are inches in diagonal display: a 17-inch monitor is about 17 inches deep. Some short-depth 17-inch monitors, however, are only 15 inches deep.

Take a Break

Before you read the next section, you might want to take a stretch break. Suggested activity: Walk the dog (or walk yourself, if you don't have a dog) and daydream about all the fun things you want to do with your computer.

Upgrades That Add New Capabilities

The rest of the upgrades I discuss in this chapter add capabilities to your system. Computers can do a lot of great stuff these days that wasn't possible a few years ago, and adding new components to your system can enable you to participate in the fun without forcing you to buy a whole new system.

Operating System Upgrades

If you have Windows 3.1, you might find it difficult to find new software that runs on your computer. Most programs being released these days are for Windows 95 and Windows 98 only. An upgrade to the latest version, Windows 98, costs about $100 and is available everywhere computers and software are sold.

But here's the Catch-22: If your computer came with Windows 3.1, the computer is probably at least five years old and lacks the processor speed and memory needed to make Windows 95 and higher run at a decent speed.

If you have less than a 90 MHz Pentium with 32MB of memory, upgrading to Window 95 or 98 makes your computer run very slowly. The same Windows programs that used to be fine become maddeningly slow.

If you have a Windows 3.1 system, consider getting a whole new computer. Your system is practically obsolete anyway. For about $600 to $1,000 you can have a brand new computer that probably comes with Windows 98, as well as some other useful software.

If you have Windows 95, there is little reason to upgrade to Windows 98. As I told you in Friday evening's session, Windows 98 and Windows 95 are very similar. Windows 98 includes support for a few of the more recent device types, such as USB, but there are few programs (actually, there are none that I'm aware of) that specifically require Windows 98 to operate.

CD-ROM Drives

In my opinion, every computer needs a CD-ROM drive because most of the good software now comes on CD-ROM. But which drive should you buy? Or should you get a DVD drive instead? The following sections offer some suggestions.

Deciphering the Xs

The most obvious feature that manufacturers advertise for in a CD-ROM drive is its speed. You see 16x, 24x, 24/32x, and so on. It's important to know what this means.

When CD-ROMs for computers first came out, they were basically big, read-only floppy disks, used to transfer large amounts of data onto your system. You could buy CDs containing programs to install, or large collections of literature, fonts, or clip art. The CD-ROM was just a data warehouse.

Then manufacturers got the idea of running programs right from the CD. The original CD-ROM drives were too slow to make this idea viable, so vendors introduced 2x drives. They were capable of reading information from the disc approximately twice as fast as the original CD-ROM drives. The race to be the fastest has spiraled ever upward—now there are 50x drives and even faster ones on the horizon.

NOTE Sometimes you might see a drive advertised with two speeds, such as 16x/32x or 16x min/32x max. This type of statement is an example of truth in advertising. Many CD-ROM drives read more quickly from the center of the disc than from the outer edges. Alhough a drive says it is a 32x drive, it can actually read only the data near the center of the disc at 32x. The outer part of the disc is read at a much slower speed (for example, 16x). If you see a drive advertised with two speeds, you can probably compare it fairly to other drives advertised at the greater of those two speeds. (Some drives have motors that vary the rotation speed depending on where the read head is working, so they can actually read the whole disc at a constant speed.)

The higher speeds make a big difference when it comes to loading programs and looking things up in an encyclopedia, but they don't do a lot for your older games. Game manufacturers tailor their video clips for the CD-ROM drive speed they expect most users to have, and spinning the drive faster than the expected rate doesn't improve them. The faster drive

doesn't do any harm to the game video; it just doesn't do any good either. So if playing older games is your goal, it probably isn't worth springing for a drive faster than about 24x at this time. Save your money for your whole new PC a few years down the road.

Software manufacturers develop their products knowing most people don't have the latest and greatest equipment, so most software in the stores today requires only an 8x or 16x CD-ROM drive. If you go to a store to buy a CD-ROM drive, however, you are hard-pressed to find anything less than 24x for sale. Consequently, you don't really need to worry about buying the highest x drive you can find, because packaged software doesn't require such a drive for many years, if ever.

The exception is if you are a serious PC game player buying the latest graphics-intensive games on a regular basis. Games are the first arena to require the higher drive speeds because they are so heavy on graphics and sound. If you plan on buying and playing all the latest games in the next few years, get the fastest drive you can afford.

CD Interfaces

When CD-ROM drives first came on the market, the most popular models were SCSI (Small Computer Systems Interface) drives. You hooked them up to a special SCSI interface card that you placed in one of your computer's expansion slots. In addition to buying the CD-ROM drive, you had to buy a SCSI interface card if you didn't have one.

The next wave of drives came with their own special interface cards. These were SCSI cards, but they were cheap models that could run only one device: that particular CD-ROM drive. Consumers liked this because they didn't have to buy and set up a SCSI card separately.

Next, someone got the bright idea of building special capabilities into sound cards so they could be used as CD-ROM controller cards. This was the birth of the multimedia kit, which was usually a sound card, a CD-ROM drive connected to it, and a set of speakers.

All those interfaces were good, and they are still fine methods. However, the dominant type of interface today for CD-ROM drives is IDE. This is the same interface your computer's hard drives hook into, so it's already in place—nothing extra to buy. Most motherboards let you have up to four IDE devices, so unless you have four separate hard disks already, you probably have an open IDE connector. IDE CD-ROM drives are also very fast; the IDE connection is used to handling the heavy data load from the hard disk, so it handles a CD-ROM's data easily.

One way to find out whether you have any IDE interfaces left on your system is to check the startup screen. It might tell you Hard Disk 1 Detected, Hard Disk 2 Detected, and so on. Most computers can have up to four, and any of these spots not taken can support a CD-ROM, a Zip drive, or some other drive. So if four devices aren't listed, chances are good that you have some IDE acreage free.

Another way to check the IDE status is to enter your computer's BIOS setup program, as you learn this afternoon. As the computer starts, watch the screen for a message such as Press F1 for Setup. Then do that. In this program, your primary and secondary IDE interfaces are listed, including what's plugged in to them. If any of them say Available or Empty, you're okay. (To exit the BIOS program, press Esc.)

NOTE Depending on your system BIOS, not all of your IDE devices might show up in BIOS. CD-ROM drives and Zip drives might not, for example, even though they work just fine.

I tell you all this just for planning and shopping purposes; you get into the actual installation this afternoon.

Internal or External CD?

Almost all CD-ROM drives are internal—that is, they run from inside your computer's case. But you also can buy an external drive that sits as a separate box on your desk and connects to the computer via a cable.

If you have an available drive bay in your PC, internal is better, because it doesn't require a separate power cable and doesn't take up space on your desk. However, if you are going to share the drive with someone else, an external model might make sense. Each of you can have a SCSI card in your computer, and whoever needs the CD-ROM drive that day can simply plug it into the card before turning on the computer.

If you can find an external CD-ROM drive to buy, it is probably SCSI, although you might also find a CD-ROM drive that works with an external parallel port.

DVD

DVD drives are like super CD-ROM drives. They can read not only regular CDs but also special DVD disks, which can hold as much as 8.5 gigabytes. That's 133 minutes of video—an entire full-length movie. That's a lot of data. DVD drives also can function as regular CD-ROM drives, so you can replace your computer's old CD-ROM drive with one.

The original DVD drives had a few quirks. They couldn't read CDs created with a CD-ROM writer, for example. They also couldn't play audio CDs. But the newer DVD drives available today can do both of these things, so you should have no problem using a DVD drive to do all the things you do with a regular CD-ROM drive.

The only thing that might give you pause about buying a DVD drive right now is the price. They cost more than $200 on the average, whereas a regular CD-ROM drive costs about $50. And as of this writing, besides playing movies, there aren't a lot of reasons to spend the extra money. (A few games have been released on DVD, but most come only on regular CDs.) If you want movies on your computer, you need a special decoder card along with your DVD drive, which adds another $100 or so to the cost. You should buy the card and the drive as a set to guarantee compatibility between them.

I just bought myself a brand-new computer with all the bells and whistles, but I opted not to get a DVD drive. Why? Because I couldn't think of a good reason to buy one now, and if I wait until I actually need it, the prices will have come down and the technology will have improved.

CD-ROM Changers

Some CD-ROM drives can hold several discs at a time in a multidisc cartridge. They can still read (play) only one disc at a time, though, so it's not like having an extra CD-ROM drive. It's more like having a stereo system that lets you load several CDs together, so you don't have to keep returning to the stereo to put another disc in.

You have to pay extra for this feature; drives like this cost more than their single-disc counterparts. In my opinion, it's not worth the money.

CD-R and CD-RW

Recordable CD-ROM drives act just like regular CD-ROM drives, except you can create your own CD-ROMs with them. If you get one of these, you will almost certainly want to keep your regular CD-ROM drive too, so you can make copies of audio and computer CDs.

I have a recordable CD-ROM drive, and I have lots of fun with it. I also use it to create CDs that contain archive copies of the final manuscript files for the books I write. These files would fill up many floppy disks, but I can put an entire book on a single CD.

There are two kinds of recordable CD-ROM drives: *CD-R,* which stands for CD recordable, and *CD-RW,* which stands for CD-rewritable.

CD-R is an older technology. With it, you can record to a disc only once. And if an error occurs while you're recording, you've just wasted a disc. (They each cost about $1.) There are two ways to write to a CD-R disc: track-at-once and disc-at-once. With disc-at-once, you write the entire CD content in one operation. With track-at-once, a recent improvement to CD-R technology, you can write to the disc in bits and pieces; however, you can't read anything from the disc until you issue a special command to close it, and after you close it, you can't write anything else to it.

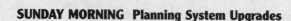

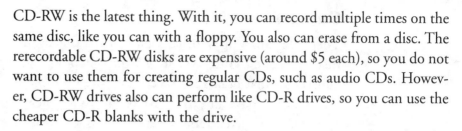

CD-RW is the latest thing. With it, you can record multiple times on the same disc, like you can with a floppy. You also can erase from a disc. The rerecordable CD-RW disks are expensive (around $5 each), so you do not want to use them for creating regular CDs, such as audio CDs. However, CD-RW drives also can perform like CD-R drives, so you can use the cheaper CD-R blanks with the drive.

Generally speaking, with any kind of recordable CD-ROM drive, you get much less x for your money. My current recordable drive cost more than $300, and it writes at 6x and reads at 24x. In contrast, my regular CD-ROM drive cost $50 and reads at 44x.

My Recommendation for CD-ROM

The average computer user doesn't need a DVD or recordable drive, just like the average driver doesn't need a touring bus with a bathroom in it. Sure it would be cool, but why spend the money on that when you can put it to better use elsewhere?

CD-ROM drives are fairly generic—they either work or they don't. For that reason, I wouldn't spend much extra money on a brand name. If you have a spare drive and IDE connection, buy a plain 24x or faster IDE internal model. It should be well under $100 and should serve you just fine.

On the other hand, if you are going to buy a DVD or CD-rewritable drive, go with a brand name drive recommended by a computer magazine. These technologies are relatively young, and well-established companies can provide better support and easier-to-use software to run them.

Removable Mass Storage

Need more storage? Besides the CD-RW drives discussed in the preceding section, there are several other types of drives that hold lots of data and have removable disks.

Super Floppies

There are now floppy drive replacements called SuperDrives (LS-120) that read and write regular 3.5-inch floppy disks, but also special SuperDisks that hold 120MB each. If you want removable mass storage but you don't have an extra drive bay in your system, you might consider replacing your current A drive with one of these. However, not all motherboards have a system BIOS that allows you to boot from this type of drive, so check with your PC's manufacturer to make sure you can use one with your system. You can put a SuperDrive in as the B drive—an extra floppy drive that you're never going to try to boot from—without worrying about the BIOS.

Removable Hard Disks

The most popular types of removable mass storage devices right now are Iomega's Zip and Jaz drives. They accept floppy-like cartridges that hold 100MB or 250MB (Zip) or 1 or 2 gigabytes (Jaz).

The cartridges cost a bit more than a regular hard disk with that capacity (about $10 for a Zip cartridge or $100 for a Jaz), so you're basically paying the $100 to $300 for the drive itself and the extra amount for the cartridges as surcharges for the extra convenience.

Although several competing brands are available, Iomega's drives seem to be winning the market-share war. Zip drives are standard equipment on many new PCs, so if being able to transport data to another computer is important, the Zip drive might be your best choice.

Iomega makes four kinds of Zip drives: SCSI internal, SCSI external, IDE, and parallel. The IDE version runs off the same IDE interface as your hard disk. If you buy a new PC with a Zip drive installed, you probably get this type because it's the least expensive to produce.

The SCSI internal version runs off your existing SCSI card if you have one; it also comes with a special limited SCSI card you can use if you

don't already have a SCSI card. Its performance is about the same as that of the IDE version.

The SCSI external version requires a SCSI interface that can be accessed from outside your computer—that is, a SCSI card you can plug in to the drive. This version is a good choice if you need high performance plus the capability to share the drive among several PCs.

The parallel version runs off your computer's parallel port, but can be extremely slow compared to the other types. I don't recommend it unless you need to share a single drive among multiple PCs.

Tape Backup Drives

Tape backup units have been around for a long time. They are used primarily for backups, as their name implies, because they are slow. They store data in a sequential order, like the songs on a cassette tape, so you can't jump easily from the beginning to the end as you can with a CD. Therefore, tape backup drives are best used for storing infrequently needed data. The oldest computers used tape drives before hard disks were invented, so the technology has a very long tradition in computers.

An internal tape drive takes up a precious drive bay in your computer; an external one requires its own power supply and takes up space on your desk.

Today's tape drives are much faster than their predecessors and hold hundreds of megabytes on each tape. If you need to do regular backups, you might like having a tape drive because you can eliminate swapping floppies in and out. However, if you don't have much data to back up (less than 100MB, for example), you might be better off backing up to a Zip drive.

Whatever tape backup unit you select, make sure it uses a standard tape type, rather than some special proprietary format, and that tapes are readily available at the computer store where you shop most often.

Modems

Until recently, having a modem was the only way most people could get online. Nowadays, there are a variety of other choices, including cable modems and network Internet connections, but modems remain the standard, especially for home users.

Modems come in both internal and external varieties. An internal modem requires an open slot in your motherboard; an external model requires a free serial (COM) port on the back of your PC, space on your desktop, and a spare power outlet to plug into.

External modems are easier for beginners to set up; I recommend them for beginner-level clients doing their own installation. Some people might tell you to always use an internal modem because an external modem would occupy one of your precious built-in serial ports; but to get an internal modem to work, you often must disable one of the built-in serial ports anyway to free up an IRQ, so that cancels out the perceived benefit. (I'll get into that this afternoon, when I talk about installation.)

NOTE   External modems are less prone to problems caused by address conflicts because the serial port (COM1 or COM2) built into the system has a preassigned address. To assign a serial port to an internal modem, you sometimes have to set jumpers on it or run special software, and it doesn't always work very well.

The current standard for modems is 56K V.90. Almost all modems available in the stores today support this standard, so it's almost a no-brainer to shop for that specification. Almost all modems you buy today are fax modems, which means they have faxing capabilities built in.

Some modems are voice modems, which means they have telephone answering machine capability. With the right software, you can use your PC as an answering machine. I have found, for myself, this feature is more trouble than it's worth, however, because it works only when the PC is on.

Some modems are advertised as For Windows Only, or Winmodems. These modems are slightly cheaper because they rely on Windows-based software to carry part of their processing load, rather than doing it all on the hardware. After it's set up, you don't notice a difference, but Winmodems can be trickier to set up on many systems. Avoid this type of modem, if possible, to save yourself some setup hassle.

With modems, name-brand does make a difference. A modem requires a driver to work with Windows, and an off-brand modem might not have a well-written driver. Further, future versions of Windows probably will not come with a driver for that off-brand modem, and you'll just have to hope the manufacturer is still in business and creates the needed driver. The difference between an off-brand modem and a well-known one is less than $50, and it's $50 well spent.

Personally, I never buy anything except U.S. Robotics/3COM modems. You can't go wrong with these. A solid company, a solid product. (And no, they didn't pay me to say that!)

Sound Cards

Sound cards have come a long way in the last several years. Creative Labs started out as and remains the industry leader, with everyone else imitating its products—its SoundBlaster is the standard. The current technology in sound is wavetable synthesis. Unless you plan on composing your own music, however, you really don't need a fancy sound card; one that simply plays your audio CDs and makes your games sound good is probably plenty.

16 bits is the standard for today's sound cards. A 16-bit sound card can process 16 bits of data at once. The more bits, the higher fidelity the sound. You might find a very old 8-bit sound card for sale somewhere, but you don't want it.

Sound cards with wavetable capability have prerecorded, built-in sounds, such as the sounds of different instruments playing different notes.

(Regular FM synthesis sound cards don't have wavetables; they simulate these notes instead, which doesn't sound as good.) You can use wavetable cards to simulate great-sounding music, playing dozens of instruments at once without having lots of recorded sound files taking up space on your hard disk. These cards are really useful for music enthusiasts who are trying to write their own music using the computer's MIDI interface (basically, an interface that can accept input from a keyboard or other instrument, or can export musical data to a synthesizer.) Wavetable cards commonly have 32, 64, or 128 voices they can play at once. (Naturally, more voices means more money.)

NOTE   If a sound card has a number 16 in its name, those numbers probably refer to 16 bits, and it probably does not contain wavetable synthesis. If, on the other hand, there is a 64 or 128 in the name, the numbers probably refer to the number of wavetable voices.

Unless you are a serious gamer or a music composer, a wavetable card isn't necessary—but if the capability comes built in to the sound card you buy, it certainly doesn't hurt anything. You also can buy an add-on card that adds wavetable synthesis to your existing sound card.

Whatever sound card you choose, make sure it is SoundBlaster or Sound-Blaster Pro compatible. Almost all games use those standards, so it is important to have this compatibility. Some newer motherboards have sound support built into them, so you don't even have to buy a sound card to have basic sound support.

Printers

You probably already have some sort of printer, so why are you thinking about getting a new one? Are you looking for more speed? Higher quality output? Color? Whatever your priorities, you can find a printer to fit your needs.

The price of a printer reflects its balance of these qualities:

- **Technology.** The newer the technology and the better the output of that technology, the higher the price. For example, laser printers are more expensive than dot-matrix printers.

- **Speed.** More pages per minute cost you more.

- **Color.** You always pay more for a printer that can print in color than the equivalent black-and-white model (if one is available).

- **Print quality.** Print quality is measured in dots per inch (dpi). For black-and-white, the higher the dpi, the nicer the output and the higher the price. For color printers, dpi is a factor but dot size and number of ink colors can make more of a difference in photographic color quality and price.

- **Memory.** Printers that compose the entire page at once (notably laser printers) need enough memory to hold the entire page. More memory means a higher up-front cost, but you probably will pay even more to add extra memory to a printer later. Memory is not an issue with ink-jet and dot-matrix printers.

- **PostScript.** The capability to print PostScript fonts and images adds to the printer's price.

You need to base your purchase decision on the balance that is right for you. For example, you might want the best possible output regardless of the speed, whereas your neighbor opts for speed (for example, for draft manuscripts) at the expense of quality. You should also consider the cost of the consumables (that is, the ink cartridge, toner, ribbon, or whatever the printer requires).

Printer Technologies

Three technologies dominate the printer market: dot matrix, ink jet, and laser. Each technology has its hybrids and subtypes, but almost all printers fall into one of these categories.

Dot Matrix

The low end printer technology is dot matrix. It works by striking the paper with a series of little pins against a ribbon (like a typewriter ribbon). In many ways, a dot-matrix printer is like an automated typewriter except that, instead of letter-shaped hammers, a group of small pins changes position to form each letter.

Dot-matrix printers are nearly obsolete. However, they offer two features other printers do not: they can print on multi-part forms, creating carbon copies, and they can use tractor-fed continuous paper. If you don't need either of those features, consider a different technology.

Ink Jet

Ink-jet printers are the current favorite for home and office use because they are inexpensive, produce nearly laser quality output, print fairly quickly, and can print in color. Their only drawback is the high cost of replacement ink cartridges, which can run $30 or more depending on the model.

Laser

Before ink-jet technology got the kinks worked out, laser printers were the only choice for serious business users. They are still very popular in business because of their razor-sharp text output and fast, quiet operation.

With a laser printer, you are stuck with black-and-white output only—unless you want to spend more than $2,000 on a color model. Upgrading laser printer technology is not a simple matter of revising the ink delivery system by adding some extra cartridges, as it is for ink-jet printers. The

innards of a color laser printer are completely different than those of a black-and-white one.

Hybrid Printers

Several manufacturers recently have introduced a new breed of printer designed mainly for small and home offices. The unit combines a printer and some other device or devices, such as a fax machine, a copier, a scanner, and so on. They go by different names; one manufacturer calls its model a Mopier; another is an OfficeJet. Others simply call them multifunction printers.

These multifunction devices seem like a great value—you get all the functions of several devices for the price (and desk space) of one. The thing to keep in mind is that you're not getting a top-quality unit in any of its categories. It can print, but not as well as a dedicated printer of the same price as the multifunction unit. It can scan, but not as well as a dedicated scanner. You get the idea. They also break down more disastrously than single-function units—the parts aren't unreliable per se, but when the scanner goes out it's apt to take the printer with it, which wouldn't be the case if they were in separate boxes. I'm not telling you to avoid these hybrids, but keep in mind that you are trading performance for size and price when purchasing one.

Printing Speed

The printer's speed depends heavily on the technology it employs. Dot matrix is the slowest, followed by ink jet, with laser at the top of the heap.

If you pay enough money, you can have a printer that prints at incredible speeds, such as 24 ppm (pages per minute). Most people have better things to do with their money, though. Home users are probably happy with a modest 8 ppm.

Keep in mind that when a printer is advertised at 8 ppm, that's the maximum speed. Your results can be lower. The 8 ppm is the speed at which the printer can print, in theory, if it doesn't have to process any graphics or wait for the computer to send data. In reality, whenever you print a page that contains fonts that are not resident in the printer, or graphics, you have to wait for the page to print. Sometimes you might wait 30 seconds or even a minute or more for the printer to begin to print a page. This is normal; don't take your printer back for a refund.

Print Quality

Print quality on a dot-matrix printer is not measured very precisely. Printers are either 9 pin (in which case the output is euphemistically called *near letter quality*, which in fact it isn't) or 24 pin (in which the output is called letter quality).

On ink-jet and laser printers, the quality is measured in dots per inch (dpi). The higher the number, the finer the quality of the image. Note that in most cases, you worry about dpi only for the sake of graphics quality; text looks good no matter now many dpi you have.

Most home and casual business users are happy with anything more than 600 dpi, the common quality of low-budget laser printers. Most ink-jet printers offer at least 720×720 resolution. On ink-jet printers, dpi is given in two separate measurements: vertical and horizontal. You might have an ink-jet printer that prints $1,440 \times 720$, for example, which means the vertical resolution is higher than the horizontal. (You won't notice the difference, except the printout looks slightly better than one from a 720 $\times$ 720 printer.)

Some printers offer resolution enhancement, which means they use one trick or another to make the printout seem like it has a higher dpi than it actually does. One such technology is Hewlett Packard's PhotoRET, which varies the ink-jet dot size to make sharper images. These technologies can make a huge difference in image quality, so don't let dpi be your only determining factor. If possible, look at some printouts to decide which has the best quality.

Color Quality

Nearly all ink-jet printers sold today are color capable, and nearly all laser printers are not. So your choice of a color or a black-and-white printer is already made for you when you decide on the technology you want.

If you plan on printing photographs, get a photographic-quality printer. Such printers usually have "photo" in their model names. These are for people who need the highest quality of printing, not for casual home and business users. If you mostly only need to print spot colors (for example, color clip art), a regular ink-jet printer is fine. Most regular color ink-jet printers can reproduce photos fairly well, certainly well enough for home use.

◆◆◆◆◆◆◆◆◆◆◆◆◆◆◆◆◆◆◆◆◆◆◆◆◆◆◆◆◆◆◆◆◆◆◆◆◆

CAUTION Some ink-jet printers require special paper to produce the highest dpi images. If you pick up a stunning color printout sample at a store, notice whether it's printed on glossy paper. If it is, you cannot duplicate that result at home unless you buy some of that paper. Such paper can cost more than $1 per sheet.

◆◆◆◆◆◆◆◆◆◆◆◆◆◆◆◆◆◆◆◆◆◆◆◆◆◆◆◆◆◆◆◆◆◆◆◆◆

To evaluate color print quality, nothing works better than taking a trip to a big computer store and actually seeing and handling the printouts from various models. You don't have to buy the printer at that store; just look at the samples and then buy wherever it's the cheapest.

Printer Memory

Printer memory serves different functions depending on what kind of printer it is.

On dot-matrix and ink-jet printers, the printer prints one line at a time on the page, as the paper moves through it. Therefore, the printer needs only enough memory to hold one line at a time. That's not much! Any additional memory the printer has serves as a buffer. When the computer tells the printer what to print on the upcoming line before the printer finishes the current line, the extra information waits in the buffer. The larger the buffer, the more data can wait in line. More memory doesn't help the printer function any better, so the memory amount in an ink-jet or dot-matrix printer is not important.

In contrast, the memory in a laser printer is very important. A laser printer composes the entire page in its memory, and then it spits it onto the paper in one pass. Consequently, the printer needs enough memory to hold the entire page. Sadly, most laser printer manufacturers cut corners and provide only 512K of memory with their printers. You have to buy memory upgrades to get more. That 512K is not even enough to hold a single full-page graphic. If you get an out-of-memory error message when printing large graphics, your printer memory is probably lacking. You should have at least 1MB of printer memory in a laser—and more is better. Why? Because the memory also has to hold any fonts the computer sends to the printer. If you are printing a page with lots of fonts and lots of graphics, you might need more than 1MB of memory for the printer to print it.

Paper Handling

A good printer should be able to accept at least 100 sheets in its paper tray so you don't have to constantly restock it. Nicer models accept up to 250 pages, and some have more than one paper tray. Models with two paper trays are good when you use two kinds of paper, such as plain and letterhead. Special trays are often available for legal-size paper or other non-standard sizes too. You also can buy special envelope feeders for some printers.

Ink, Toner, and Other Consumables

Most people don't think about the cost and availability of ink until it's too late. If you buy a well-known printer brand, such as Canon, Epson, or Hewlett-Packard, you should be able to buy consumables (ink, toner, or

ribbons) in almost any office supply store. If you go with an off-brand printer, you might have to order consumables by mail.

Dot-matrix printers and their replacement ribbons are inexpensive. However, it is becoming difficult to find them in office supply stores.

Although ink-jet printers are cheap, the ink cartridges for them can be rather expensive. A typical cartridge costs around $15, but might only print 1,000 pages. In contrast, a toner cartridge for a laser printer might cost $100, but might print 20,000 pages.

Some of the best ink-jet printers use four separate ink cartridges: one for each of the three colors that make up all the other colors (magenta, cyan, and yellow), and one for black ink. This is great because you can replace only the cartridge that is empty, without wasting any ink. Other models (slightly lesser ones, in my opinion) have two cartridges: one color cartridge containing each of the three colors in compartments, and one black cartridge. Both cartridges can be loaded in the printer at the same time.

A third type of ink-jet system uses separate color and black cartridges but only one or the other can be in the printer at once. When you want to switch between black-and-white and color printing, you must manually switch the cartridges. What a pain! In addition to the extra work of switching the cartridges, they produce very poor copies of photographs. They have to simulate black while printing in color by combining the three colored inks, and the result is a sort of nasty brown. Such printers aren't a good deal no matter how cheap they are.

Laser printers must periodically have their toner cartridges replaced (and sometimes other parts, such as the drum). These parts are rather expensive, up to $200 in some cases, but they do not need to be replaced very often. I have had to replace the toner cartridge in my laser printer only once this year, whereas my friend with an ink-jet printer has gone through six or more ink cartridges.

Scanners

If your business requires you to take photos and insert them into computer documents or Web pages, you legitimately can justify a scanner. Otherwise, it's just a toy. But what a wonderful toy! And at under $200 for a good quality one, why not?

A scanner digitizes pictures so you can use them in your computer. Some scanners also come with optical character recognition (OCR) software, which allows you to scan text and translate the picture of the text into real text in a word processor. This feature sounds great, but in practice the OCR software that comes with most scanners makes so many mistakes, you can spend as much time correcting the typos as you would have spent retyping the entire article. If you really need OCR, you can usually upgrade to a professional version of the software; the upgrade is preferable to retyping the original, but it's still not perfect.

The resolution of a scanner's scanned image is measured in dots per inch, or dpi, just like printer output. You want a scanner that can scan in at least 300 dpi. (This should not be difficult to find.)

Scan Quality

Scanners used to come in both black-and-white and color models, but nowadays it's hard to find anything but color for sale. You might hear the quality of the scanner expressed as a number of bits. Low-end scanners are 30-bit, whereas higher end models are 33- or 36-bit or more. This refers to the number of data bits needed to store the information on each pixel, or dot, in the image.

For home use, you cannot tell much difference in quality among the various scanner models, so go with one of the cheaper ones. Umax, Visioneer, Epson, and Hewlett-Packard are reliable brand names.

Scanner Interface

Some scanners come with their own interface cards; others require you to have a SCSI card. A third category attaches to your parallel port, which

means you don't need an extra interface card. It provides a pass-through for your printer, so you can connect your scanner and printer at the same time to share the port. (This works in theory; in practice, often it doesn't, especially if you have an ink-jet printer. An alternative is to install a circuit card containing an additional parallel port.)

If your system has a USB port, consider a USB interface for your scanner. USB, or Universal Serial Bus, is the wave of the future, the newest and most convenient way to connect devices to your PC. You will likely see more and more USB devices available in the years to come. Be careful, however, not to buy a USB scanner if your computer doesn't have a USB port. (Computers made before 1998 probably do not.) Also, the original version of Windows 95 did not support USB. Later versions do, and Windows 98 does.

Video Capture and Digital Cameras

Video capture refers to hooking up a video camera of some sort to your PC and capturing live motion video. You can buy a number of different devices that do this in varying degrees of quality. One such device is a Connectix camera. It's a little round ball with a camera lens in the middle and a cord that attaches to your PC. You can point it at whatever you want to record. You also can get interface cards or external adapters that you can attach to your home video camera and feed the video into your PC.

A digital camera, in contrast, captures still images and feeds them into your PC. Unlike the video capture devices, digital cameras are not attached to your PC, so you can take them out into the world with you, just like a regular camera. You bring them back to your PC and transfer the pictures you took. Some digital cameras (notably the ones in the Sony Mavica line) hold disks you can pop out and insert in your PC; others have interface cards they hook into via a cable.

Both of these can be a lot of fun, but the models priced for home users are not professional quality, and you might be disappointed if you plan to use the images for business. For example, the images taken by a digital camera are fairly low resolution compared to the much sharper images you get when you use a regular camera to take a picture, and then scan in the results. And a simple video capture device you buy at your local computer store cannot substitute for a real video camera for videoconferencing.

When shopping for a digital camera, look at these factors:

- **The maximum image size.** Try to find one that saves images in at least 640 × 480 resolution.

- **The zoom.** Zoom lenses are useful in capturing closeups; look for a camera with an adjustable zoom of at least 3x.

- **Flash.** If the camera doesn't have a built-in flash, some pictures might turn out too dark.

- **Special features.** Some cameras have features that allow you to see the stored images through the camera itself, or to take pictures in black-and-white or sepia-tone modes.

- **Connectivity.** Different cameras interface with the PC in different ways. Make sure your PC can handle whatever way a particular camera requires. For example, if the camera hooks up to transfer images via the serial port, make sure you have one free on the back of your PC.

Mouse Variants

Besides a normal mouse, you can use various nontraditional devices for pointing on the screen. Just go to any computer hardware store and take a look at the vast display of options:

- **Cordless mouse.** The cordless mouse is a regular mouse that communicates with your PC through an infrared beam or radio waves (or other technology) so you don't have to deal with the unsightly and awkward mouse cord.

- ⚙ **Trackball.** Trackballs are like upside-down mice. The base stays stationary, and you roll a ball with your thumb or hand to move the mouse pointer onscreen. My favorite model is the Kensington Expert Mouse, which runs about $100. You really need to try out the model you want to buy to make sure it feels comfortable in your hand.

- ⚙ **Touchpad.** These small rectangular pads are built into many laptop computers, but you can also buy them to plug into a desktop computer's mouse port. You just glide your finger across the pad to move the mouse pointer, and tap the pad to click or double-click. I have one of these on my laptop and I like it a lot.

- ⚙ **Light pen.** These devices never really caught on, but the general idea is that you move a pen across a grid of wires, and the light from the pen shines on the grid to indicate a position on the screen. Light pens are supposedly good for drawing, but not many applications support them.

Special Keyboards

Special keyboards fall into two categories: those with extra keys and those with unusual shapes that supposedly prevent wrist problems. Some models have both features.

My favorite special keyboard is the Microsoft Natural keyboard. It has some special Windows keys that open menus with a touch of a key, but the best part is that the keyboard is split slightly so your hands can come in at a natural angle to type. It also has a built-in wrist rest at the bottom. Generic keyboards with the same features cost slightly less, but if the price difference is small, I prefer the name-brand product.

You also can get keyboards with cordless mice, keyboards with trackballs attached, and keyboards with touchpads. There are keyboards that are split into two separate pieces, and keyboards that slant up or down. Walk through the computer store's keyboard aisle sometime and marvel at the variety.

TV and Radio Cards

Now you can watch television right on your computer screen. A TV card is an interface card that enables you to open a window in Windows and watch your favorite television shows. I don't own one of these, so I can't attest to how well they actually work, but it sounds like an interesting idea.

CAUTION

If you're shopping for a TV card, read the box carefully. Another kind of interface card—also sometimes called a TV card—does not contain a TV tuner. Instead, this card enables you to use your television set as a computer monitor, an entirely different function. You won't be happy with it if you went shopping for a card for watching television on your PC.

Although Windows 98 touts its support for TV cards, it currently supports only the ATI All in Wonder Pro card. When you shop for a TV card for Windows 98, check carefully to be sure it will run when you get it home.

Joysticks and Game Controllers

If you're a serious game player, you can rack up higher scores in your favorite games with the right equipment. All kinds of game controllers are available, from simple game pads to complex steering wheels and gas pedals for driving games, flight yokes for flight games, and rapid-fire joysticks for shoot-em-up action. By the time you read this book, you might also be able to buy virtual reality gloves and helmets at your local computer store, along with games to play with them.

If you're just beginning to explore the world of games, don't overbuy. I bought a simple joystick for under $20 and have yet to find a game that requires a fancier controller.

On the other hand, if you often play a particular type of game—let's say, flight simulators—you owe it to yourself to have a good controller. Go to the stores where these devices are available for demonstration and see which ones feel the best to you.

Name-Brand or Generic Parts?

Name-brand parts cost more than generics, just like name-brand canned food costs more than the store brand equivalent. You might be able to find a great sale and pick up a really good name-brand component at a discount, but it doesn't always work out, so leave that what-if out of your thinking for now.

When you buy a name-brand part, what are you getting for the extra money?

- **Higher quality.** Name-brand parts are usually (but not always) made from better quality materials. A name-brand computer case might be made of higher-grade, thicker metal than a generic one. Depending on the component, the quality difference can be small or great from one brand to another.

- **Fewer defective units.** In general, name-brand parts are manufactured under stricter quality control, resulting in a smaller percentage of returns due to defects. Generic parts are apt to come from some unregulated foreign factory.

- **Advertising.** A name brand becomes that way through advertising. By buying the product, you are helping pay for that advertising.

- **Better drivers.** Generally speaking, brand-name components that require Windows drivers have better-written drivers that install more easily and work more smoothly in Windows than their generic counterparts. This is especially true for modems and sound cards.

- **Customer support.** A name-brand company usually provides more service after the sale, perhaps a toll-free number you can call with questions.

- **Warranty.** Even if a generic part comes with a warranty, it might be difficult to contact the company and get the company to honor the warranty. Large name-brand companies have well-established systems for honoring warranties.

Are all those factors worth paying for? Usually. Every time I buy cheap generic parts, I end up regretting it and telling myself not to be such a penny-pincher the next time. Ultimately, the decision is up to you. Perhaps your budget doesn't allow you to go with name-brand parts. But if you have the extra money, you can save yourself some headaches by going with the good stuff.

A quick scan through a computer magazine can give you an idea of the big, successful brand names. Begin by leafing through the first 100 pages or so, looking at the full-page ads for a particular product. These are ads placed by the manufacturers for a particular model or line of component, such as sound cards, hard disks, or monitors. If a company places a full-page ad in the front of the magazine, chances are that it's a well-known and successful brand-name company.

Now look at the vendor ads in the back. These are ads for mail-order stores that sell components. You can recognize them by the prominently displayed toll-free number and the long columns of tiny type listing the parts they sell. Look for the brand names that appear in these ads. Mail-order vendors carry only the most popular brand names, so if several vendors advertise a particular brand name, you can be sure it is a big name.

Making Your Buying Decision

Here is the strategy I use to pick a component to buy:

1. What is the overall best brand and model available today, regardless of price? What features make it the best? I get this information from reading computer magazines and from information on Web sites and Usenet newsgroups.

2. Which features of that best model can I do without?

3. Which alternative models offer the features I care about without the features I don't need? Again, I research this information in magazines and on the Internet.

4. Of the products from question 3, which can I afford?

If the answer to question 4 is "None of them," I go back to question 2 and try to reduce the list of features I care about until I can find a product I can afford.

The computer world frequently debates the objectivity of the reviews in computer magazines. These magazines rely on hardware manufacturers to buy ads and to supply free parts for their tests, so the publications don't want to anger the manufacturers with bad reviews. The editors of these magazines walk a difficult line between serving their readers and maintaining friendly relations with the manufacturers. In general, though, they do not give their Editor's Choice awards to total dogs. Although you can't be certain the award-winning model is the absolute best, you can be assured it is at least in the top half of the group in quality.

Where to Buy Upgrades

After you decide how much extra you are willing to spend for high-quality parts, you need to decide how much extra you are willing to spend for a full-service sales experience.

You make decisions like this in every day life—it's no different with the computer equipment. Let's say a coffee maker costs $55 at a fancy department store in the mall. The identical coffee maker costs $42 at a local department store. Some people are willing to pay the extra $13 at the mall for shopping in a carpeted store with classical music playing and for dealing with a polished, well-dressed salesperson who puts the item in a colorful shopping bag with tissue paper. Other people would rather keep the $13; they don't mind dodging screaming children with a plastic shopping cart and having their purchase rung up by a gum-chewing teenager in a polyester uniform.

You can buy computer equipment at any of the following places, depending on how much you want to pay for the extra services you receive with your purchase.

Locally Owned Computer Store

If you go to a real computer store, one that employs professionals who love and know about computers, you probably pay close to the manufacturer's suggested retail price. These "Dwayne and Gilbert" operations are too small to make large-quantity buys from the distributors, so they're forced to pay higher prices. They must, in turn, pass these prices along to their customers.

Although you don't find many discounts at these stores, you do find knowledgeable, helpful clerks who can confirm you're purchasing the right part for your upgrade. You can also expect quick and painless returns and exchanges, and possibly some advice on installation. Some local shops have their own on-site repair and installation facilities where you can have someone else install the upgrade if you chicken out.

NOTE Be a decent human being. Don't go to a locally owned computer store, pick the guy's brain for an hour, and then go across the street and make your purchase at the Mega-SuperWarehouse. If you are going to use the knowledge found in a local store, pay for it by making your purchase there.

Computer Superstore

In the last five years, a whole lot of computer and electronics stores have sprung up in big cities. Some of them, like CompUSA, sell only computer hardware and software. Others, like Best Buy, sell a variety of things—not only computers, but also appliances, televisions, and so on. Given the choice, I prefer the computers-only stores, because the sales staff seems to be more knowledgeable and the selection seems better.

You can expect to find some decent bargains in these national chain stores because they buy in bulk and pass on some of the savings to you. You also can find a fairly knowledgeable sales staff (typically computer-techie teenagers who like their jobs) and a well-established policy on returns and

exchanges. Some of these stores also have on-site repair and upgrade facilities. You might have to hunt for someone to help you, though; these stores are sometimes understaffed. You might also have a hard time finding the exact brand and model you want here, unless you are looking for one of the most popular products in the category. These stores cater to the low-end user and carry mostly the economy models from name-brand manufacturers.

Office Supply Stores

Increasingly, national chain office supply stores are offering computer equipment. Their salespeople are usually not computer focused, although they normally are friendly and mature. Their prices vary, usually on the high side except for special sales, which can be very good.

I have noticed that office supply stores typically cater to the nonexpert. They assume their customer is a busy person who just wants a piece of hardware that can do the job and that their customer is not picky about models or features. In keeping with this philosophy, these stores usually carry older models, rather than the latest thing. A recent trip to a local office superstore, for example, turned up six laser printers, four of which I knew were last year's models and on sale at clearance prices at most computer stores. However, this store was selling the printers at full price, as if they were still the latest thing. The newer models that replaced them in the manufacturer's lineup were not on the shelves.

Department Stores

Department stores in malls, such as Sears, J.C. Penney, Marshall Fields, and so on, sometimes have computer departments. These usually are small and are stuck in the corner of the TV and VCR department. You seldom find components for sale; these places deal mainly in new systems.

I would avoid these types of stores for buying computer hardware. The prices are typically not very good and the salespeople are usually not computer experts.

Discount Stores

Discount stores—Target, Wal-Mart, K-Mart, and so on—do not usually have a wide selection of computers or parts. However, if you happen to find what you want, and it is on sale, you can get a great deal. I got some inexpensive speakers, for example, for my nephew's computer. There was only one model for sale, but it was $10 less than the same model at the local computer superstore. Watch the weekly ads for bargains, but don't expect to walk in and find exactly what you want.

Direct from the Manufacturer

Can't find the product for sale in any store? You can order it directly from the manufacturer in some cases. Most manufacturers have toll-free sales lines; some also take orders on their Web sites.

The telephone salesperson should be extremely knowledgeable about that brand and might even be able to suggest a model better for your needs than the one you had in mind. This type of buying experience is usually very pleasant. However, you probably won't get any kind of discount. Expect to pay full price plus shipping.

TIP   If you can't find the product in stores, visit the manufacturer's Web site and look for a page called Where to Buy or Vendor List. Manufacturers often provide lists of stores that carry their products, and you might be able to get a better price from one of those stores.

Mail Order Vendors

Mail order companies deal in deep discounts. The best price almost always comes from a mail-order source. They can afford to offer the best prices because they buy large quantities from the distributor and have very low overhead (no showroom or well-dressed salesmen).

Drawbacks? You don't get much advice here; you need to know exactly what you want before you call. Also, if the merchandise arrives damaged, you have to mail it back; you can't just drive over to the store like you can with a local vendor. Most vendors require you to call first and get a special return-authorization code to put on the package.

I make most of my purchases through mail order vendors, simply because the prices are so good. Rather than calling on the phone, I usually shop from their Web sites.

To find a mail order vendor, pick up a computer magazine and look at the ads in the back. Or try some of these popular Web sites:

- **Individual vendors**. These companies have large online catalogs of computer hardware for sale, and you can even place your order online.

  www.buy.com

  www.cdw.com

  www.microwarehouse.com

  www.pczone.com

  www.egghead.com

- **Price comparison sites**. These sites let you look up a particular product make and model, and the various prices for it, and dozens of individual vendor Web sites appear. This makes comparison shopping very easy.

  www.pricewatch.com

  www.computershopper.com

Some Final Shopping Recommendations

Shopping for computer equipment is a lot like shopping for anything else. You can bargain hunt, but don't be too stingy to pay a little extra for the best quality if that's what you need. Here's a quick summary of my shopping advice:

- ✿ If you are uncertain as to whether you are buying the right thing, pay the higher price to get the part from the friendly local computer store. The extra service is worth it.

- ✿ If you know exactly what you want and you need it today, go to your local computer superstore chain.

- ✿ If price is the most important factor and you know what you want, buy through mail order.

- ✿ If you shopped and shopped and cannot find the item you want, call the manufacturer and ask where it is sold.

Take a Break

Now you know what parts to buy and where to buy them, so take a break from the book and go get those parts! Treat yourself to lunch at your favorite restaurant, and then pay a visit to the local stores, or spend some time shopping mail order Web sites. When you have your new hardware in hand, go on to this afternoon's session.

Installing Upgrades

- ✿ Do You Need Professional Help?
- ✿ Installing a New Version of Windows
- ✿ Hardware Installation Tips
- ✿ Making Windows Recognize a New Component

You have now chosen, shopped for, and purchased upgrade components for your PC, and it's time to put them to use.

You can install the upgrades yourself, or you can pay someone else to do it. (Bribing a techie friend with food sometimes works too!) In the following sections, I help you make that decision and guide you through some installation basics if you decide to go the do-it-yourself route.

Need Professional Help?

Everyone has certain things they would rather pay others to do. My list includes changing my car's oil, unclogging the dryer vent in my crawlspace, and trimming my cat's claws, for example. So don't feel like you have to install your own computer upgrades. There's absolutely no shame in not wanting to try it.

The rest of this chapter is devoted to the do-it-yourselfers, but if you're not one of them, here are some ideas for finding installation help:

✪ **In-store installation**. If you buy a component at a local store, that store might offer free or reduced-price installation. It never hurts to ask. Of course, you need to take your computer to that store.

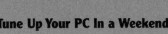

- ✿ **Computer repair shop**. Most cities have a variety of businesses that repair computers; most of these places also install upgrades. They might even sell you the parts more cheaply than a retail store. You can look for an Authorized Service Center for your brand of computer if you want, but it's not necessary for an upgrade.

- ✿ **In-home computer consultants**. You might be able to locate a computer consultant who comes to your home and works on your computer. (That's what I do for a living, besides writing books!) This is great because you don't have to pack up your computer and take it anywhere.

For in-store installation or a repair shop, you probably pay a fixed price. For example, one popular computer superstore chain installs hard disks for $65 and CD-ROM drives for $45. With an in-home consultant, you probably pay by the hour.

Installing a New Version of Windows

The latest Windows versions have a very slick, automated upgrade procedure. Just pop the new CD in your drive; a message appears saying the disc contains a newer version of Windows than you have and offering to upgrade you. Click Yes, and then follow the onscreen prompts to install the new version of Windows. (See "Installing Windows" in Saturday Evening's session for details.) You are prompted to enter a key code at some point, which is on a sticker on the back of the CD's case, so make sure you have it handy.

If you put the CD in the drive and nothing happens, it's possible that your CD-ROM drive's Auto Insert Notification is turned off. Do the following to start the setup program:

1. Double-click on My Computer on the desktop.
2. Double-click on your CD-ROM drive.

3. Locate the file Setup.exe and double-click on it.

If you put the CD in the drive and a window appears offering such options as Interactive CD Sampler, Cool Video Clips, Browse This CD, and so on, you already have that version of Windows installed on your PC.

Hardware Installation Tips

I can't make you a hardware expert in a single chapter, but in the following sections, I tell you some of the most important dos and don'ts for installing certain kinds of new hardware. For more detailed information, pick up my book *Upgrade Your PC in a Weekend*, also published by Prima.

General Tips

Your work area should be a clean, well-lit table with plenty of room and an electrical outlet nearby. If the table you choose is made of finished wood, you might want to cover it with a piece of cardboard or some newspapers. Computer cases sometimes have sharp edges that can mar the finish.

Here are the tools you should assemble for an upgrade:

- A pad of paper and a pencil for taking notes
- A startup disk (see Saturday Morning's session)
- A small, nonmagnetic Phillips-head screwdriver
- Any available manuals for the computer

Depending on the upgrade, you might also find the following helpful to have:

- An antistatic wrist strap (available at your local Radio Shack)
- A small, nonmagnetic flat-head screwdriver, or other screwdriver if required for your PC. (Compaq computers often require a six-pointed Torx screwdriver, for example.)

- A large pair of nonmagnetic tweezers (in case you drop a screw inside and need to fish it out)

Don't rip the packaging of the upgrade component, in case you need to return it later. Unpack the item as if you are doing so on the sly and want to be able to put it all back in the box later with no evidence of it having been unpacked.

If the component is memory or a circuit board, don't remove it from its antistatic plastic bag until the last minute. The longer the part is exposed, the great the chance of something bad happening to it.

Locate the instructions that came with the component and keep them handy, along with any extra pieces that came with it, such as a cable or a knob.

Read the instructions carefully! If anything in the instructions contradicts what's in this book, follow those instructions, because they're specific to that device, whereas the advice in this book is general.

Monitors

With the PC and monitor both turned off, unplug the old monitor from the back of the PC and plug the new one into the same socket.

Your old monitor's plug might be fastened to the PC by plastic screws that you can turn with your fingers (the more modern way), or with actual metal screws that require a screwdriver. Loosen the screws enough to pull the connector free; you don't need to remove the screws completely (see Figure 6.1). Then plug the new one into the same spot and tighten its screws down.

To take full advantage of your new monitor, you might want to change the video mode in Windows or the refresh rate. I explain that in the Saturday Afternoon session.

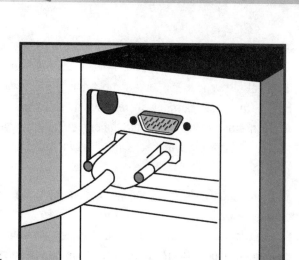

Figure 6.1

Loosen the connector's screws and pull it out of the socket.

Printers

After unpacking the new printer, you might need to prepare it in one or more ways. Read the documentation that came with the printer. Depending on the model, you might have to do any of the following:

- Remove cardboard or plastic inserts or protectors from inside the printer.

- Install a toner or an ink cartridge or a print ribbon. Pay close attention to the documentation; every printer's toner or ink installs a little differently.

- Attach any knobs or stickers that were packaged separately from the main unit.

NOTE   For a laser printer, you install a toner cartridge while the printer is *off*. Depending on the model, you might also have to install some sort of drum cartridge, which might look like a big metal roller. On a toner cartridge, there is usually a plastic strip that you need to pull away before inserting the cartridge into the printer. The cartridge might also come with a felt strip on a plastic piece that fits somewhere in the printer to clean the transfer wire.

For an ink-jet printer, you usually install the ink cartridge while the power is *on*. In some printers, you must press a button to move the cartridge holder into view. *Read the directions!* Most ink cartridges have some sort of plastic sticker you remove before installing, but pay close attention because many of them have two plastic labels—one you remove, and one you must not remove.

⚙ If possible, print a test page. The printer's documentation should explain how to perform this test. On some printers, for example, you hold down a certain button on the printer while you turn on the power.

NOTE   Some printers don't have any mechanism for printing a test page except through Windows. If that's the case, you cannot print a test page until after you finish the printer's setup in Windows.

Next, you need to hook up the printer to the computer (with both of them turned *off*). If you already had a working printer, just disconnect the printer cable from the old printer and connect it to the new printer.

A printer cable attaches to the printer with two wire loops, as shown in Figure 6.2. To disconnect the old printer, push the loops away from the connector and unplug it. Plug the connector into the new printer, and push the wire loops toward the connector until they snap into place.

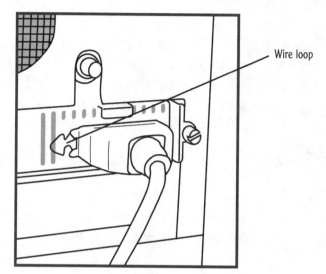

Wire loop

Figure 6.2

Push back the wire loops to disengage the printer cable from the back of the printer.

NOTE Most printers do not come with a printer cable. If you did not have a printer before, you need to buy a cable. They cost less than $10 at most computer stores. Make sure you get one labeled Bi-Directional Parallel Printer Cable.

If you did not have a printer before, you need to attach the other end of the printer cable to your PC. Just find the socket that matches the end of the printer cable (25 holds for its 25 pins) and plug it in. Then secure it with the screws built into the connector.

NOTE Some newer printers are coming out with USB connectors, either instead of or in addition to the parallel connectors. You can connect your printer to your PC with a USB cable if you have a USB connector on your PC and if you have Windows 98 or higher (or a version of Windows 95 that supports USB).

You probably also have some software to install. Most printers come with an installation program you can run in Windows. Windows might automatically detect the new printer, but it is better to run the software that came with the printer to get the full installation. If you see a message when you start your PC that the new printer has been detected, click on Cancel, and then run the setup program on the disk that came with the printer.

Scanners

Scanners are available with different interfaces—notably USB, SCSI, and parallel—and each hooks up differently. Read the instructions to see which kind you have.

A USB scanner hooks up to a USB port using a special cable that comes with the scanner. A USB port looks like a small rectangular hole, about the size and thickness of two stacked pennies. Just plug the USB cable into it.

A SCSI scanner typically comes with its own SCSI circuit card, so you need to install that card first. Then connect the scanner to it using the cable provided. I tell you about installing circuit cards in the "Circuit Cards" section later in this session.

If you have a parallel scanner, you probably set it up to share your parallel port with your printer; just follow these steps:

1. Turn off the power on all devices.
2. Unplug the printer cable from the back of the computer.
3. Plug the scanner's cable into the parallel port on the computer.
4. Plug the printer's cable into the extra port on the scanner.
5. Plug the power cord for the scanner into the wall outlet, and plug the other end into the scanner.

When you finish the physical installation, you must run the installation software that came with the scanner.

If you have problems with either the printer or the scanner when they are sharing a port, you might be able to solve them by changing the mode setting parallel port in your BIOS setup program. (See "Understanding the System BIOS" in the Saturday Morning session for help with your BIOS setup program.) You can experiment there with the mode for your parallel port (Normal, ECP, or EPP). Try each mode, restarting the computer and testing the printer and scanner to see if any of them make a difference.

Some ink-jet printers do not share the parallel port very well. If you are unable to resolve your problems, you might need to buy and install an extra parallel port on a circuit card. See the "Circuit Cards" section later in this session for help with that.

Keyboards

In most cases, you can simply unplug your old keyboard and plug in your new one. (Make certain the power is off before you do this!) The only glitch might be that you have the wrong kind of plug on the new keyboard. AT-style motherboards have 5-pin, AT-style keyboard plugs (big ones), whereas ATX-motherboards have 6-pin, PS/2 style keyboard plugs (small ones). If you get your new keyboard home only to find that you have the wrong type, you can either return it for an exchange or buy an adapter like the one shown in Figure 6.3. Adapters like this are relatively inexpensive (under $10) and allow you to use a different keyboard type.

Upgrade Processors

A processor upgrade is like a brain transplant, but not nearly as gory and complicated. The difficulty depends a lot on your present system. You learned about the various types of processor upgrades this morning, when you were deciding what to buy.

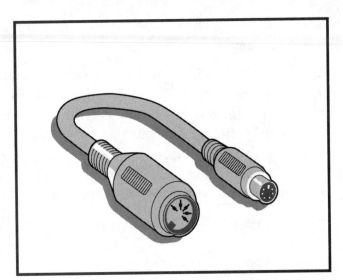

Figure 6.3

This keyboard
adapter plugs into
a PS/2 style
keyboard slot on a
computer, allowing
you to use an
AT-style keyboard.

Before beginning a processor upgrade, do the following:

○ Triple-check that you bought the right model before you rip open the package.

○ Read all the instructions from start to finish, both the ones that came with the upgrade and the ones in your original computer manual.

○ Check your computer's manual to see whether you need to change any DIP switch or jumper settings.

DIP Switches and Jumpers

Generically speaking, a jumper or a DIP switch allows a component to be used in different ways. For example, if your motherboard can accept several different types of processors, the switch or jumper settings tell the motherboard which type of processor you have. Some older motherboards require you to do this when you add or remove memory too, although most newer ones do not. You also sometimes find DIP switches or jumpers on circuit cards, such as modems or sound cards, to set a

particular memory address or IRQ for the device. Figure 6.4 shows a sample set of switches; Figure 6.5 shows a sample jumper.

DIP switches are like tiny light switches. They are usually white on an orange or red plastic block. Like a light switch, each one has two positions: on and off. The documentation that came with your new component (or your motherboard) specifies the correct switch settings for a particular configuration.

Sometimes manuals can be cryptic about switch settings. For example, suppose your manual tells you that, for the configuration you have, you need to set the bank of switches shown in Figure 6.4 to 124. That means switches 1, 2, and 4 should be on, and switch 3 should be off, just as is shown in Figure 6.4.

Figure 6.4

DIP switches are small on/off switches.

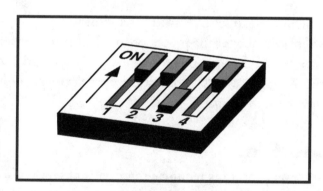

Figure 6.5

Jumpers provide another way to configure a device.

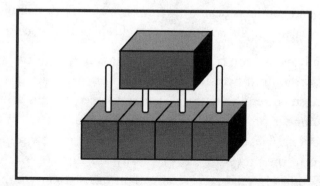

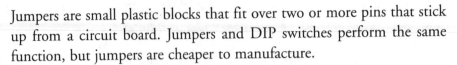

Jumpers are small plastic blocks that fit over two or more pins that stick up from a circuit board. Jumpers and DIP switches perform the same function, but jumpers are cheaper to manufacture.

For example, suppose the documentation for your motherboard specifies that for your new processor, you must set the jumpers shown in Figure 6.5 to the 3-4 position. That means the jumper should cover pins 3 and 4. In Figure 6.5, it is at the 2-3 position, covering the middle two pins, so you would need to move the jumper over.

● ●

NOTE   If you need to set a jumper to None, do not remove the jumper cap completely; you might misplace it. Instead, attach it to only one pin, leaving half of it dangling. This arrangement has the same effect as removing the jumper cap entirely.

● ●

You might need to set DIP switches and/or jumpers on the motherboard in two places: one for the processor speed and another for the processor's voltage. Read the motherboard manual carefully, and compare its charts to the new processor's speed and voltage specifications, to see what changes need to be made.

Heat Sinks and Fans

Most newer processors require either heat sinks or fans to help them stay cool. A heat sink is a porcupine-like plastic square that sits on top of the chip and conducts heat away from it. A fan is a small plastic device that spins whenever the computer is on, keeping the processor cool.

Usually, when you buy a processor, it comes with the appropriate heat sink or fan, but occasionally it does not. Read the instructions for the processor carefully. If the instructions recommend a heat sink or fan, but none is provided, buy one separately and install it according to its directions. Heat sinks are usually glued or otherwise permanently fastened to the processor; fans typically are clipped or screwed into place with some kind of bracket. Some fans have two pieces that sandwich the processor.

◆ ◆

CAUTION Different chip classes require different sizes of cooling fans. The fan for a 486-type chip does not work with a Pentium chip, and vice versa. Both the Pentium II and Pentium III also require their own specific size and type of fan.

◆ ◆

Most fans have power connections that must be hooked into the computer's power supply. The exception is the Intel OverDrive processors; these come with built-in fans that take their power from the processor socket so they don't require a separate power supply connection. Depending on the motherboard, there might be some pins on it that the fan's power cord fits on, or you might need to plug the fan directly into one of the power supply's plugs.

Installing a New Processor

Here is the general procedure for installing an upgrade processor:

1. Read all the instructions. Also, check your computer's manual for any information about using a different or upgrade processor.
2. Turn off your computer and unplug it. Remove the cover. If you have an antistatic wrist strap, attach it to the PC's case to ground yourself.

● ●

NOTE An antistatic wrist strap is a simple wristband with a cord attached to it. They cost about $10. You attach the end of the cord to a grounded metal object, such as your computer's power supply unit (the big silver box inside the case), provided the PC is plugged into an electrical outlet. It prevents parts from being damaged by static electricity. Some people find its use excessively paranoid, but better safe than sorry.

You can achieve the same grounding effect for free by frequently touching the power supply to ground yourself as you work.

If you are working on an ATX motherboard, you must unplug the system before working on it, so your grounding strap attached to the PC won't have much effect. Ground yourself in some other way when working on an ATX system, such as by attaching your wrist strap to some other plugged-in metal object.

● ●

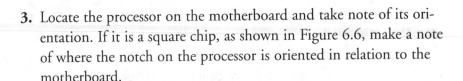

3. Locate the processor on the motherboard and take note of its orientation. If it is a square chip, as shown in Figure 6.6, make a note of where the notch on the processor is oriented in relation to the motherboard.

NOTE The socket shown in Figure 6.6 is called Socket 7. The Pentium II and III cartridges fit into a long, narrow socket called Socket 1. A motherboard has one or the other, but not both, so you can't use a Pentium chip in a Pentium II or III motherboard, and vice versa. I show you the older kind here because people with the newer processors aren't likely to be installing an upgrade to them.

4. If there is a cooling fan attached to your current processor, unplug the fan's power cable and, if possible, remove it from the processor.

5. Lift the handle next to your current processor, releasing it from its socket. Then lift it out.

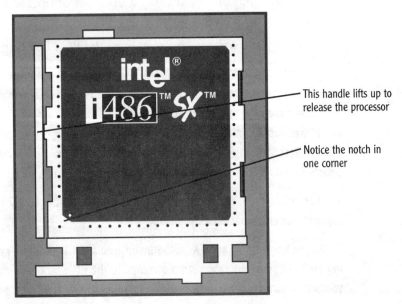

Figure 6.6

A typical processor on a motherboard.

6. Set any jumpers or DIP switches on the motherboard required to accommodate the new processor.

7. Straighten any bent pins on the bottom of the new processor. Be very careful and use a nonmagnetic tool, such as tweezers, and make sure you are grounded to prevent static electricity damage.

8. Install any fans, heat sinks, or adapters that came with the new processor if they are not already installed. Refer to the instructions.

9. Insert the new processor in the socket, making sure to orient the notch in one corner the same way as with the old processor. (This corresponds with a notch or a missing hole in one corner of the socket.)

10. Lower the handle to secure the new processor.

11. Double-click the jumpers or DIP switches.

12. Plug in the new processor's fan if it has one.

13. Plug in everything and start the computer (without replacing the computer cover). Watch the opening screen to see whether the new processor's information appears.

14. If the computer appears to start correctly, turn it off and replace the cover. You're done. If not, review this procedure, and the instructions that came with the processor, to find out what is wrong.

Circuit Cards

Lots of different upgrades require circuit cards. (Other names for a circuit card include *expansion card*, *adapter*, and *circuit board*.) A card can be an internal modem, a sound card, a video card, an input/output port, a SCSI card for plugging in a drive or scanner, an FM radio tuner, or any of dozens of other components.

Depending on the upgrade, installing the card might be the only thing you need to do, or it might be one step of a larger procedure. For example,

if you're installing an internal modem, you basically just install the card and go. On the other hand, if you're installing a card to function as an adapter for a CD-ROM drive, you must not only install the card but also install the drive and run a cable between them.

To install a card, you need a small Phillips-head screwdriver. Also, if you need to set any jumpers or DIP switches, you might need a pointed object to move the switches or some tweezers to help you grab the jumper caps.

Here are some precautions to take when working with a circuit card:

- Read the instructions that came with the part before you begin the upgrade.
- Handle circuit cards only by the edges.
- Do not attempt to straighten anything sticking up out of a circuit board that looks bent. You can only make things worse.
- Do not force a card into an expansion slot in the motherboard. If it doesn't fit, check to make sure you are putting it in the right slot.
- On the other hand, don't be afraid to exert moderate pressure. Some cards fit very tightly into a slot. Push only by the top edge of the card.

Setting Jumpers on the Card

Before installing a card, check the manual to see whether there are any jumpers or DIP switches to set. They are much easier to set when you can hold the board in your hands; after it is installed, you might not be able to reach or see the jumpers or switches. Figure 6.7 shows some jumpers on a modem, for example.

If the card you are installing is Plug and Play, and yet it has jumpers on it that seem to indicate a particular OCM port or IRQ, check the documentation to see whether you should remove them. Some devices (notably modems and sound cards) can operate in Plug-and-Play mode or out of Plug-and-Play mode, depending on the status of certain jumpers.

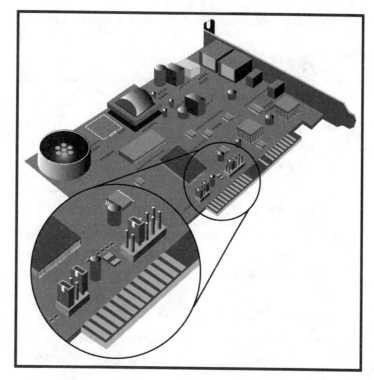

Figure 6.7

Set the jumpers on the card before you install it.

Selecting a Slot for the Card

All the expansion slots with the same connector work equally well; you can pick any of them. However, there are probably several kinds of slots on your motherboard. The long and short of it: Pick a slot that matches the metal strips at the bottom of the card. Then remove the screw holding the metal cover over that slot's back panel. Save the screw; you need it to secure the card.

That said, here are a few practical tips for selecting a slot, assuming you have a choice of two or more of the same type available:

✿ If you think you might have to change the jumper settings after installation, install the card in a slot with plenty of room on that side so you can get your fingers in there.

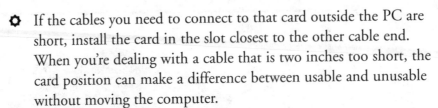

- If the cables you need to connect to that card outside the PC are short, install the card in the slot closest to the other cable end. When you're dealing with a cable that is two inches too short, the card position can make a difference between usable and unusable without moving the computer.

- If some slots in your motherboard have two kinds of connectors, avoid using these slots until you fill up all the single-purpose slots. That way you have flexibility for future expansion.

- Use the smallest socket that can accommodate the card you are installing.

- If the card you are installing has two sections of connectors in a row, don't put it in a too-short slot into which only the first section fits. The card won't work that way, trust me.

Seating the Card in a Slot

After you select the slot, you have to place the card in it. This step is not a zero-force activity; you really need to apply some pressure. The fit is intentionally tight.

The best way to put a card in a slot, I have found, is to see-saw it. Start with one corner and push firmly on the top edge until you feel the slot give way slightly. Then push on the other end until it goes in slightly. Keep pushing one end and then the other until the card is completely seated (see Figure 6.8).

How do you tell when the card is in as far as it will go? Check out the metal plate at the back of the PC. When a card is fully seated, the top lip of its plate rests on the PC's bracket, and you can attach its mounting screw. If the lip is not resting there, the card is not completed seated.

Memory

This morning, I made a rather big deal about picking out the correct memory (RAM) for your system. That was necessary. If you don't have

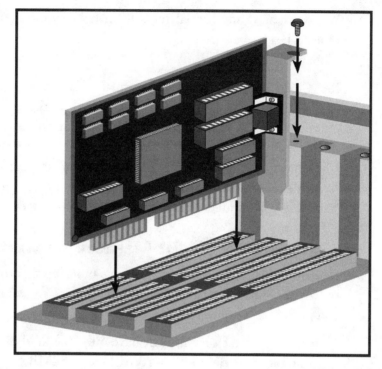

Figure 6.8

Push the card completely into the slot and secure it with a screw.

the right kind, installed in the right banks, it won't work. Some systems are extremely picky about the RAM they accept.

RAM can be a really easy upgrade if everything goes well. On most newer systems, assuming you bought the right kind, you simply plug it in and go. The system detects the new amount of RAM automatically.

On older systems, you might have to do one or both of the following for the system to recognize the new RAM:

✪ Set jumpers or switches on the motherboard to tell it how much RAM it has.

✪ Enter the new amount of RAM in the BIOS setup program, or at least enter the BIOS setup program so it redetects the RAM itself.

You don't need any special tools to install memory. (Well, you need a Phillips-head screwdriver to remove the computer's cover, but you've probably done that already.)

RAM can't hurt you, but you can hurt it. Leave it in its protective bag until you are ready to install it. Otherwise, you risk exposing it to static electricity zaps. And when installing RAM, don't force it. If you break off the little clips that hold the memory in place on the motherboard, you have ruined your whole motherboard (unless you can find someone to repair the clip for less than a new motherboard costs.) Handle RAM the same way you handle any circuit board—by the edges only.

Choosing the Right Memory Banks

Remember that chart I showed you this morning that told what capacity of RAM should go in each bank? Haul yours out for your system, because you need it to determine where to put the new memory.

Remember that each bank must have only one kind of memory in it—for example, you can't mix a 16MB and a 32MB SIMM in the same bank. In most 486 systems, a bank can consist of either four 30-pin SIMM slots or one or two 72-pin SIMM slots. Pentium systems always have two 72-pin SIMM slots per bank, but 168-pin DIMM slots (in Pentium and later systems) each stand alone as a bank.

Inserting the Memory Correctly

After you get the hang of inserting and removing memory from a PC, it's not difficult. However, beginners often fumble with it simply because the pieces are small.

Memory can fit into its slot facing in only one direction; if you try to put one in the wrong way, it doesn't fit. SIMMs have small notches in them that must be aligned correctly for them to be inserted. DIMMs have a gap on the bottom that is slightly off-center, so they only go in one way.

Small clips (usually metal) hold SIMMs in place; DIMMs have clips (usually plastic) that push down over their tops. To install most SIMMs, you slide them into the slot at a 45-degree angle to the motherboard and then push them upright into a 90-degree angle (see Figure 6.9). DIMMs, in contrast, drop straight down into their 90-degree angle slots.

NOTE If you are inserting a DIMM, you might have to press it down very hard to get it into a tight DIMM slot. This can be scary, pressing so hard on something so expensive! Just remember to press only by the edge and not to touch any of the chips on it. You'll know when the DIMM is fully inserted because the retaining clips will hold it in place. If you can lift either end of the DIMM with your fingers, it's not in all the way.

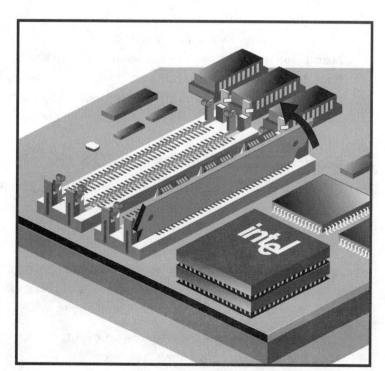

Figure 6.9

Insert a SIMM at a 45-degree angle and then push it up perpendicular to the motherboard.

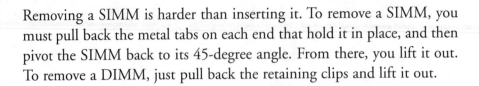

Removing a SIMM is harder than inserting it. To remove a SIMM, you must pull back the metal tabs on each end that hold it in place, and then pivot the SIMM back to its 45-degree angle. From there, you lift it out. To remove a DIMM, just pull back the retaining clips and lift it out.

Setting Jumpers for New Memory

On some motherboards (mostly 486 and earlier), you must set jumpers or DIP switches to tell the system how much RAM is installed. If this is the case on your system, there should be information in your motherboard's manual that shows the proper switch or jumper settings.

If you do not have the manual for the computer and the new RAM doesn't work, call the PC manufacturer and ask the technical support person to look up the motherboard settings for you. If the PC manufacturer is out of business, try to identify the motherboard manufacturer (the name is sometimes printed on the motherboard) and call that company. If that fails, try the Internet; look for an archive that contains pictures of generic motherboards. You might be able to match your board to a picture and get the settings that way. Realistically, however, if your motherboard is old enough to require jumper changes for different amounts of RAM, you might be better off getting a whole new PC or at least a new motherboard.

Making the BIOS Recognize the New Memory

On a very few systems, when you install new RAM, you must enter the BIOS setup program and tell it how much RAM it now has. On many other systems, when you start the PC with new RAM, you see some sort of memory error and a message about pressing some key to enter the setup program. When you do so, the BIOS setup program automatically detects and displays the new RAM amount. You then exit from the BIOS setup program, saving your changes, and the new RAM is ready to go.

The newer systems do not require you to interact with the BIOS setup program at all when installing new memory. When you start the computer, it automatically detects and uses all the available RAM.

Batteries

All PCs have a battery (somewhat like a watch battery) that keeps the memory chips in the ROM-BIOS charged. This battery enables the computer to keep track of the current date and time, among other things.

These batteries typically last at least two years, but after that, they begin to weaken. You can tell when a battery is dying when the computer forgets the date and time or forgets other BIOS settings, such as drive types. You can enter the BIOS setup program and remind the computer of these essentials as a stopgap measure, but the only way to permanently correct the problem is to replace the battery.

Before removing the battery, go into your BIOS setup program, as described in "Understanding the System BIOS" on Saturday morning, and make notes of all the settings you can find. In particular, note the specifications for your hard disk. That way, you can restore the settings after the replacement. Then turn off the PC's power and unplug the machine.

The battery is somewhere on the motherboard, so your first challenge is to remove the computer's cover and locate it. Computers use several different types of batteries, and most of them don't look like any batteries you have ever seen before. You need to find the battery, remove it, take it to a computer store to buy a replacement, and then install the new one.

Here are some tips for locating and replacing various kinds of batteries:

- The battery is usually along an edge of the motherboard rather than in the middle.

- Some batteries look like little barrels or oil drums on their sides. These are usually encased in a plastic sheath with writing on them, such as 3/V60R. These are held in place by friction; simply pull them out, like you would pull out the batteries in a portable radio. Then wedge the new battery into place.

- Most batteries on more modern computers are flat metal discs lying flat against the motherboard, like a watch battery. A metal clip over

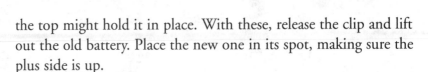

the top might hold it in place. With these, release the clip and lift out the old battery. Place the new one in its spot, making sure the plus side is up.

✿ Some batteries look like flat metal disks held at a 90-degree angle to the motherboard by two fasteners (one on either side). Release the fastener if needed (some are held in place by friction), and then replace the battery.

✿ Some batteries look like any other microchip on the motherboard but with some special writing on them to indicate their battery function. (Such batteries seldom wear out, so you should not have to replace this kind.)

NOTE On some old motherboards, the battery is soldered into place. You can't remove the old battery here; if it dies, you must buy an external replacement battery. It comes in a plastic-encased pack with a three- or four-hole connector that plugs into pins on the motherboard. Your computer's manual should contain installation directions; at the minimum, it should tell you which pins on the motherboard a replacement battery should plug into. After installing an external battery, you might need to set some jumpers on the motherboard to tell it to use the external battery. Again, check the manual.

If you have your computer's documentation, it should show you where the battery is located and give directions for replacing it. If you have such documentation, follow it.

If you replace the battery and the PC starts perfectly sometimes and refuses to start other times, you probably installed the battery backwards or upside-down.

After changing the battery, you need to go into your BIOS setup program and reset all the non-default values. For example, the default in most BIOS programs is to have one floppy drive; if you have two, you need to configure it there. See "Understanding the System BIOS" in the Saturday Morning session for help.

Drives

I talk about drives generically first, as in hard drives, floppy drives, CD drives, tape drives, and so on, because they have some things in common. Then I tell you about some quirks of each of the major drive types separately.

With any drive, you slide it into an empty drive bay and then connect the drive to the rest of the computer and to a power supply. Next, you usually have to use the computer's BIOS setup program to tell the computer that the new drive exists.

To install a drive, you need a Phillips-head screwdriver for the screws on the drive, and possibly a flat-head screwdriver (or something similar) to pry off the plastic plate from the front of the drive bay. If you need to set jumpers on the drive, you might want a pair of tweezers to help you grasp and pull off the jumpers, although some people can do this handily with fingers.

Here's the basic procedure; I explain many of these steps more fully in the upcoming sections:

1. Set any necessary jumpers, switches, or settings on the new drive.

2. Set any jumpers, switches, or settings on any existing drives that share a cable with this drive.

3. If needed, remove the plastic cover plate over the drive bay into which the drive goes.

4. Slide the new drive into the bay from the back, so you can see and reach where the power and interface cables need to be connected.

5. Plug a power cable into the power socket on the drive. Notches on either side of the socket prevent the connector from going in the wrong way.

6. Plug the ribbon cable (the interface cable) into the interface socket on the drive. Make sure the striped edge of the cable goes to pin 1 and that it is firmly seated.

7. Plug any special cables into the drive as needed (for example, a cable from a sound card to a new CD-ROM drive). Refer to the directions that came with the drive.

8. Attach the other ends of the cables to the proper places if needed.

9. Slide the drive into its final location in the bay, aligning the front with the front panel of the PC if it is externally accessible.

10. Use screws to mount the drive in place.

11. Start up the computer and test the new drive. Set it up in the BIOS setup program if needed.

Tips and Tricks for Drive Installation

Installing a drive is actually one of the more fumble-prone tasks. You need to fiddle with cables and connectors, align a lot of holes, and tighten many screws. Here are some of the tricky parts, so you can be prepared for them (or avoid them entirely!).

Locating an Appropriate Drive Bay

A computer case can house two kinds of drive bays: internal and external. Your PC has a certain number of internal drive bays, which hold drives but have no front access. These are for hard disks. If you have a hard disk in an externally accessible drive bay, you are wasting that bay. (An exception is if your system has only external bays, as is the case in some older systems.) Using an external bay for the hard disk doesn't really matter until you need to use that bay for something else; then you must move the hard disk into one of the internal bays.

External bays are available in two sizes. Most floppy and hard drives are 3.5-inch drives. (That measurement refers to the width of their media.) They fit in the smaller drive bays in a PC's case. Most CD-ROM and tape backup drives are 5.25-inch drives. They fit in the larger drive bays.

You can't put a large drive in a small bay, obviously, but the reverse does work. If you don't have a large enough bay available, check your existing

drives and make sure none of them are small drives sitting in large bays. If you have any of those, you can switch them with the new equipment so everything fits.

If you have a small drive to install but only a large bay free, you can buy a mounting kit from your local computer store that provides the supports and faceplate needed to center the smaller drive in the larger hole, as shown in Figure 6.10. Follow the directions that come with the kit to install it. Some good quality drives even come with their own mounting rails and hardware for this purpose, so you don't have to buy a kit separately.

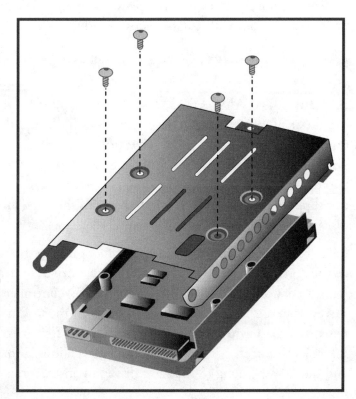

Figure 6.10

If you need to mount a small drive in a large bay, install a mounting bracket around the drive to hold it in place.

Removing the Bay Cover from the Case

If you have an open external drive bay, it probably has a plastic plate covering it in the front of your PC. When you're ready to install a new drive in that bay, you must remove that plate.

It's often easier to remove plates from the inside. If the plate is attached to the computer cover, work from the inside of the removed cover. If the plate is attached to the PC itself, work from the inside of the drive bay. The plate usually has some kind of lip or edge that holds it in place; sometimes you can pull these back with your fingers and pop the plate through the hole.

Sometimes, when you remove a plastic plate, you find a metal plate right behind it. Unpleasant surprise! If there are screws holding the metal plate in place, remove them; often the plate edges are partially perforated, so you can pop it out with a flat-head screwdriver.

Setting Master/Slave Relationships (IDE Drives Only)

IDE drives (and ATA, ATA-2, EIDE, and so on fall into this category) run on an IDE controller. This controller is built into the motherboard on newer computers; on older ones, an IDE interface card in an expansion slot controls them. Each IDE interface can control a maximum of two drives. (Most motherboards today have two IDE interfaces, so they can support a total of four drives.) Drives of this type include IDE hard disks and some CD-ROM drives and Zip drives.

Each IDE controller has a single cable running from it, with two connectors. (If your cable does not have two drive connectors, replace it with a new IDE cable.) Because each IDE controller can have two drives, it needs a way to distinguish between them. One drive is designated the master, the other the slave. The master drive is the one the PC talks to directly; it receives all the instructions from the controller, and then passes along to the slave drive any instructions that are meant for it.

The interface cable runs from the controller to one disk to the next in a chain. On most systems, it doesn't matter which drive is plugged into which connector. The disks rely on jumpers you set for one of the following situations:

- The drive is the only drive on that controller and therefore, by default, is the master.
- The controller has two drives, and this drive is the master.
- The controller has two drives, and this drive is the slave.

You might see an additional setting on some drives called Single. It is used, if available, as an alternative to Master when the drive is the only drive on the controller.

Some newer systems use CSEL or CS, which stands for cable selection. With such systems, the drive's position in the cabling determines whether it is the master or the slave. For example, suppose you have a cable that starts the controller, runs to disk 1, and then runs to disk 2. Disk 1 is the master because it comes first in the chain. If you want disk 2 to be the master, you simply swap the connectors.

Let's look at an example. Suppose you see the jumpers shown in Figure 6.11 on the back of your new CD-ROM drive. MS stands for master, SL for slave, and CS for cable select. If this drive is the only drive on the controller, you can leave the jumper set to MS, as shown in Figure 6.11. If it is going to be the slave (for example, on the same cable as your original hard disk), you should move the jumper to the SL pins. If you are using cable select, you need to move it to the CS pins. (Cable select requires a special cable; you can't do this with a regular ribbon cable that comes in the average PC.)

Some drives have jumpers that are not so self-explanatory. They might not have any labeling on them. In that case, you need to refer to the instructions that came with the drive. The jumpers also might not be on the back of the drive; they might be somewhere else, such as on the circuit board on the bottom of the drive.

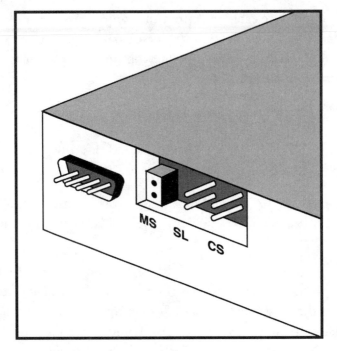

Figure 6.11

These jumpers on a drive control whether it is the master or slave.

If you add a second drive to the controller, you might also need to change the jumpers on the existing drive. For example, suppose you add a CD-ROM drive to a controller cable that already runs your hard disk. You set the jumpers on the CD-ROM drive to slave, of course. But then you need to check the hard disk's jumpers too. Some hard disks require different settings for being the master all alone and being the master with a slave.

TIP

If you no longer have the instructions for your original hard disk and you aren't sure whether you need to change the jumpers, you can call the manufacturer and ask. Have your drive model number ready. You also can get the jumper information for drives at many manufacturer Web sites.

Using the correct jumper settings is extremely important. If two drives are both set for master, or both set for slave, neither works. Similarly, if your primary hard disk is set for Single (also called Master, No Slave) and you add a slave, the drive won't know that the slave is there. Carefully study the documentation that came with both drives to determine the correct settings.

Setting Termination (SCSI Drives Only)

If you add a SCSI drive, some special rules apply. SCSI devices run on a SCSI interface (which is probably a circuit card in one of your expansion slots). If you already have a SCSI interface card, you don't need to add another; a single SCSI card can support up to seven devices. (Some can support even more.) However, if this is your first SCSI device, you should first install the new SCSI circuit card, as explained earlier in this session in "Circuit Cards."

SCSI devices work in a chain fashion. A cable runs from the controller card to the first device. Another cable runs from the first device to the second device. If you have more devices, cables run from one to the next, and so on. Each device has a single-digit ID number (which is just an identifier; it does not reflect its place in the chain). The controller sends a message down the cable, along with the device number that the message is for, and the appropriate device listens to the message. All other devices ignore it.

The last device in the chain needs to be terminated, meaning that a stopper prevents the signal from going any further. The stopper reflects the message back to the controller: Your message has reached the end of the line.

As you can imagine, it is very important that each device be assigned a unique ID number and that the last device be terminated. (It's also important, of course, that no devices be terminated other than the last one; otherwise, the signal would go no further.)

You set the SCSI ID on a device with DIP switches, jumpers, or some other special control. Some devices have a really nifty little window and a button. Each time you press the button, a different number appears in the window, indicating the device's new ID number.

Termination varies according to the device. On some internal SCSI devices, such as circuit cards, you have to install a special resistor (which comes with the device, along with instructions). External SCSI devices usually have some type of plug that plugs into the socket where the cable would go to the next device if you had one. Or, you might get some of the really modern devices, which have an auto-terminate setting—if they have anything plugged into the outgoing plug, they know that they're not at the end of the line; if the outgoing plug is empty, a built-in terminator takes effect. Check the documentation to see what you have.

Not Enough Power Supply Plugs?

See the colorful wires coming out of the power supply, in sets of four? These are the power plugs, and each drive must have one plugged into it. (The motherboard has two of them plugged into it, which is how the circuit cards, processor, and memory get their power.) An average system's power supply has about eight power plugs.

If your system already has many devices, you might be out of power plugs. An easy workaround is to buy a splitter, which is like an extension cord. It plugs into a single plug and has two or more outlets.

In addition to the sheer number of power plugs, you also need to consider the sizes. A power supply typically has both large and small plugs. The large size gets the most use; almost all devices use large plugs. The small plugs are for floppy drives. Figure 6.12 shows the difference. If you need a small plug but have only large ones available, you can buy an adapter.

Connecting the Ribbon Cable Correctly

The ribbon cable is the interface cable between the drive and the computer or a circuit card. A ribbon cable has a red stripe on one edge; this corresponds to the position on the connector known as Pin 1. You must

Figure 6.12

Power supplies have two connector sizes to accommodate devices with differing power requirements.

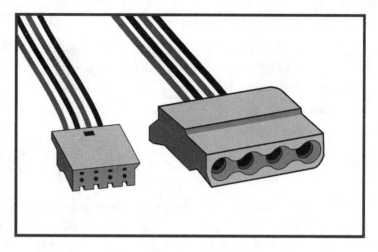

make sure that you plug in the connector so that Pin 1 matches the little 1 notation on the drive; otherwise, the drive can't work right because the cable will be backwards.

The same goes when plugging the other end of the ribbon cable into the motherboard or circuit card; make sure that the red stripe goes toward the 1. If you don't see a 1, perhaps you can see a 25; this is the opposite end from the 1.

Securing the New Drive with Screws

When you mount a drive into a bay, you secure it to the inside of the PC with two screws on each side. Some case designs make it very hard for you to reach the far side with a screwdriver. You then have two choices: You can say, "Forget it," and secure the drive as well as possible with screws on only one side, or you can go to the trouble of removing other components until the screw holes are accessible. I recommend the latter if possible, even though it's more work.

If you are removing an old drive to make room for the new one, you might have no choice but to completely disassemble the PC to get to the screws holding the old drive in place. Just remember how everything fits together.

Extra Cables to Attach

Almost all drives require you to attach two cables: the power cable (which runs to the power supply) and the interface cable (a ribbon cable that runs to the controller). With a few drives, however, you might have an additional cable or two.

For CD-ROM drives, you might have a cable to run from the drive to your sound card. This enables you to play audio CDs through your sound card's speakers.

If you buy a CD-ROM drive, it probably *does not* come with the audio cable you need. It looks like a cluster of three or four colored wires bound together with small connectors on each end. A sound card is more likely to include such a cable, but some cheaper models and brands omit it to cut costs. If you find yourself without the proper cable, you can pick one up at a computer store inexpensively.

For hard disks, you might have a drive light cable that runs to the small light in the front of your computer case. This light illuminates whenever the hard disk reads or writes. This light is not necessary, strictly speaking, but it is handy and not difficult to hook up.

Setting Up a Drive in the BIOS Setup Program

The newer systems detect the new drive automatically when you turn on the computer, so you don't have to do anything special. However, on most older computers, you must enter the BIOS setup program to let it know that you have installed a new drive. Some BIOS setup programs can automatically detect the type of drive you have when asked to do so; others require you to enter a string that includes the new drive's number of sectors, landing zone, and other specifications.

Floppy drives are easy to set up in the BIOS setup program because the BIOS typically supports only five or six floppy types. IDE CD-ROM drives are easy too, especially if your BIOS setup program has an Auto

Detect or Auto Configure drive type you can choose. Some BIOS setup programs automatically detect CD-ROMs without your making any changes to the settings at all.

After installing your new drive, start your computer and enter the BIOS setup program. (See the section "Understanding the System BIOS" on Saturday morning for BIOS basics.)

If your BIOS has an Auto setting for drives, you're in luck. Choose this option for the hard drive type, and the BIOS setup program makes all the choices for you. Exit the BIOS setup program, and your computer restarts, automatically detecting the new drive.

In some other BIOS setup programs, there is a drive detection utility, but it's not automated. For example, in the BIOS program shown in Figure 6.13, you choose Detect IDE from the Utility window. When you do so, you see a list of the drives that the system detected, as shown in Figure 6.14.

Notice in Figure 6.14 that you can change three of the settings: PIO, Block, and LBA. I explain more about these settings in the following bulleted list. The program determines the rest of the settings automatically.

After you run an Auto Detect utility, the BIOS setup program may ask whether it should transfer the new settings to the BIOS's setup for that

Figure 6.13

The opening screen of a typical BIOS setup program.

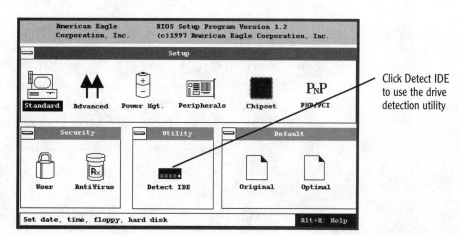

Click Detect IDE to use the drive detection utility

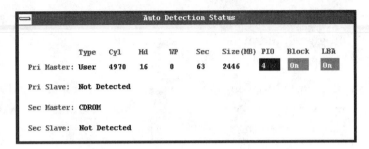

	Type	Cyl	Hd	WP	Sec	Size(MB)	PIO	Block	LBA
Pri Master:	User	4970	16	0	63	2446	4	On	On
Pri Slave:	Not Detected								
Sec Master:	CDROM								
Sec Slave:	Not Detected								

Auto Detection Status

Figure 6.14

In this example, the detection program found one hard disk and one CD-ROM drive.

drive. You should answer Yes. However, most BIOS setup programs automatically transfer the settings for you. If you go back to the main setup screen and display the settings for the drive you just Auto Detected, the correct settings are there.

If your BIOS setup program does not automatically detect the hard disk type, or does not detect it correctly, you must configure the drive manually. This method requires you to know a little more about the drive you're installing than you normally need to know. Before you start, check the drive's documentation or the label on the outside of its casing to determine the correct settings for the following:

- **Type**. The type of the drive. If this is one of the older drive types, it has a type number from 1 to 46. If you have this number, you do not need any of the other settings described next. Most likely, though, your drive does not have a type number. Only very old drives have this.

- **Cylinders (Cyl)**. The number of cylinders that the drive has. It should be a number in the thousands for most modern drives; my 2.4 gigabyte drive has 4,790 cylinders. A sticker on the drive should list the number of cylinders, heads, and sectors.

- **Heads (Hd)**. The number of read-write heads that the drive has. This value is a single- or double-digit number. My 2.4 gigabyte drive has 16.

- **Sectors (Sec)**. The number of sectors per track.

- ✿ **Landing zone**. This setting is nearly obsolete on newer drives; it's the position where the heads rest when the drive is off. On all modern drives, it is 65550.

- ✿ **PIO**. New enhanced IDE drives support fast data transfer with Programmed I/O (PIO) modes. If your drive supports this feature, you should use the highest mode it supports (0 through 4). Don't use too high a mode, though, because you might get lost or corrupted data. If you aren't sure whether your drive supports PIO, leave the setting at its default.

- ✿ **Translation**. Translation converts the physical disk locations into logical addressable units. If your drive is over 604MB, it probably uses some extended translation method, such as Logical Block Addressing (LBA). You might also see this method referred to as Extended Cylinder Head Sector (ECHS) or just plain Large. In contrast, a translation method of Normal refers to the standard Cylinder Head Sector (CHS) translation.

- ✿ **Block mode**. Not all BIOS programs ask about Block mode, but some do. If it's enabled, the computer can transfer data to and from the drive in blocks rather than in bytes, so it can perform better. Enable this mode only if you are sure that your drive supports it. (If your drive uses something other than Normal translation, it's a safe bet that it also supports Block mode.)

- ✿ **32-bit mode**. This setting allows 32-bit access to the drive through the BIOS. Most IDE drives support this setting, but you can use it only if your motherboard has a local bus. (Almost all 486 and later systems do.)

From your BIOS setup program, and with your drive information in hand, do the following to set up your drive:

1. Select the interface on which the drive is installed (Primary Master, Secondary Master, Primary Slave, or Secondary Slave). Its current setting is probably Not Installed.

2. Choose User Defined (or User) as the drive type. The setup program opens some sort of box through which you can enter the settings. Figures 6.15 and 6.16 show examples from two different BIOS setup programs.

3. Enter the settings in the appropriate fields.

4. Exit from the BIOS setup program, saving your changes.

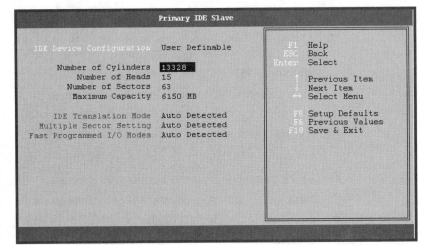

Figure 6.15

Text-based BIOS programs typically have simple fields for you to fill in.

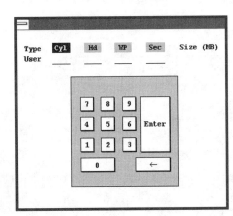

Figure 6.16

Some graphical BIOS programs provide an onscreen keypad to enter numbers.

Modems

Installing an internal modem is just like installing any other circuit card (see "Circuit Cards" earlier in this session). Make sure you set any needed jumpers or DIP switches before you install.

An external modem connects to one of your computer's serial (COM) ports using a cable that (probably) comes with the modem. If not, you can pick up the needed cable at any computer store inexpensively. Follow the diagram in the instructions that come with the modem; it's easy.

Both kinds of modems usually have two phone jacks on them: one labeled LINE and one labeled PHONE. LINE connects the modem to the wall outlet; PHONE connects the modem to the phone. If you are sharing your phone line between a telephone and the modem, unplug the phone cable from your telephone and plug it into the LINE port on the modem. Then run another phone cable from the PHONE port on the modem to your phone. That way, your telephone can use the same line whenever the modem is not in use.

In theory, you shouldn't have to change anything in your BIOS setup for an internal modem. Your computer's BIOS supports two built-in COM ports: COM1 and COM2. When you install an internal modem, it is usually configured as COM3 or COM4, so you shouldn't have a conflict. Unfortunately, some things don't work in reality as well as they work in theory, and internal modem installation is one of them. If you are having a problem getting Windows to see your new modem, you might try disabling one of the built-in COM ports in your BIOS program, so that the new modem can use that COM port designation. For example, if you aren't using COM1 on your system, you could disable it in BIOS, so that your new internal modem could call itself COM1. Figures 6.17 and 6.18 show a COM port being disabled in two different BIOS setup programs.

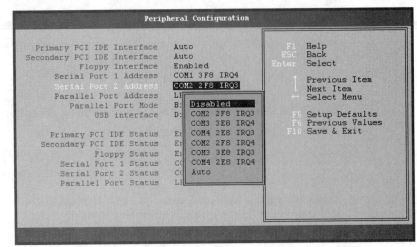

Figure 6.17

In text-based BIOS programs, the Peripheral Configuration is usually a full-screen display. Select the COM port, and then choose Disabled as its setting.

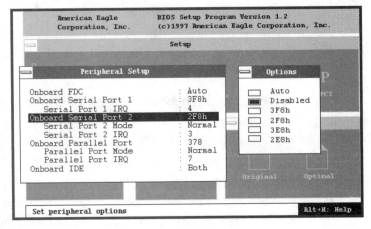

Figure 6.18

In graphical BIOS programs, you select ports to enable or disable from a pop-up box.

Take a Break

Gee, this break is coming pretty late in the afternoon! But you've been doing some important stuff, getting the hardware installed. Before you take a deep breath and turn on your PC to see if the new device works, take a few minutes for a stretch and a snack.

Making Windows Recognize a New Component

When you turn your computer on after installing a new program, Windows might detect the new component and automatically install drivers for it. That's the best case scenario. The worst case is that the device doesn't work at all or crashes Windows every time you turn on your computer.

Here's how Plug and Play is supposed to work:

1. You physically install the hardware.
2. You turn on the computer and Windows starts. Windows sees the new device and installs its drivers.

   Windows might prompt you for a setup disk or the Windows CD; if so, you insert it and click on OK to continue.
3. You install any special software that came with the device.
4. You test the device and find that it works flawlessly.

If it indeed works like that, you're done! If not, see one of the following sections.

If You Have a Setup Program

If Windows didn't detect the device at startup, but you have a setup disk that came with the device, now would be a good time to run that setup program:

1. Place the disk or CD into the drive on your PC.
2. Double-click My Computer, and then double-click the icon for that drive.
3. Look in the file listing for a file that is likely to be the setup program (anything with Setup or Install in the name).
4. Double-click on that file. The setup program runs.

5. Follow the onscreen instructions to complete the setup program's work. If asked whether you want to restart, click on Yes.

6. Test the new device to make sure it works. If it doesn't, see the section "If Windows Fails to Detect the Device" later in this session.

Telling Windows to Detect a New Device

Sometimes, for whatever reason, Windows doesn't immediately notice the new device. If you don't have a setup program—or you have one and running it didn't help—here's how to prompt Windows into noticing the new device:

1. Choose Start/Settings/Control Panel. Then double-click Add New Hardware.

2. The New Hardware Wizard opens. Click on Next.

3. If you are using Windows 98, it informs you that it will look for Plug-and-Play devices. Click on Next to let it do so. If it finds the new device, great. Follow the onscreen prompts to continue the installation. If Plug-and-Play detection fails to find the device, you're asked whether you want to search for a device that is not Plug-and-Play compatible (see Figure 6.19). Select Yes and then click on Next.

Figure 6.19

Let Windows try to detect the hardware before resorting to manual configuration.

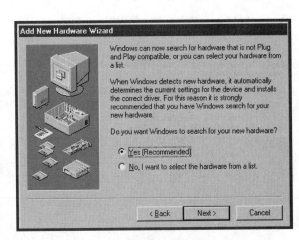

4. Read the warning message and click on Next to begin.

5. Wait for the progress indicator to reach 100 percent and for another dialog box to appear. It might take several minutes. If Windows finds the new hardware, you see a box like the one in Figure 6.20; otherwise, you see the box shown in Figure 6.21.

   If Windows detects the hardware (see Figure 6.20), continue to step 6. If not, go on to the next section of this chapter, "If Windows Fails to Detect the Device."

Figure 6.20

Windows was able to identify the new hardware.

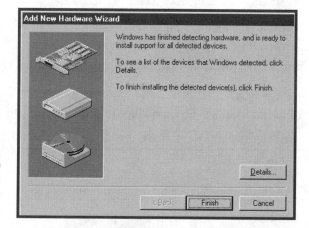

Figure 6.21

If Windows fails to detect your hardware, you are stuck with manual configuration.

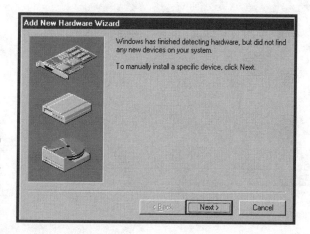

6. Click on Details to see what Windows found.

7. Do one of the following:

   ✪ If the device on the list is the device you were expecting, great. Click on Finish.

   ✪ If the device is not the one you want to install, Windows did not detect it correctly. Click on Cancel, then repeat steps 1 and 2. When you get to step 3, select No, and then jump to step 2 of the steps in the following section.

If Windows Fails to Detect the Device . . .

If you're reading this section, Windows wasn't able to find your device. Starting from Figure 6.21 (where Windows reports it can't find your hardware), follow these steps to install the device's driver manually:

1. Click on Next. The Add New Hardware Wizard displays a list of hardware types, as shown in Figure 6.22.

2. Click the device type you are installing (for example, Modem), and then click on Next.

Figure 6.22

Choose the type of hardware you are trying to install from this list.

3. If you are installing a modem, a box appears offering to search for the modem. (You don't see this box with any other device type.) Select the Don't select my [device type]; I will select it from a list box, then click on Next.

   A list of manufacturers and models appears for that device type. The one for modems is shown in Figure 6.23.

4. Do one of the following:

   ❂ If the device came with a setup disk, place it in your floppy drive and click on Have Disk. In the Install from Disk dialog box, confirm the drive letter for the floppy (A is the default) and click on OK. Windows finds the driver and installs it. If the disk contains drivers for more than one device model, Windows displays a list; double-click on the one you have.

   ❂ If you do not have a setup disk, or you have one but you have already tried it and it doesn't contain the right files, select the device's manufacturer from the list. Then select the model number from the list on the right. Click on Next to continue.

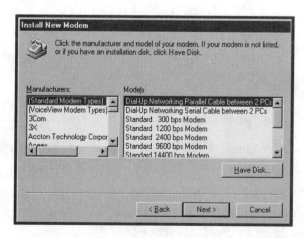

Figure 6.23

You can choose your device's make and model from a list of devices that Windows supports.

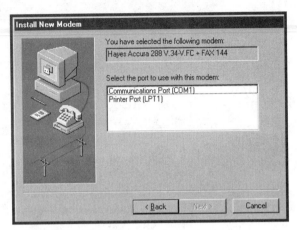

Figure 6.24

For some devices,
such as modems,
you must
specify a port.

5. If you are installing a device that requires you to select a port, a new dialog box asks you to do so. For example, Figure 6.24 shows the dialog box for a modem. If you see such a box, do one of the following:

- If the port that the device is connected to appears on the list, select the port and then click on Next.

- If the port does not appear on the list (for example, if you have a new internal modem set for COM3 but COM3 does not appear), click on Cancel. You're running out of things to try here; call the technical support number for your new device to see if the manufacturer can help you.

- If you see some other kind of information request other than port, select whatever setting is appropriate and click on Next.

6. Click on Finish when Windows tells you that your device has been set up. If Windows asks to restart, click on Yes.

7. Test the device to make sure it works. If it doesn't, try the technical support phone number for the device manufacturer. (The number should be in the documentation.)

NOTE   My book *Upgrade Your PC in a Weekend* has an extensive troubleshooting section that can help you figure out why a particular device doesn't work in Windows; check out that book for more information.

Take a Break

Congratulations, you made it through the entire weekend of training! At this point, your PC is error-free and working to its full potential, and probably running better than ever with the new upgrade parts you have bought and installed. Way to go! I hope you had fun and learned a lot this weekend. Now take a well-deserved break and have some fun!

GLOSSARY

8.3 filename. A filename that consists of no more than 8 characters followed by an extension of no more than 3 characters. For example, TESTFILE.DOC. Some operating systems, such as MS-DOS, do not support long filenames as Windows does; these operating systems limit filenames to 8.3.

Accelerated Graphics Port. See *AGP*.

Adapter. Generically, this can refer to any card in a motherboard slot, but it usually refers to the video card.

Address. The location, or path, to which you save or from which you open a file or folder. Can also refer to a *memory address*.

AGP. Stands for Accelerated Graphics Port. A new, very fast motherboard slot for connecting a video card.

Allocation error. An error in which the file's size being reported by the FAT does not match its size on the disk. ScanDisk can identify and repair this error.

America Online. A popular online service and Internet service provider (ISP).

Antivirus. A program that identifies and removes computer viruses from your system and prevents reinfection.

Aperture grille. A monitor technology that uses an array of stretched wires to create images. These monitors have superior brightness and contrast, but their poorer horizontals make them less suited for displaying text.

Application software. Software that helps you accomplish a specific task. Contrast with *operating system*.

Archive attribute. An attribute for a file that indicates it has been changed since it has been backed up.

AT motherboard. A motherboard in which the card interface slots run parallel to the wide edge of the board. Compare to *ATX motherboard*.

ATA-2. See *IDE*.

ATX motherboard. A motherboard in which the card interface slots run parallel to the narrow edge of the motherboard. Compare to *AT motherboard*.

AUTOEXEC.BAT. A startup file that processes its batch of commands whenever the computer starts.

Average access time. A hard disk performance measurement of the time it takes for the drive head to reach and read the average bit of data. It's measured in milliseconds (ms). The lower the number, the faster the drive.

Base address. See *IO address*.

Basic Input/Output System. See *BIOS*.

Beep codes. Patterns of beeps heard when starting up a non-working PC that can help a technician diagnose the problem.

BIOS. Stands for Basic Input/Output System. An automatically executed startup routine that runs tests and allocates resources before Windows loads. Sometimes called *ROM-BIOS*.

BIOS setup program. A built-in program in a PC that enables you to configure the PC's base-level settings. See *BIOS*.

Block mode. A data transfer scheme set up in BIOS that enables a computer to transfer data to and from the drive in blocks rather than in bytes, so it can perform better.

Bookmarks. See *Favorites list*.

Boot. To start up a computer.

Boot disk. A disk (hard or floppy) that contains the startup files needed to boot a computer. Also called *startup disk*.

Boot sequence. The order in which your computer tries the disk drives on your computer at startup, looking for the files it needs to start. The standard boot sequence is A, then C.

Browser. A program that enables you to browse the Web. See *Web browser*.

Buffer. A holding area in memory for data that is waiting to be processed or sent to an output device.

CAB file. Short for cabinet file. The compressed setup files that install Windows 95/98.

Cable modem. A device that interfaces with a PC and a cable TV system to provide Internet access, if the cable company provides it.

Cable select. A mechanism by which a hard disk or other IDE device can tell whether it is the master or the slave according to its connection position on a multi-device cable. See *Master* and *Slave*.

Cache. Blocks of memory set aside to temporarily store data that the process has just used and may need again soon.

Card. A circuit board that you plug in to a slot on the motherboard to add hardware capability. Can also refer to a *PCMCIA card*.

Case. The metal box that holds the computer's internal parts.

CD-ROM drive. A drive that reads CD-ROM discs. Most programs come on CD-ROM these days, so a CD-ROM drive is almost a necessity for any computer. Some CD-ROM drives have extra features, like the capability to play DVD movies or hold more than one disc at a time.

CHKDSK. A command run at the DOS prompt to check for errors on a disk.

Churning. See *Thrashing*.

Clean install. The process of wiping out your hard disk's contents (or just the Windows folder and related folders) and reinstalling all your software from scratch. A clean install is usually performed to eliminate a tough-to-troubleshoot system problem.

Clock speed. The speed, in MHz, at which a processor's internal clock operates. For example, some of the Pentium III processors operate at 700MHz.

Cluster. A small physical section of a disk. An organizational unit for storing data on a disk.

CMOS. Stands for Complementary Metal Oxide Semiconductor. A microchip on the motherboard that stores the BIOS setting changes you make with the BIOS setup program.

Color depth. The number of colors that comprise the Windows display in a particular video mode. 256 colors (8-bit) is a common color depth.

Complementary Metal Oxide Semiconductor. See *CMOS*.

COM port. Short for communications port. A method for a peripheral to connect to the computer, in which data is sent serially (one bit after another, one at a time). Also called serial port. Compare to *LPT port*.

Compression. A method of making a file or a group of files fit into a smaller disk space by storing them more compactly. Two kinds of compression are *file compression* and *disk compression*.

CONFIG.SYS. A startup file that lists the drivers and system settings the PC should load when it starts. This is important with DOS-based systems—less so with Windows 95/98 systems.

Convergence. A measurement of how well the three guns inside the monitor—red, blue, and green—align to paint the color onto each dot. If one of the guns is misaligned, the colors are not true.

Cookie. A bit of information that a Web page leaves behind on your hard disk to identify you in the future if you return to that page.

Cooling fan. A small round fan that straps onto a processor to keep it cool.

Cross-linked files. An error in which a conflict in the FAT keeps the system from knowing to which of two files an area of the disk belongs. ScanDisk can detect and repair this error.

Data error. An error reading from or writing to a disk. Usually the result of a physical error on the disk.

Data transfer rate. A measurement of how quickly data moves from the hard disk to memory. The higher the number, the faster the rate.

Defragment. To reorder the files stored on a disk so that all files are stored contiguously, rather than in multiple, noncontiguous pieces (fragments).

Device conflict. A struggle between two devices over which will control the use of a particular system resource, such as an IRQ or a DMA channel.

Device driver. A file that controls the interaction between a specific device and Windows.

Digital camera. Like a regular camera, except instead of film, it saves images in electronic format and feeds them into your PC.

Digitize. To scan an image or record it with a digital camera so that it becomes a computer file.

DIMM. Stands for Dual Inline Memory Module. A newer kind of memory (RAM) for PCs that is faster and better than the older SIMM type. The most popular type is S-DRAM DIMMs.

DIP switches. Small switches, like light switches, on a circuit board, that control low-level settings (much as *jumpers* do).

Directory. An older, MS-DOS name for *folder*.

Disk Cleanup. A Windows utility that helps identify and delete non-essential files to save disk space.

Disk compression. An alternative method of storing files on a disk so that they can be stored more compactly, saving disk space. Applies to the entire disk. Compare to *file compression*.

Diskette. See *Floppy disk*.

Disk Operating System. See *DOS*.

Display resolution. The number of pixels (dots) that make up a particular video mode in Windows. Common resolutions are 640×480 and 800×600.

DMA. Stands for Direct Memory Access. See *DMA channel*.

DMA channel. A path for communicating with the processor used by some devices, such as sound cards and floppy drives. Each device that requires a DMA channel must have a unique one assigned. Windows typically assigns DMA channels automatically through *Plug and Play*.

DOS. Stands for Disk Operating System. For many years, the definitive operating system for PCs. The most popular brand is MS-DOS. Newer systems that use Windows 95 or Windows 98 do not need DOS.

DOS Compatibility mode. A Windows operating mode in which performance is sacrificed for backward compatibility with certain DOS utilities. To be avoided if possible.

Dot matrix. A printer technology that works by striking the paper with a series of little pins against a ribbon (like a typewriter ribbon). In many ways, a dot matrix printer is like an automated typewriter except that, instead of letter-shaped hammers, a group of small pins changes position to form each letter.

Dot pitch. The measurement of how far apart the dots are that make up a monitor's picture. Lower is better.

Dot trio shadow mask. The most common monitor technology. Three colored guns (red, green, and blue) shine light through a grille of round holes to form the picture. These monitors deliver clean edges and sharp diagonals, which is important for showing text on-screen.

DoubleSpace. See *DriveSpace*.

Download. To transfer a file from another computer, usually on the Internet, to your own computer.

Driver. See *Device driver*.

DriveSpace. A program that compresses your hard disk so that you can store more files on it. Some older versions of this program were called *DoubleSpace*. See *Disk compression*.

Drum. The big metal cylinder inside a laser printer that transfers the image onto the paper.

Dual Inline Memory Module. See *DIMM*.

DVD drive. Stands for Digital Versatile Disc (or Digital Video Disc). A type of super CD-ROM drive. This can read not only regular CDs but also special DVD discs, which can hold as much as 8.5 gigabytes of data. DVD drives can also function as regular CD-ROM drives.

EDO memory. An improved type of non-parity memory (compared to FPM, or Fast Page Mode, memory). Many Pentium-class systems use it.

EIDE. See *IDE*.

E-mail. Short for electronic mail. A message sent or received over the Internet or a network.

Explorer. Can refer to Windows Explorer, a file management tool, or Internet Explorer, a Web browser.

Extended Data Out. See *EDO memory*.

Extended partition. In hard disk partitioning, the portion of the physical drive not allocated to the primary partition.

Extension. See *File extension*.

Fast page mode memory. FPM is generic memory. It works in just about any system that requires non-parity memory and doesn't mention anything about EDO. Look for a *32* in the specifications for this, as in 16×32-60ns.

FAT. A system chart stored on your hard disk that keeps track of what files are using which physical spots on the disk. Accessible only by the operating system.

Favorites list. In Internet Explorer, a list of saved Web addresses that you can easily access to return to those pages. Some other Web browsers call these *bookmarks*.

FDISK. The utility program used to partition a hard drive.

File Allocation Table. See *FAT*.

File attribute. One of four attributes that a file can have: Read-Only, Hidden, System, and Archive.

File compression. A method of storing an individual file or group of files more compactly on a disk by compressing them. Compressed files cannot be used until they are decompressed. Compare to *disk compression*.

File extension. The three-letter code following the period in a file's name. The file extension indicates the file type. For example, a file with a .txt extension is a text file.

Find Fast. A Microsoft Office utility that indexes files for fast access to them. It can interfere with utilities such as ScanDisk and Disk Defragmenter in Windows if not paused before those utilities are run.

Floppy disk. A thin plastic square (usually 3.5-inch in size) that fits into a floppy drive. Standard floppy disks hold 1.44 megabytes of data. Also called *diskette*.

Floppy drive. A drive that uses floppy disks. The term floppy refers to the thin, flexible plate enclosed in the hard plastic diskette casing.

FM Synthesis card. A type of sound card that does not include *wavetable* support.

Folder. An organizing unit into which files can be placed on a disk.

Format. To prepare a disk for use by running a formatting utility. Can also be a noun referring to a file's format.

FPM memory. See *Fast page mode memory*.

Fragment. A part of a file that is stored noncontiguously with the rest of the file. File fragmentation slows down system performance. See *Defragment*.

Freeware. Software that can be freely distributed without charge. Compare to *Shareware*.

FTP. Stands for File Transfer Protocol, a method of transferring files between computers on the Internet.

General protection fault (GPF). A type of error message in Windows that indicates a program has a problem or has stopped working.

Gigabyte. Approximately one billion bytes. Abbreviated as GB or G.

Hardware. The physical parts of the PC, usually made of some combination of metal, plastic, silicon chips, and electronics.

Hard drive. The non-removable storage drive mounted inside your computer, where you store most of your files. A hard disk consists of a series of stacked metal platters with a read/write head that reads them like a phonograph needle reads a record or a laser reads a CD. Contrast with *Floppy drive*.

Hard drive type. Older hard disks have a type number from 1 to 46. Hard disks manufactured in the last several years, however, do not use this typing scheme.

Heat sink. A grid of black spikes mounted on top of a processor to keep it cool. Heat sinks are common on newer 486 and older Pentium systems. Newer systems use cooling fans instead.

High color. A 16-bit color depth.

IDE. The most popular type of hard disk interface. Each motherboard has two IDE interfaces that can each support two devices apiece. Other devices that can be plugged in to an IDE interface include some CD-ROM drives and Zip drives. Enhanced versions of the IDE specification include EIDE and ATA-2.

Inkjet. A type of printer that works by squirting tiny blobs of ink onto the paper with an ink nozzle.

Input device. A device used to enter data into a computer. Examples include keyboards, mice, and scanners.

Interlacing. A display monitor scheme that refreshes every other line on the screen rather than every line in order to create acceptable video performance on cheap hardware. Interlacing can cause eyestrain, and the inability to display in non-interlaced mode is the mark of a poor-quality monitor.

Internet. A vast interconnected network of computer networks all over the world.

Internet Explorer. The popular Web browser software that comes with Windows. It is also available separately for other systems, such as the Macintosh.

Interrupt Request. See *IRQ*.

IO. Stands for input/output. See *IO address*.

IO address. The specific address in the computer's memory used to help a specific device communicate with the processor. Each device must have a unique IO address assigned. Also called *base address*.

IRQ. Stands for Interrupt Request. A path from the processor to a device on the motherboard. Each system has 16 IRQs (0 through 15), and each device must be assigned its own IRQ. Under certain circumstances, devices can share IRQs, but this often causes problems.

ISA. Stands for Industry Standard Architecture. One of the 8-bit or 16-bit slots on a motherboard that can accept ISA expansion cards. ISA is old technology; a newer kind of slot is *PCI*.

ISP. Stands for Internet service provider. The company that you use to connect to the Internet.

Jumpers. Small plastic blocks that fit over two or more pins that stick up from a circuit board to change a low-level setting on it (such as its IRQ or its operating mode). Like DIP switches, but cheaper to manufacture.

K6. An AMD (Advanced Micro Devices) brand processor that competes with the Pentium.

K6-2. An AMD (Advanced Micro Devices) brand processor that competes with the Pentium II. The K6-2 has a built-in 3-D technology called 3DNow! that boosts performance for 3D graphics and other multimedia in applications that support it.

Kbps. Stands for kilobytes per second. A measure of data transfer.

Kilobyte. 1,024 bytes of data or storage space. Abbreviated KB or K.

LAN. Stands for local area network, a network confined to a small area such as a single building.

Laser printer. A printer that prints by fusing toner onto a page using a drum and transfer wires, much like a photocopier. Laser printers provide superior-quality images to inkjets, but print only in black-and-white, except for a few very expensive color models.

LCD monitor. A very thin, high-quality monitor found mostly on laptop computers. LCD stands for Liquid Crystal Display. Some manufacturers are beginning to use LCD in large desktop monitors with stunning results.

Line in and line out. Jacks on a sound card. A line in jack provides a way to route sound from another amplifier, such as your home stereo system or a boom box headphone jack. The line out jack provides a way to route the sound card output to an amplifier, such as your home stereo system.

Local bus. Expansion slots on a motherboard that have high-speed connections to the processor for fast performance. Types of local bus include *VLB*, *PCI*, and *AGP*.

Logical drive. A drive letter assigned by partitioning the drive. Compare to *physical drive*.

Logical error. An error accessing the files on a disk that results from faulty information in the File Allocation Table (FAT). Compare to *physical error*.

Lost cluster. An error in which an address contains data but the FAT does not know to which file the data belongs. ScanDisk can identify and fix this error.

Low-insertion force (LIF) socket. A processor socket in which the processor's pins are wedged into little corresponding holes and held in by the tension. An older technology; *Zero-insertion force (ZIF)* is newer.

LPT port. A parallel port, usually used for connecting printers and scanners. As the name parallel indicates, data is sent several bits at a time, in parallel with one another. Compare to *COM port*.

LQ. Stands for Letter Quality. Generically, any printout that is as good or better than that achievable with a typewriter. Also refers specifically to the output of the 24-pin kind of dot matrix printer.

Mail server. A computer that handles e-mail distribution. When setting up your PC to send and receive e-mail, you must specify the address of the incoming and outgoing mail servers to use.

Maintenance Wizard. A series of dialog boxes that help you set up routine tasks such as disk defragmenting to occur automatically.

Master. The IDE device that controls the device chain. Each IDE port on a motherboard can support two devices. The primary device is the master; it talks directly to the processor. The secondary device is the slave; its orders come from the processor through the master device. IDE devices usually have jumpers that determine master or slave status.

Megabyte. Approximately one million bytes of data or storage space. Abbreviated MB or M.

Memory (RAM). The workspace in which your computer operates. The more memory you have, the more and bigger programs you can run at the same time. If you don't have enough memory, your programs may run more slowly or not at all. Physically, memory consists of chips or small circuit cards installed on the motherboard. The most common types are SIMMs and DIMMs.

Memory address. The specific part of memory being used by a particular file or device.

MIDI input. This port enables you to plug in a keyboard or other instrument to put sounds into the computer for manipulating or saving.

M-II. Cyrix's Pentium II equivalent processor.

MMX. Stands for Multimedia Extensions. A capability of some processors to handle multimedia processing better than others. Built in to most newer Pentiums and all Pentium IIs. Lacking in the Pentium Pro.

Modem. A device that allows you to communicate with other computers through phone lines by translating digital data (PC) to analog (sound) and then back again on the other end.

Motherboard. The big circuit board inside the case that everything else plugs into. The motherboard you have determines the processor (or processors) you can use, the type and amount of memory, the video card type, and more.

MS-DOS. See *DOS*.

Multimedia. An activity involving more than one medium, such as a game that includes both visuals and sounds. Can also refer to certain hardware components that make such activities possible (sound cards, CD-ROM drives, speakers, and so on).

Multimedia Extensions. See *MMX*.

My Computer. A window containing icons for each drive on your system, along with several other special-purpose icons. You can access it by double-clicking on the My Computer icon on the Windows desktop.

Net. See *Internet*.

Netscape Navigator. A popular Web browser; a competitor to Internet Explorer.

Network. A group of computers connected with cabling and network interface cards or through the Internet. One popular type is a local area network (LAN).

NLQ. Near Letter Quality. A description of output quality of a 9-pin dot matrix printer. The term *near* means it is not quite as good as the output from a typewriter.

Non-DOS partition. In partitioning a drive, an area of the drive set aside for some special use other than storing files. For example, on some laptops, a small non-DOS partition is used to save system settings in the event of a battery failure.

Non-interlaced. See *Interlacing*.

Operating system. Software that keeps the computer running and accepts user commands. Windows 98 is the most popular operating system today; others include MS-DOS, Linux, and OS/2.

Output device. A device that receives information coming out of a computer. Examples include monitors, printers, and speakers.

Parallel port. See *LPT port*.

Partitioning. Setting up a hard disk in preparation for formatting, assigning drive letters to one or more sections of it.

Path. The full location of a folder, file, or other object. For example, C:\Windows\System is the path to many of the files that run Windows 95/98.

PCI. Peripheral Component Interface, a very popular type of local bus slot on newer motherboards.

PCL. Stands for Printer Control Language. A language used for communication between the computer and certain types of printers. Originally developed by Hewlett-Packard.

PCMCIA card. A credit-card-sized hardware device that plugs in to a laptop computer, providing additional functionality. PCMCIA stands for Personal Computer Memory Card International Association, the group that developed the standard by which it operates.

Pentium. A processor made by Intel. The original Pentium is no longer being made. It is succeeded by the Pentium II, and more recently the Pentium III.

Peripheral. A device that is not physically located inside the main computer case. Examples include printers and scanners.

Physical drive. The drive hardware. Compare to *logical drive*.

Physical error. A bad spot on a disk from which data cannot be read or written. Compare to *logical error*.

PIF. Stands for program information file. A shortcut to a DOS-based program, containing the special settings needed to make that program run under Windows.

Pincushion. A monitor adjustment that controls how wide the image is near the vertical center of the image compared to the top and bottom. If your image looks like it has a waistline drawn in near the middle of each side, reduce this setting; if it bulges in the middle, increase it.

PIO. Stands for Programmed I/O. A scheme of enhancing data transfer on a hard disk. There are five available PIO modes (0 through 4), that can be set in the BIOS setup.

Plug and Play. A method of identifying and configuring new hardware. If your motherboard and the new device are both Plug-and-Play–compatible, when you add your upgrade components to the system, Windows 95/98 detects and configures them automatically.

PostScript. A language used for communications between the computer and certain types of printers.

PostScript printer. A printer that uses the PostScript language to communicate with the computer.

Primary partition. The main partition on a drive. See *Partitioning*. Compare to *Extended partition*.

Processor. The brain of your computer. The types include 286, 386, 486, Pentium, Pentium Pro, Pentium II, and Pentium III. Your processor has a speed—given in megahertz (MHz)—at which it operates.

PS/2. An obsolete type of IBM PC that introduced the PS/2 port. Even though the computers are no longer produced, PS/2 ports have become the standard for mouse connection in almost all new PCs made today.

Pull. A piece of equipment that has been removed from an old system. Buying one is like going to a junkyard to buy a part from a wrecked car.

Quick Launch toolbar. The row of shortcut icons to the right of the Start button in Windows 98 and some versions of Windows 95.

RAM. Stands for random access memory. See *Memory*.

RAM disk. A temporary disk made out of extra memory in your computer. The startup disk you make in Windows, for example, contains commands that create a RAM disk and copy utilities to it.

Reformat. See *Format*.

Refresh rate. Refers to how often the video card sends updated instructions to the monitor. If you have ever seen a videotape of someone working at a computer and the computer screen seemed to be blinking or flickering, the computer screen's refresh rate was lower than the videotape's frame rate. Both monitors and video cards can be bottlenecks to improving refresh rates.

Regedit. A utility program for editing the Registry in Windows.

Registry. A configuration file for Windows 95/98 and Windows NT that holds all your Windows settings, preferences, and information about installed programs.

Registry Checker. A utility that finds and repairs some errors in the Registry. If it detects an error as Windows is starting up, it automatically runs.

Repartition. See *Partitioning*.

Resolution. The number of pixels (dots) that make up a display on a monitor. Common resolutions are 640 × 480 and 800 × 600.

Resource conflict. A situation in which two or more devices are trying to use the same base address, DMA channel, or IRQ.

Resources. See *System resources*.

Right-click menu. See *Shortcut menu*.

ROM. Stands for read-only memory. A small amount of non-volatile memory (that is, it doesn't blank out when you shut off the PC) that stores important startup information for your PC. See *BIOS*.

ROM-BIOS. See *BIOS*.

Root directory. See *Root folder*.

Root folder. The top-level folder on a disk, in which all other folders reside.

Safe mode. A troubleshooting mode of Windows. If Windows will not start normally, sometimes it will start in Safe mode, and you can fix the problem there.

ScanDisk. A utility program that runs in DOS 6.0 or later or in Windows 95/98 to check a disk for errors. Replaces the older *CHKDSK*.

Scanner. A device for digitizing pictures so that you can use them in your computer. Some scanners also come with optical character recognition (OCR) software, which allows you to scan text and then translate the picture of the text into real text in a word processor.

SCSI. Stands for small computer system interface. A type of device interface that runs a variety of devices, such as hard disks, scanners, and CD-ROM drives. Its primary benefit is that you can plug up to 7 devices into a single chain, without using separate IRQs. SCSI is common on high-end systems and servers, but has not caught on in the mainstream PC market because it requires buying a special interface card in which to plug the SCSI devices.

S-DRAM DIMMs. This newer, faster kind of memory comes in a 168-pin DIMM package. The performance is great, but the cost per megabyte may be higher than it is for non-parity EDO SIMMs.

Self-extracting Zip. A Zip file that can be decompressed and its contents extracted without using a Zip utility program.

Serial port. See *COM port*.

Shareware. Software that is freely distributed in trial form; users are honor-bound to pay for it if they like it and continue to use it. Compare to *freeware*.

Shortcut. An icon in Windows that provides quick access to a file or program.

Shortcut menu. A menu of commonly used commands that appears when you right-click on any file, folder, or object in Windows.

SIMM. A type of memory found in 486 and some Pentium systems. SIMMs were the standard type of memory for many years, but are now being superceded by *DIMMs*.

Single inline memory modules. See *SIMM*.

Slave. The secondary device in a two-device IDE chain. See *Master*.

Slot mask. A hybrid type of monitor that integrates features of both shadow mask and aperture grille technologies.

Slot pitch. A measurement, like *dot pitch*, of the quality of a slot mask type monitor.

Socket 1. A long, thin slot on a motherboard designed for a Pentium II cartridge.

Socket 7. A square processor socket on a motherboard designed for 486 or Pentium CPUs or their competitors.

Sound card. An interface card that plugs into the motherboard and enables you to hear sound through speakers (typically sold separately). If you don't have a sound card, you miss out on the sound effects associated with most games and also on the audible warnings your computer issues from time to time.

Standoffs. The supports (some plastic and some brass) that hold the motherboard off the floor of the case. (They make the motherboard "stand off" the floor.)

Startup disk. A floppy disk containing the files needed to start your computer in the event of a hard disk failure.

Subfolder. A folder within another folder.

Swap file. See *Virtual memory*.

System.ini. A configuration file, along with win.ini, that specifies Windows settings. Windows 95/98 primarily use the Windows Registry for this purpose, but System.ini continues to exist for backward compatibility.

System File Checker. A utility, run through the System Information utility in Windows, that makes sure the Windows system files have not become corrupted.

System resources. Generically, this means the memory available for running the operating system and your programs. In Windows, it also includes *virtual memory*.

System tray. The area to the left of the clock in the lower-right corner of the Windows 95/98 screen. Icons appear in the system tray for programs running in the background.

Task Scheduler. The utility in Windows that manages your scheduled maintenance tasks.

TCP/IP. The communication protocol used in Windows to connect your computer to your ISP so that you can use the Internet.

Temporary file. A file that Windows or some other program creates to hold data as it calculates; it deletes the file automatically when it is finished with it. Sometimes temporary files do not get deleted; the Disk Cleanup program can delete them for you.

Termination. In a SCSI device chain, the switch, plug, or other indicator on the last device that tells the PC that there are no more devices in the chain.

Thrashing. Continual hard disk spinning caused by the PC accessing its swap file. This can indicate that the PC could benefit from more memory being added. Also called *churning*.

Toner. The dry ink used by laser printers.

Trapezoid. A monitor adjustment that controls how wide the image is at the top versus the bottom of the screen. If you have more black space on the sides near the top of the monitor than near the bottom, or *vice versa*, adjust this setting to even it out.

Trojan horse. A variant of a *virus*. A program that appears to do something useful, but in fact infects your computer system with a virus.

True color. A 24-bit color depth.

True parity memory. A type of memory for systems that require parity memory. Many older 486 systems require true parity memory.

TweakUI. A free utility for Windows, originally developed by Microsoft engineers, that assists in some system configuration tasks.

UART. A chip in a serial port or an internal modem that controls the throughput. If you want to use a high-speed serial device, you might want to buy a high-speed serial port interface card that contains the top-of-the-line UART, which is the 16750.

Universal Serial Bus. See *USB*.

Upload. To transfer a file from your own computer to another, usually through the Internet. Compare to *Download*.

URL. Stands for Uniform Resource Locator. Synonymous with *Web address*.

USB. Stands for Universal Serial Bus, a kind of connector that PC manufacturers began including on their systems in

mid-1997. You can plug several USB devices into a single USB port (chaining them together) and you don't have to do any special configuring for them.

Video card. The interface between your PC and your monitor. The card interprets the PC's instructions and sends codes that tell the monitor which pixels (dots) to light up with which colors.

Video driver. A file that tells your operating system (such as Windows 98) how to work with your video card.

Video mode. The combination of a particular *color depth* and a particular *display resolution*. Some people also include a particular *refresh rate* in this specification.

Video RAM. Memory built in to your video card.

Virtual memory. A portion of the hard disk set aside to be used as a temporary holding tank for information that doesn't fit in the computer's memory as it operates. Also called a *swap file*.

Virus. A malicious computer code that attaches itself to your existing programs. From that point, it can infect other files, cause damage to your system, or do something embarrassing to you, such as send an X-rated e-mail to everyone in your address book.

VLB. Stands for VESA Local Bus, an older kind of local bus slot found on 486 computers. See *Local bus*.

Volume label. The name you give a disk when formatting it. That name appears under the drive's icon in Windows. Using a volume label is optional.

Wavetable cards. Interface cards (usually sound cards) that have pre-recorded, built-in sounds, such as the sounds of different instruments playing different notes. Regular FM synthesis sound cards don't have wavetables; they simulate these notes instead, which doesn't sound as good.

Web address. The address by which you access a Web page. Most Web addresses begin with http://. Also called *URL*.

Web browser. A program designed to view Web pages.

Web page. A file created in the HTML programming language that can be made available on a Web server and viewed with a Web browser.

Web server. A computer connected to the Internet full-time that serves up Web pages to other computers that request access to them.

Web site. A collection of Web pages tied together with hyperlinks and organized around a common subject.

Windows Explorer. A program in Windows that helps you view and manage files.

Windows Registry. See *Registry*.

Windows Update. A utility that works with Internet Explorer to download updates to Windows through the Internet.

win.ini. An initialization file, along with System.ini, that tells Windows what settings to use when it starts. A holdover from Windows 3.1; Windows 95/98 primarily use the Windows Registry for this same purpose. However, win.ini continues to exist for backward compatibility.

Wizard. A series of dialog boxes that help you accomplish an otherwise tricky task by asking you a series of questions.

World Wide Web. An interconnected network of Web pages available on the Internet.

Write-protected disk. A disk that has been set so that no changes can be made to it. To write-protect a floppy disk, slide the black plastic tab to expose the hole.

Zero-insertion force (ZIF) socket. A type of processor socket found in newer 486 computers and all Pentiums and Pentium-equivalent computers. The processor appears to be sitting on a small platform (usually white) with a handle alongside it. You lift the handle, and the chip then lifts easily out of the socket.

Zip drive. A type of drive that accepts removable disks that store between 100 and 250 megabytes of data apiece.

Zip file. A file compressed with a utility called PKZip (or a similar utility). Zip files have .zip extensions. You cannot use the content of a Zip file until you decompress it with an unzipping utility.

INDEX

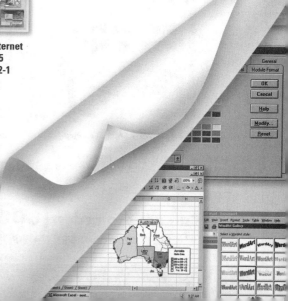